RELIGION
AND THE
DEMISE OF
LIBERAL
RATIONALISM

J. JUDD OWEN

# Religion

THE FOUNDATIONAL CRISIS

# and the

OF THE SEPARATION

# Demise of

OF CHURCH AND STATE

# Liberal

THE UNIVERSITY OF CHICAGO PRESS

# Rationalism

CHICAGO & LONDON

J. JUDD OWEN is
assistant professor of
political science at
Emory University.

THE UNIVERSITY OF CHICAGO PRESS, CHICAGO 60637
THE UNIVERSITY OF CHICAGO PRESS, LTD., LONDON
© 2001 by The University of Chicago
All rights reserved. Published 2001
Printed in the United States of America
10  09  08  07  06  05  04  03  02  01    5  4  3  2  1
ISBN (cloth): 0-226-64191-0
ISBN (paper): 0-226-64192-9

Library of Congress Cataloging-in-Publication Data

Owen, J. Judd.
    Religion and the demise of liberal rationalism : the
foundational crisis of the separation of church and
state / J. Judd Owen.
        p.    cm.
    Includes bibliographical references and index.
    ISBN 0-226-64191-0 (cloth) —
    ISBN 0-226-64192-9 (pbk.)
    1. Liberalism.    2. Church and state.    3. Dewey,
John, 1859–1952—Contributions in political
science.    4. Rawls, John, 1921—Contributions in
political science.    5. Rorty, Richard—Contributions
in political science.    6. Fish, Stanley Eugene—
Contributions in political science.    I. Title.
JC574.094    2001
323.44'2—dc21
                                        00-012232

*To my mother*

*and to the memory*

*of my father*

CONTENTS

## ACKNOWLEDGMENTS

Portions of chapters 6 and 7 appeared in the *American Political Science Review,* which kindly gave permission for their reprinting here. For financial support while revising the manuscript, I thank the Earhart Foundation, the Bradley Foundation, and the departments of political science at the University of Toronto and Boston College. I thank the members of my dissertation committee for their questions, comments, and corrections: Clifford Orwin, Ronald Beiner, Stanley Fish, Donald Forbes, David Novak, Melissa Williams, and especially my supervisor, Thomas Pangle. Professor Fish has shown generosity on several occasions besides that of his service on my dissertation committee. I have profited from conversations and exchanges on the subject of this book with Mark Lloyd, Linda Rabieh, Robert Bartlett, Keith Whitaker, Nassar Behnegar, Christopher Bruell, Robert Faulkner, Susan Shell, Ruth Grant, Michael Gillespie, Steven Kautz, Peter Lawler, and Stephen Macedo. Peter Ahrensdorf is due special thanks for his guidance as a teacher as well as his support and friendship. Special thanks is also due to Peter Busch, who patiently helped me think through many problems and commented on much of the manuscript. I thank John Tryneski, my editor; Richard Allen, my copyeditor; the anonymous reviewers of the manuscript; and Daniel Slater, my research assistant at Emory University. I thank my dear wife, Marion Kaylor Owen, for her unflagging encouragement, and my brother, John M. Owen, for much good counsel. I am especially indebted to my entire family — John, my sister Tricia Palardy, and above all my mother Pat Owen and my late father J. Malloy Owen, for preparing me to take seriously the most serious things.

# 1

## IF LIBERALISM IS A FAITH, WHAT BECOMES OF THE SEPARATION OF CHURCH AND STATE?

The liberal institutions concerning religion — the separation of church and state, religious pluralism, religious freedom — were originally justified on the basis of a revolutionary comprehensive philosophic doctrine, covering human nature, the purpose of political society, and the proper domain of religious faith. The liberal doctrines concerning religion were the product of the Age of Reason, or the Enlightenment. These doctrines were the cornerstone of the Enlightenment's political philosophy, as well as its political project. Today, belief in the comprehensive philosophic teaching of the Enlightenment appears to lie in ruins, and few hope that any other comprehensive philosophy could successfully replace it. This despair is, to a considerable extent, due to a radical critique of reason as such. According to this critique, there are no evident and certain principles in either natural, moral, or political science. The belief in the very possibility of science and of a life and society guided by rational norms must therefore be said to be rooted in a prejudice or faith. This critique may thus seem to cut to the heart of the Enlightenment. And yet we follow in the Enlightenment's wake. We carry on practices begun in the Age of Reason, but without the confidence that our practices are moored to timeless principles. The separation of church and state remains. But can any justification be offered for it after the demise of liberal rationalism? Does it remain secure, as a matter of deeply entrenched tradition, as part of a "faith community centered on the Constitution" (Levinson 1988, 52)?[1] Or is it especially vulnerable, lying close to the Enlightenment's rationalist core?[2]

Challenges to liberalism's original self-understanding as the most rational and enlightened achievement of humankind are as old as liberalism itself. Arguably the most fundamental of these challenges began over a hundred

1

years ago when Nietzsche attempted to undermine liberalism's rationalist grounding by a radical critique of reason as such. The critique that Nietzsche began has a complicated history, but never before has it been so pervasive and influential in the West and particularly in the United States. The form of this critique that has gained such currency in political theory as elsewhere in the academy commonly goes by the name of antifoundationalism, which asserts that no claim to knowledge is founded in the one truth. All claims to knowledge are from a particular human, all too human perspective, or are socially constructed. There is nothing to which we can appeal in order to settle the most profound human disagreements, and thus there is no possibility that the awesome variety of conflicting opinions about the things most important to human beings, including the best political order, can be transcended toward universal and objective knowledge. The original claim that liberalism is grounded in natural right and reason and therefore the claim that it is universally legitimate are naive and even arrogant fictions.

Sanford Levinson speaks of the "death of constitutionalism" to describe the ever spreading skepticism regarding the theoretical underpinnings of the prevailing liberal order. He warns that "the 'death of constitutionalism' may be the central event of our time" (1988, 52), an event comparable in magnitude (and not unrelated) to the death of God for the previous generation. This book takes that warning with the seriousness it deserves, by focusing on the question of liberalism's relation to religion — in particular nonliberal religion — in the wake of the apparent demise of liberal rationalism to which Levinson alludes. Our attention is not narrowed arbitrarily. The problem posed by what today might be called religious "difference" is not only liberalism's original but also its most enduring and even its defining problem.

We can approach the problem liberalism confronts today in the following way: Levinson speaks of our "constitutional faith" and of liberal principles as our "civil religion." But the liberal state cannot adjudicate rationally or impartially among the various faiths, as it claims to do, if it itself rests on one of the competing faiths. If liberalism deserves to be called a "civil religion," then the separation of church and state is in danger of becoming incoherent and disestablishment of becoming meaningless. We cannot simply embrace liberalism as a faith, as a civil religion, and then speak intelligibly of the separation of church (faith, religion) and state. But is the claim that liberalism rests on faith warranted?

I mean to offer a limited defense of liberal rationalism, insofar as I aim to show that antifoundationalism has misunderstood it and therefore failed to refute it decisively. Antifoundationalism can, however, do us the service of making us aware that a rationalism taken for granted is no rationalism, but instead a faith. And a liberalism that rests on faith is inherently problematic, being vulnerable vis-à-vis the perennial challenges of nonliberal religion in particular. The confrontation with antifoundationalism calls us to reconsider the arguments for and against liberalism's claims to rationality and all it entails. Yet, while as a friend of liberalism I wish to see it defended, my chief aim in this book is not to offer such a defense but to issue a call for the serious theoretical reexamination of our situation respecting the relationship between religion and politics and to make some contribution to that end. Such a reexamination is made especially urgent in light of the recent turn of much political theory, including liberal theory. But it is a perennial necessity for thoughtful liberals who take seriously for themselves liberalism's orientation toward rational enlightenment.

The three thinkers on whom I focus — Richard Rorty, John Rawls, and Stanley Fish — are united in their turn away from political theory's need to address itself to fundamental, or "foundational," questions. In the case of Rorty and Fish, political theory is said to be incapable of addressing fundamental questions — incapable, that is, of doing so theoretically or rationally. Rawls's position is ambiguous in this respect, but he joins Rorty and Fish in claiming that political theory, regardless of its capacities, does not *need* to address itself to fundamental questions. I argue as follows: It has not been shown by our leading critics of "foundationalism" that rationally addressing the questions that are fundamental for human beings is impossible, however herculean a task it surely is. But, even though we cannot be assured of success at the outset, it is nonetheless *necessary* for us as human beings to address such questions. This book therefore may be said to be a defense of "foundationalist" political theory, though it should become evident that I take what Rorty and Fish describe as foundationalism to be a caricature that in fact has more in common with their own theoretical stances than with genuine rationalism.

I would not wish to be interpreted as attempting to shield liberalism from the serious challenges it faces. On the contrary, I suppose that liberals must confront those challenges and that they must do so ultimately on a "foundational" level. The anti- or non-foundational liberalisms of Rorty and Rawls, in contrast, would absolve us of the responsibility of facing those challenges by relegating all such challenges to the plane of assertion or private faith. Perhaps not coincidentally, by relegating liberalism also to the plane of assertion or private faith they would absolve us liberals of the responsibility of justifying our principles before liberalism's opponents, and even before ourselves. I aim to set liberal theory back on its proper plane. If liberalism cannot ground its institutions and principles with rational arguments, liberalism is reduced to an illiberal dogmatism. Fish faces this possible consequence squarely and concludes that the liberal posture to religion lacks a coherent justification. We must confront the possibility that the "death of constitutionalism" spells the death of the separation of church and state and the corresponding principle of religious freedom.

### Antifoundationalism in Religion Clause Jurisprudence

Stepping back for a moment from such a grave possibility, one finds that most constitutional scholars who have approached our topic do not foresee or seek the overturning of liberal institutions, or even seriously entertain the possibility. Instead, they typically seek to open a greater space in the political sphere for expressly religious participation, or what jurisprudents call greater "accommodation," of religion. The case for greater accommodation of religion can, of course, be made on liberal grounds.[3] Indeed, as Fish points out, the very notion of "accommodation" is a liberal one (1999b, 257). A growing number of scholars, however, make the case for accommodation by questioning the very foundations of liberalism. These scholars have appropriated the antifoundationalism of theorists like Rorty and Fish in an attempt to win renewed intellectual and political respect for religious faith qua faith.[4]

The most notable — but by no means the most radical — among antifoundationalist proponents of accommodation is Stephen L. Carter. Carter's book *The Culture of Disbelief* (1993) received widespread attention (including in the popular press), generally rave reviews, and even an endorsement from President Clinton (Levinson 1994, 1873). Carter's criticism of liberalism in his book is much more muted than it was in an earlier article in the *Duke Law Journal* (1987).[5] In that article, Carter states that his aim is "to expose the contradictions at the heart of the liberal theory of neutrality toward religion" (978). Carter states that "liberals display a single-minded fanaticism in upholding the right of free speech" (987). This is because liberals have a "faith in the ability of individual humans to create themselves and their world through dialogue" and in the "power of reason to move others to action"

(988). He asserts that "without a faith in the faculty of reason, liberalism has nothing whatever to recommend it." Carter uses the debate between "creationism" and "evolutionism" to argue that the liberal faith is indeed without warrant. The dispute over creation and evolution is ultimately a dispute between two competing faiths. The faith in science or reason, Carter asserts, can claim no epistemological superiority over any religious faith. More precisely, each faith presupposes its own "epistemology" — its standard of evidence and rationality — which is not itself susceptible to rational scrutiny.

Carter warns that if "the liberal refuses to accept the claim that the devout religionist knows rather than simply believes, then the argument that religion is nevertheless cherished stumbles near the edge of a frightening and perhaps unbridgeable precipice" (993). What Carter means is suggested in the subtitle of his book: "American law and politics trivialize religious devotion." This trivialization, Carter claims, poses a threat either to American law and politics (liberal constitutionalism) or to religion. For either the deeply religious people of the United States will rebel against the liberalism that denigrates their faith, or else religious faith must erode. One or the other must give. And it would be rash, according to Carter, to bet against religion. Carter finds this tension between religious faith and liberalism extremely troubling and is unprepared to abandon either one. Both article and book are pleas for a solution. Yet, Carter admits, "to transcend these difficulties" may be "to transcend liberalism itself" (1987, 995). Carter does not hint what this may mean.

The focus of Carter's criticism of liberalism is its claim to be neutral to religion. That claim seems to be implicit in the separation of church and state. The liberal state is neutral to religion because its own purposes are distinct from religious purposes. If religion is occasionally "burdened" by the actions of the state, it is burdened not qua religion but simply as a group of citizens, who qua citizens are burdened no more or less than citizens of any other faith. In other words, so long as the state acts with a view to its own strictly secular ends, its actions are neutral to religion. This claim can be found as early as Locke's *Letter Concerning Toleration* ([1689] 1963, 60) and as recently as the Supreme Court's controversial decision in *Employment Division v Smith* (1990). Phillip Johnson has claimed: "That in some sense the federal government and the states ought to be 'neutral' in religious matters is undisputed" (1984, 818).

As Steven D. Smith suggests, however, determining precisely what this neutrality means is no simple matter: "Scholars have offered myriad explications of the ideal of religious neutrality" (1995, 77). But while Carter continues to harbor hope that some resolution to the problem of liberal neutrality may yet be found, Smith declares the quest for neutrality a "foreordained failure." According to Smith, this failure means that there can be no coherent constitutional principle of religious freedom. For in the jurisprudence of religious freedom, "neutrality is not merely one major theme among others, or one attractive theoretical option, but rather an essential theoretical requirement" (77).

Smith's powerful argument can be summarized as follows. Every doctrine of religious freedom must presuppose what Smith calls "background beliefs" about such things as the nature of religious belief, what counts as coercion, and the purpose and therefore the limitations of religious freedom. Yet "background beliefs" as such are not neutral. For example, Locke takes for granted in his *Letter Concerning Toleration,* as Smith points out, several things concerning religion about which there was (and to a considerable extent continues to be) widespread disagreement. Locke depends on a strictly voluntarist notion of faith, where coercion has no effect on belief. Indeed, only belief that is uncoerced, according to Locke, counts toward salvation. This fact, Locke claims, "absolutely determines this controversy" ([1689] 1963, 52). Smith objects:

> Augustine affirmed, as did Locke, that ultimately only a genuine faith can save; but also recognized (as parents do, and as our modern system of compulsory schooling arguably does) that coercive measures *can* sometimes put a person in a position from which he can favorably consider, and perhaps come to embrace, a true idea. Augustine cited the example of the Apostle Paul. . . . God "not only compelled Paul . . . by word but He also prostrated him with power, and in order to lead him from the savagery of his dark unbeliefs to the desire of the light of the heart, he first struck him with bodily blindness." (1995, 67)[6]

Locke's case for religious toleration is persuasive only to those who already agree with some specific and controversial notions of the character and purpose of religious belief as distinguished from the character and purpose of the state. However, once "Locke's background beliefs are seen as dubious, his argument for religious tolerance loses force" (66).

Locke's *Letter,* of course, may not be intended to stand on its own. Locke's "background beliefs" may be brought to the fore and demonstrated as true elsewhere (for example in the *Reasonableness of Christianity,* the *Essay Concerning Human Understanding,* and the *Two Treatises on Government*). Smith argues, however, that it does not matter with respect to the success of the doctrine of religious freedom if Locke's "background beliefs" are sound or unsound. For the soundness of such background beliefs is precisely what Locke's doctrine of religious freedom is supposed to leave for each to determine for himself. In sum, a doctrine of religious freedom must be neutral to background beliefs, but background beliefs are necessarily already at work in any doctrine of religious freedom. Smith, unlike Carter, is willing to conclude unambiguously "that the quest for neutrality . . . is an attempt to grasp an illusion" (1995, 96).

Such an analysis does not necessarily depend upon a critique of rationalism as such, and perhaps not even of liberal rationalism in particular. After all, Smith does seem to admit that the background beliefs of the liberal rationalist Locke (presumably *liberal* background beliefs) may be sound. Such an analysis need not, therefore, depend upon antifoundationalist presuppositions, which repudiate rationalism as such. While Smith, a professor of law, admits that he is no student of philosophy, evidence of antifoundationalist influence nevertheless occasionally shines through. He states:

> Upon reflection, th[e] failure [of liberal neutrality] should not be surprising. The failure of a truly "neutral" theory of religious freedom is analogous to the impossibility, recognized by modern philosophers, of finding . . . a "God's Eye View" . . . from which to look down on and describe reality. . . . There is no neutral vantage point that can permit the theorist or judge to transcend these competing positions. (1995, 96–97)

Smith's statement of what "modern philosophers" have "recognized" could well be found in the writings of Richard Rorty or Stanley Fish as shorthand for the antifoundationalist critique of rationalism.

When it comes to prescribing a course of action, Smith admits to being at a loss. Prescription, however, is not his purpose. He is "simply trying to illuminate our present situation" (1995, vii). One scholar who both embraces antifoundationalism more emphatically than Carter and Smith and who claims to see more clearly the political direction in which we should head is Frederick Gedicks. Gedicks echoes Carter's and Smith's critique of liberalism's sham neutrality to religion. Liberal neutrality, Gedicks contends, is in reality merely a specious gloss covering an unbelieving secularism. Secularism is the dominant "discourse," or mode of thought, in the courts and among Western cultural elites — i.e., among a small minority. Secularism arose as a solution to what Gedicks admits was a politically problematic pluralism arising in Europe after the Reformation. But, he argues, "secularism has not solved the problem posed by religion in public life so much as it has buried it" (1991, 139). The political dominance of secularism represents not enlightenment but an ideological exercise of power.

According to Gedicks, "such a 'solution' can remain stable only so long as those who are ignored [the religious believers] acquiesce in their social situation" (1991, 139). But, he warns, the recent resurgence of the "religious right" — not only in the United States, but around the world[7] — suggests that "acquiescence in a secularized public life . . . is vanishing, if it has not already disappeared." Thus "there remains the possibility that the conflict between religion and secularism in public life could end with the triumph of religion." Even though Gedicks is a believing Mormon, he is sure that any such triumph would mean merely the establishment of some "religious ideology," which would rest ultimately on power alone.

Gedicks's solution to this conundrum is a "post-secular" politics. According to Gedicks and Roger Hendrix, this means replacing the "metaphor" of separation of church and state, which "force[s] one into a confrontational mode of thinking about religion in public life" (Gedicks and Hendrix 1991, 161). Church and state are not "separate and mutually exclusive realms." They write: "What public culture needs are ways of talking about religion and politics, church and state, and public and private life which unify rather than divide." There is, of course, a name for the complete unification of church and state: theocracy. Gedicks and Hendrix would not be misunderstood as even contemplating theocracy. Gedicks states that "public discourse in a post-secular, post-modern society must evolve from the current view that secularism is the departure point and limit on public debate, and it must accomplish this without substituting religion in its place" (Gedicks 1991, 115). Precisely what he and Hendrix have in mind, however, remains vague: "In our view, the ideal relation between religion and public life — the religious and the secular — is one that ensures that all voices are heard with seriousness and respect" (162). They seem to propose, not a sham neutrality, but a *real* neutrality; not sham liberalism, but *real* liberalism.

Yet they offer no indication of how a "post-secular" neutrality can succeed where liberal neutrality as Carter and Smith describe it has failed. Gedicks admits that in one sense, a "post-secular" politics will continue to be "a threat to religion or, at least, to conservative religion" (144). For "if there is really no neutral position from which to discern the Truth, as post-modern critiques generally argue, then there can be no coherent claim to the exclusivity of Truth." It seems that not *all* voices will be heard with seriousness and respect. More than this, if a "post-secular" politics has already determined that there is no "exclusivity of Truth," then it seems that there must be an essential limitation to the "seriousness and respect" with which "all voices are heard." No one will be heard with the seriousness and respect with which one hears the Truth.

We see from this brief survey of Carter, Smith, and Gedicks what is perhaps only the seed of a radical critique of the separation of church and state. The fact that none of the three turns his back on liberal institutions should not make us sanguine. The fact that persons of generally moderate, and indeed liberal, sentiments can entertain such serious doubts about the most basic constitutional principles should sound a tocsin for serious liberals. For Carter, Smith, and Gedicks are not fully attuned to the full implications of the critique of liberalism they begin. If their critique should prove sound, would the liberal separation of church and state lose its ultimate justification?

Before we reach a conclusion of such magnitude, however, we are obligated to cross-examine liberal rationalism's accusers. Is the critique of liberal rationalism that has gained such currency today sound? However sophisticated Carter, Smith, and Gedicks may be, we cannot get to the heart of the matter without turning to the theoretical sources of the most radical elements of their writings. We must turn to those antifoundationalist theorists who have thought most seriously about the questions before us.

### Rationalism and Neutrality

Many important difficulties for liberal rationalism must remain in the background of our discussion — such as the charge that the liberal conception of human beings as desiring primarily only comfortable self-preservation and material accumulation is reductionist and blanches too much spiritual and social meaning from human life. There is also the charge that liberalism has shaped our aspirations and moral opinions to an extent that liberalism itself — with its individualism and social contract doctrines — is unable adequately to explain. These are serious issues, and by no means irrelevant to my theme. Yet this book obviously cannot survey all criticisms of liberal rationalism. The difficulty with liberal rationalism that will reemerge throughout this book is its purported neutrality. Richard Rorty and Stanley Fish claim that neutrality is a problem of rationalism as such — preliberal, natural scientific, etc. This is a seemingly technical or abstract criticism. But underneath the critique of neutrality lies the human dissatisfaction with the inhumanly cold and dispassionate calculation that may seem to be a part of rationalism as such. Reason desires to be above the fray. It desires to be impartial and objective. As Aristotle makes clear in the *Politics,* it is the task of the political scientist to adjudicate among the contending political parties, investigating what is the best regime in the circumstances as well as what is the best regime simply. That is, even Aristotle's preliberal political rationalism may seem somehow impartial and neutral. In Book 7 Aristotle speaks of the life of the rationalist as "the [life] of the foreigner and separated from the political community" (1324a17–18, my translation). He articulates the objection of the political human being that the life of rational analysis is inactive (1325a), or, we might say, disengaged from life. Aristotle, obviously a partisan of rationalism, responds to this objection: rational study is an activity, and the most complete and humanly satisfying one. But such promises of happiness have been overwhelmed for us by the fruits of the cultural dominance of rationalism brought about through the Enlightenment. The knowledge capable of producing modernity's awesome technological power is different from the knowledge of how to use that power wisely. Wisdom is harder to come by. Cold, calculating, detached, even morally irresponsible, analysis and technological reasoning are in the foreground of the rationalism of the modern world, so that the promises of happiness associated with the life of reason seem naively hopeful.

As powerful as such objections may be, the antifoundationalism that will be featured in this book goes further in denying that the impartiality that reason claims for itself is humanly possible. Antifoundationalism, being a variety of historicism, teaches that all of our thinking is bound up in some "worldview," a horizon that varies from society to society and age to age. No worldview is rooted in timeless principles, nature, or divine decree. All have their sources only in the vagaries of history, in "sheer contingency." There is no rational or natural viewpoint that transcends all such partial viewpoints. No single perspective could hold all worldviews in its scope without distorting them. It seems that the political rationalist therefore cannot adjudicate impartially. It is, moreover, impossible to *live* neutrally. The life guided by reason's authority necessarily excludes competing claims to authority concerning how to live. Could there be such a thing as a partisan of rationalism? How could such a rationalism avoid dogmatism, which is fatal to rationalism's self-understanding?

Antifoundationalism concludes that reason is always dogmatic — the function of some more basic assumption that cannot itself be defended or examined rationally. And while this conclusion is fatal to the life of reason from its own point of view, it is not simply fatal from the point of view of antifoundationalism. For, according to the antifoundationalist, dogmatism of some form or other is unavoidable. Yet the antifoundationalist does tend to accuse rationalism of distracting us from the world of primary human concern — our immediate moral and social bonds — by calling us to some "higher," abstract purpose. Thus in one sense reason is one viewpoint among many. But it is also uniquely pernicious, since it pulls us away from our historical, but real or authentic, human commitments.

Yet reason's questions cannot be wholly suppressed. Did the commitments of the Athenians, for example, to the gods and the nobility of the polis and empire satisfy the needs that the Greeks hoped they would? Their commitments to Zeus were "real," but, to raise a prosaic question, is Zeus real? Aristophanes illustrates in the *Clouds* why Athenians were angry with Socrates: his rationalism threatened their "commitments." But who was right? And does not Athenian anger at Socrates indicate that reason's questions are not artificially abstract but touch (literally, are *contingent* upon) what matters most within the "historical worldview"?

Although antifoundationalism repudiates rationalism as such, this book, as its title indicates, is concerned particularly with liberal rationalism, and by extension with modern scientific rationalism — Enlightenment rationalism's more successful half. We may not take for granted that liberal rationalism is the standard for political rationalism. Nor, therefore, may we assume that the failure of liberal rationalism would mean the failure of political rationalism as such. To state the reason for this reservation simply, liberal rationalism defined itself in opposition to all preliberal political rationalism. But if liberal rationalism becomes questionable, then its critique of preliberal rationalism also becomes questionable. But, as Rorty says, "we have to start from where we are" (1991a, 29), and that means with the contemporary crisis of liberal rationalism.

*The Plan of the Book*

In the course of the present study, we will consider the political thought
of Richard Rorty, John Rawls, and Stanley Fish, with brief excursions considering John Dewey and John Locke. The majority of the book is occupied with
the work of Rorty and Fish on account of both their extensive similarities and
their profound differences. Their common critique of liberal rationalism may
be summarized as follows. Both Rorty and Fish repeatedly criticize attempts
and aspirations to apprehend and demonstrate timeless truths, which they
regard as truths that necessarily appear the same from each of the infinite
variety of historical human perspectives. We could recognize a timeless truth
only from a vantage point outside of time — from a "God's eye view" — a
vantage point that no human being can occupy or even imagine. All descriptions of the world and all alleged political and moral principles are irreducibly
historical. The awesome variety of conflicting human opinions about the
whole cannot be transcended toward a universal knowledge. Fish's shorthand expression for this situation is "irreducible difference." Neither modern science nor liberal democracy represents the triumph of knowledge over
ignorance, enlightenment over prejudice; they represent instead a change of
radically controversial assumptions. More than this, Rorty and Fish agree
that liberalism, like modernism generally, is ultimately secular and deeply
suspicious of, if not hostile to, religion. But liberalism is no less based on a
radically contestable interpretation of the human situation for that reason
than is traditional religion. Such, they maintain, is the "insight" of antifoundationalism.

The disagreement between Rorty and Fish regarding the consequences of
this line of argument is serious and profound. The most obvious point of
disagreement between Rorty and Fish lies in the status of liberalism in light
of the antifoundationalist insight. Rorty believes that liberalism can divorce
itself from its rationalist origins and stand aloof from disputes over the status
of its foundations, just as it stands aloof from theological disputes. Rortian
liberalism continues to define for itself a limited sphere of political cognizance. Rorty believes that liberalism not only can survive the demise of rationalism, but that it is strengthened by it, since "ethnocentric" sentiments (the
true basis of liberalism) allow for greater liberal solidarity than an abstract
rationalist humanism ever could do. Moreover, neopragmatist indifference to
"matters of ultimate importance" (such as God, nature, and the highest hu-

man obligations) encourages an easygoing tolerance that is, to Rorty's mind, most suitable for liberal citizenship.

Fish, on the other hand, contends that the belief in the possibility of standing aloof from such disputes in the hope of managing or overcoming "irreducible difference" is precisely the hope of liberal rationalism. Liberalism must enter into the fray of such disputes in order to define its "limited" sphere of cognizance. But having entered into the fray, it no longer stands aloof and, revealed as the partisan agenda it is, can no longer lay claim to the name of liberalism. Once it is admitted that liberalism is, as Rorty puts it, "ethnocentric," the essential liberal aim of transcending and mediating deep moral and religious differences must be abandoned. Fish concludes that by its own self-understanding, "liberalism doesn't exist." He argues that the most basic liberal principles, such as free speech, the distinction between public and private (limited government), and above all the separation of church and state, depend upon an incoherent theoretical justification.

This leads us to another, less obvious, but more important disagreement: the consequences of the critique of rationalism for religious belief. Rorty understands his critique of rationalism to be an extension or deepening of the Enlightenment's critique of religion. Rorty accuses rationalism (including natural science) of a latent religiosity. The rationalist has merely substituted Reason or Nature for God — some superior nonhuman power before which human beings must bow. Antifoundationalism, according to Rorty, "de-divinizes" all of reality. It permits human beings not to worship or revere anything (including themselves or others), freeing them to creatively reshape "reality" according to their own ever-changing desires. Rorty (who identifies pragmatism with antifoundationalism) states that "the Enlightenment thought, rightly, that what would succeed religion would be better. The pragmatist is betting that what succeeds the 'scientific,' positivist culture which the Enlightenment produced will be better" (1982, xxxviii).

Fish's analysis cuts deeper. According to Fish, rationalism represents the failed attempt to transcend the need for faith, originally and most importantly religious faith. Fish's antifoundationalism does not necessarily revive religious faith, for we are not in control of what we believe. Yet it can help free religious conviction from its self-subordination before a supposedly "objective" reason, in both its modern scientific and liberal adjudicative forms. Put otherwise, recognition of the "fact" of the "irreducible difference" among worldviews offers no guidance whatsoever in revealing the "difference" to which one ought to be committed. Nothing, so to speak, can be ruled out — not even religious orthodoxy and theocracy — in light of the antifoundationalist critique.

The sections on Rorty and Fish are divided by a chapter on Rawls. This requires some explanation, since Rawls does not engage in an explicitly antifoundationalist or antirationalist critique, as Rorty and Fish do. Yet Rawls, especially in his recent doctrine of "political liberalism," has also left rationalism behind. Rawlsian liberalism does not claim to be grounded in reason, nor is it oriented toward rational enlightenment. Rawlsian liberalism is thus an episode in the demise of liberal rationalism. What is more, Rawls claims that the abandonment of political rationalism is necessary in order to embrace nonliberal religious believers in a framework of mutual toleration and respect. According to Rawls, it is Enlightenment liberalism's inability to deal fairly and reasonably with nonliberal religion that makes clear the need for non-"metaphysical" or merely "political" liberalism.

The chapter on Rawls ties together my treatment of Rorty and Fish in what some may find a surprising way. Rorty claims that Rawls's nonmetaphysical liberalism is in accord with his own antifoundationalist moral project. From Fish's point of view, however, Rawlsian liberalism, precisely in its attempt to stand neutrally above what Rorty calls "matters of ultimate importance," is the antithesis of antifoundationalism, which reveals that every opinion is embedded within some perspective on matters of ultimate importance. Fish's critique of Rawlsian neutrality is devastating. Yet the similarity between Rawls's doctrine and Rorty's antifoundationalism serves to reveal a hidden fatal difficulty with Fish's own antifoundationalism — its own metaphysical-theological neutrality. Liberal rationalism as it was originally understood was not neutral but presented a doctrine of natural right, which was supported by a decidedly nonneutral philosophic understanding of human nature, including moral and religious belief. Thus the critique of liberal neutrality does not constitute a decisive or fundamental critique of liberalism, as Fish supposes, but is at best preparation for such a critique.

# 2

PRAGMATISM, LIBERALISM,

AND THE QUARREL BETWEEN

SCIENCE AND RELIGION

Richard Rorty finds that "in our century, th[e] rationalist justification of the Enlightenment compromise [with religion] has been discredited" (1991a, 176). This "compromise" was found in the liberal toleration of religious belief; citizens were allowed to hold any religious beliefs whatever, so long as their beliefs were kept private. Liberals discovered that political society could get along well, indeed better than ever, if religion was kept separate from politics. This separation was made possible, it was believed, owing to the discovery of a more universal, natural, and therefore more solid basis for political society than religion — plagued by intractable and impassioned disagreement — could ever reasonably hope to provide. According to Rorty, the separation of church and state was thought to be justified by the claim that, despite our various accidental differences of faith, all human beings share a common rationality. This rational human essence was thought to "ensure that free and open discussion will produce 'one right answer' to moral as well as scientific questions." Today, however, "contemporary intellectuals" — from philosophers such as Heidegger, Gadamer, and Quine, to anthropologists and psychoanalysts — have collectively managed to "erase the picture common to Greek metaphysics, Christian theology, and Enlightenment rationalism: the picture of an ahistorical, natural center, the locus of human dignity, surrounded by an adventitious and inessential periphery" (1991a, 176). Reason was thought capable of transcending this "adventitious and inessential periphery," littered with the products of mere "cultural bias," which include "religion, myth, and tradition." Such was the Enlightenment's rationalist justification for pushing religion to the private sphere. Religion may perhaps be tolerated as "relevant to, and possibly essential for, individual perfection"; but it must nevertheless be considered "irrelevant to social order" since it is not "common to all human beings qua human be-ings" (175, 176).

The growing consensus among intellectuals today is that liberalism itself, like everything else human, is the product of a "cultural bias." Rorty agrees. We are "without a skyhook with which to escape from the ethnocentrism produced by acculturation" (1991a, 2). Liberal democracy does not transcend ethnocentrism; it is a form of ethnocentrism. Rorty remains devoted to the liberal democracy to which he was acculturated. Liberalism, however, is in need of updating in light of the new intellectual climate. The spreading loss of faith in Enlightenment rationalism could lead to a spreading loss of faith in liberalism, unless liberalism can be "redescribed" so as to make it appear consonant with the intellectual and spiritual tenor of the day.

Rorty takes as his model in this project of "redescription" John Dewey, who, in a different context, also saw the need to update liberal theory. Rorty's updating of liberalism follows (and is indeed often indistinguishable from) his updating of the American school of thought known as pragmatism. Rorty is known for tying together trends in Anglo-American philosophy with trends in Continental philosophy, highlighting common doubts in such thinkers as Quine, Davidson, Wittgenstein, Heidegger, and Derrida about Western phi-losophy's tradition of rationalism. Rorty, however, believes that his philoso-phy is, in its most important respects, a continuation of American pragma-tism, above all the philosophy of Dewey. He has had to defend this contention against an obvious objection. Dewey was a most enthusiastic proponent of science as the authoritative and objective guide of human life. For Dewey, the spread of the "scientific attitude" throughout society was crucial to the con-tinued progress of liberal democracy. Rorty, in contrast, denies that science is a "standard setting area of culture" (1991a, 162). Indeed, Rorty believes that "we need a redescription of liberalism as the hope that culture as a whole can be 'poeticized' rather than as the Enlightenment hope that it can be 'rational-ized' or 'scientized'" (1989, 53). According to Rorty, the notion of reason as a guide for life is "one of [the new pragmatism's] principal targets" (1991a, 62).

The theme of this chapter is Rorty's alteration of Deweyan pragmatism and its consequences, first for liberal democracy and second for what Rorty calls the warfare between science and theology. Rorty says that "the scientis-tic, method-worshiping side of Dewey, his constant exaltation of something called 'the scientific method,' was the unfortunate legacy of Dewey's youth, a youth spent worrying about the warfare between science and theology"

(1991a, 17). Rorty supposes that taking pragmatism in the direction he does marks a transcendence of the plane of that warfare — the plane of objective truth. If liberals can wean themselves from their concern for "objective truth" and such things as "inalienable rights," they may find that the human, all too human basis of liberalism is enough to win their admittedly contingent loyalty. In order to make clear the significance of Rorty's alteration of pragmatism, it is necessary to begin with a brief exposition of the place of science within Dewey's pragmatism.

### Dewey on Science and Liberal Democracy

Dewey, like Rorty, was deeply devoted to liberal democracy but found liberal rationalism to be in crisis. Unlike Rorty, Dewey understood the crisis of liberal rationalism to be a result of the progress of rationalism, including new scientific discoveries. (In Rorty's scheme, the very notion of scientific discovery or progress becomes unintelligible.) The most massive difficulty liberal rationalism faced in Dewey's estimation was the unbelievability of the liberal doctrine of natural right. Natural right had become unbelievable because the notion that there is a fixed human nature seemed to have been repudiated in natural science by Darwinism and in philosophy by Hegelian historicism. Darwinism revealed that species, as well as their specific needs, are continually evolving. Hegel revealed the extent to which all philosophies are products of their times. Dewey concluded that "the alleged unchangeableness of human nature cannot be admitted" (1939, 112). Moreover, "the views about human nature that are popular at a given time are usually derived from contemporary social currents" (113). Dewey recognized that these conclusions led to a crisis for liberalism:

> The old doctrine about human nature was . . . tied up with the ethical belief that political democracy is a moral right and that the laws upon which it is based are fundamental moral laws which every form of social organization should obey. If belief in natural rights and natural laws as the foundation of free government is surrendered, does the latter have any other moral basis? (1939, 5)

The fact that the crisis of liberal rationalism is in part the result of the progress of science was significant for Dewey, for he was not tempted to turn his back on rationalism on the basis of scientific, and therefore rational, discovery. The crisis, to Dewey's mind, was therefore not a crisis of rationalism as such, but only of rationalism as it applies to human things. Dewey claimed that modern physical science had from its inception turned its attention away from the permanent and universal and toward the changing and discreet.[1] But, until Darwin, "the gates of the garden of life were barred to the new ideas; and only through this garden was there access to the mind and politics" ([1910] 1965, 8). Thus political rationalism remained possible if it took natural science as its model. The human sciences should not focus on the eternal, which in truth is merely a fixation on past events. All science should be oriented toward the future, toward consequences, and concern itself with past events only as "the bases for organizing future observations" ([1931] 1963, 25). Science should focus "not upon the precedents but upon the possibilities of action" (24). Such a transformation of the human sciences would be "almost revolutionary in its consequences." For "an empiricism which is content with repeating facts already past has no place for possibility and for liberty" (24). We can say that, according to Dewey's analysis, the crisis of liberal rationalism was precipitated by adherence to outdated modes of scientific thinking, i.e. by pseudo-scientific, or unscientific, thinking. Dewey's solution to the crisis of liberal rationalism thus lay, not with the repudiation of rationalism as such (the path Rorty takes), but with the unprecedented advance of modern science into psychology and social and political science.[2]

The great ambition of Dewey's project will become clearer as we consider more closely how what he calls "classic Liberalism" went astray. Liberalism, according to Dewey, had ignored the crucial role of socialization, or education, in the formation of democratic citizens. Dewey associates "classic Liberalism" with "the theory of *laissez-faire* and the limitation of government to legal and police functions" ([1931] 1963, 278). Dewey is not opposing "individualism" with what we today would call "communitarianism." Instead, Dewey argues that liberalism has mistakenly assumed that individuals are liberated by simply removing governmental restraints on their thoughts and actions. This error is the result of the belief in a fixed human nature, which was assumed to be sufficient for democratic citizenship without further ado:

> The real fallacy lies in the notion that individuals have such a native or original endowment of rights, powers and wants that all that is required on the side of institutions and laws is to eliminate the obstructions they offer to the "free" play of the natural equipment of individuals. (281)

The result was a philosophy that "assisted the emancipation of individuals having a privileged antecedent status, but promoted no general liberation of all individuals." Thus economic reform was crucial, in Dewey's eyes, for the genuine development of liberal democracy. The economic fruits of the wondrous technology made possible by modern natural science were not yet widely accessible.

The Enlightenment unleashed enormous technological power, but it placed that power in the hands of human beings whose beliefs and attitudes had been molded by prescientific society. Dewey follows Rousseau in arguing that when the Enlightenment philosophers supposed they were describing human nature, they were really describing only the socially shaped characteristics of contemporary human beings. But Dewey does not follow Rousseau in the quest for the true, pristine, presocial human nature. Neither Rousseau nor the early liberals had yet seen the radical evolution of human nature. The human species has (or had) no pristine nature to discover. Following Bacon's prescription, the power to manipulate nature with a view to human purposes had been exercised to remarkable effect. But the belief in a fixed human nature meant that the power unleashed by science had not yet been applied in a thorough fashion to our essentially plastic human nature and political society. Dewey believed that when the apparent crisis of liberal rationalism was seen in the proper light, there was greater reason for hope than despair for the Enlightenment's emancipatory project. Not a scaling back of modern science was called for, but an unprecedented and wholesale advance.

In thus promoting the continued advance of science, Dewey was well aware that the burden of proof was on himself. Dewey was not simply naive in his hopes for science. Natural science — understood in a Baconian manner, as the human mastery of nature — was already, to be sure, well advanced: "The power over Nature which [Bacon] expected to follow the advance of science has come to pass" (1939, 141). But the success of Baconian science had had, Dewey confessed, the opposite effect of what Bacon intended. The effect of the advance of science had been only "to increase, instead of reduce, the power of Man over Man." In the face of massive political and economic oppression, to say nothing of a world war fought with unprecedentedly deadly weapons, the steadfast faith in the benevolent effect of an even further advance of science — in effect, a continuation of the belief in Enlightenment — ran the risk of being the height of naiveté or irresponsibility.

Awareness of this difficulty led Dewey to an apparently great qualification of his endorsement of modern science: "at least we know that the earlier optimism which thought that the advance of natural science was to dispel superstition, ignorance, and oppression, by placing reason on the throne, was unjustified" ([1931] 1963, 319). But to blame science for the ill effects its advance has wrought is as simple-minded as to place an overweening trust in it. Dewey states:

> To [blame science] is to mythologize; it is to personify science and impute to it a will and an energy on its own account. In truth science is impersonal; a method and a body of knowledge. It owes its operation and its consequences to the human beings who use it. It adapts itself passively to the purposes and desires which animate these human beings. It lends itself with equal partiality to the kindly offices of medicine and hygiene and the destructive deeds of war.

Science doesn't kill people; people kill people. For this reason, "it is silly to talk about [the] bankruptcy [of science], or to worship it as the usherer in of a new age." The blaming of science merely repeats, albeit in an opposite manner, the mistake of the Enlightenment. Both fail to recognize the essential neutrality of science. Science is essentially indifferent to its use for good or evil. The recognition of the "neutrality of science" is "the beginning of wisdom."

The neutrality of science, then, forms in the first place part of Dewey's apology on the behalf of science. But it also opens the possibility of a renewed, less naive, attachment to and hope for science. If science has in fact been used to increase oppression and the scale of warfare, and if science is "an instrument which is indifferent to the external uses to which it is put" ([1931] 1963, 320), then the possibility remains of using science for gains comparable in scale to the losses we have suffered through it.

But does such hope in the future use of science not appear foolish in the light of the historical facts, as Dewey himself presents them, which seem clearly to recommend the gravest doubts concerning the continued advance of modern science? If human beings and not science are to blame, is this any less reason to fear an advance in technological power? Do not the facts of human behavior precisely as modern science observes them speak against the possibility of the social progress Dewey hopes for?

It is here that the full significance of Dewey's disbelief that human nature is fixed and immutable begins to emerge. If human history is the authoritative tutor concerning human possibility, then Dewey's hopes for science would be radically unscientific, even antiscientific, not to say foolish. But because human nature evolves, the opportunity is open to human beings to master their own evolution. This would appear to mean that human beings are capable of jumping the evolutionary track, signaling a radical movement of pragmatism beyond Darwinism. Be that as it may, science, according to Dewey, has yet to affect the human soul so as to enable human beings to use the instrument of science for good. Dewey believed that it is "possible for the scientific attitude to become such a weighty and widespread constituent of culture that, through the medium of culture, it may shape human desires and purposes" (1939, 142). The alternative is too grim: "Denial that [desires] can be influenced by knowledge points emphatically to the non-rational and anti-rational forces that will form them" and have formed them from man's origins to the present (140):

> The entrenched and stubborn institutions of the past stand in the way of our thinking scientifically about human relations and social issues. Our mental habits in these respects are dominated by institutions of family, state, church, and business that were formed long before men had an effective technique of inquiry and validation. It is this condition from which we suffer to-day. Disaster follows in its wake. ([1931] 1963, 328–29)

The situation today is made urgent owing precisely to the merely partial progress of technology:

> It is impossible to overstate the mental confusion and the practical disorder which are bound to result when external and physical effects are planned and regulated, while attitudes of mind upon which the direction of external results depends are left to the medley of chance, tradition, and dogma. ([1931] 1963, 329)

Fortunately, Dewey assures us, "just as soon as we begin to use the knowledge and skills we have to control social consequences in the interest of shared abundant and secure life, we shall cease to complain of the backwardness of social knowledge."

Reason, then, is not yet on its throne. Reason can and must be the authoritative guide of human life. Dewey thus may be said to be one of the prime exemplars of the liberal rationalism Rorty claims has been thoroughly discredited. Dewey defined pragmatism as "the formation of a faith in intelligence, as the one and indispensable belief necessary to moral and social life" ([1931] 1963, 35). Dewey appears to have been so impressed with the power of technology that he believed modern science able to master any human problem — even the problems posed by the constitution of the human soul — if only it were faithfully applied. In the same essay in which he says that "it is silly to worship science as the usherer in of a new age," he writes:

> In spite, then, of all the record of the past, the great scientific revolution is still to come. It will ensue when men collectively organize their knowledge for application to achieve and make secure social values; when they systematically use scientific procedures for the control of human relationships and the direction of the social effects of our vast technological machinery. ([1931] 1963, 330)

The great scientific revolution will mean the correction of "[mankind's] halfway and accidental use of science."

This seems, however, only to beg the question concerning the fear of the advance of technology. Could not the manipulation of human attitudes and desires be used for either good or evil? If science is morally neutral, must not human beings undergo a moral transformation *prior* to their acquisition of still greater technological power in order to use it wisely? But that transformation, in Dewey's scheme, is supposed to be the *product* of advanced technological control. Dewey shows signs that he is aware of the potential danger: "A more adequate science of human nature might conceivably only multiply the agencies by which some human beings manipulate other human beings for their own advantage" (1939, 171). Grave though this danger is, no solution, or even full awareness of the problem, is available to us unless we continue on scientifically: "Improved science of human nature would put at our disposal means, now lacking, for defining the problem and working effectively for its solution" (171). Dewey does not, however, see siding with technological science as a dangerous gamble, though one worth taking. Dewey does not maintain consistently the moral neutrality of science: "Save as [an improved science of human nature] should reinforce respect for the morale of science, and thereby extend and deepen the incorporation of the attitudes which form the method of science into the disposition of individuals, it might add complications similar to those introduced by improved physical science" (171–72). The advance of science carries with it a moral advance, because the practice of science is characterized by a new morality: the scientific morale. If there is to be hope for the improvement of society, science must be capable of "the creation of new desires and new ends" ([1931] 1963, 147). Evidence that it can do so can be found in the "new morale" of "the great body of scientific inquirers."

What is the scientific morale? The new morale is marked by "fair-mindedness, intellectual integrity, . . . [the] will to subordinate personal preference to ascertained facts and to share with others what is found out" ([1931] 1963, 148). At present, the new morality — the scientific attitude — is a preserve of the band of natural scientists, which is small relative to society as a whole. The spread of science comes to mean, for Dewey, the spread of the "scientific attitude." While it is absurd to imagine that everyone could become a scientist proper, it is not absurd to hope that the scientific attitude could be extended to every human pursuit and disseminated into the culture generally. Hence we arrive at the importance of scientific education for Dewey.[3] By scientific education Dewey does not mean mere training in this or that special technical body of knowledge. Rather scientific education should feature the importance of scientific method as such for the achievement of the desired results in all pursuits, whatever they may be. Scientific method appears be the equivalent of, or at any rate the preparation for, the scientific attitude or morale. Scientific method is not only "the method of all effective mental approach and attack in all subjects" ([1931] 1963, 326). It is also "the chief means of developing the *right* mental attitudes" (my emphasis).

In particular, scientific training develops the right mental attitudes for democratic citizenship. Democratic citizenship requires fair-mindedness, integrity, cooperation, and the capacity to judge intelligently for oneself. The scientific attitude "is the sole guarantee against wholesale misleading by propaganda" (1939, 148–49). The alternative to citizens who "have their beliefs formed on the ground of evidence [and] procured by systematic and competent inquiry" is citizens who "should have them formed by habit, accidents of circumstance, propaganda, personal and class bias" (148).

### Religion and the Scientific Attitude

In order to receive some indication of the fate of religion in Deweyan liberalism, it is necessary to consider the scientific attitude toward religion.[4] Like his fellow pragmatist William James, Dewey was not antireligious (though to a considerably lesser extent than James) but wished rather to retain and emphasize those parts of religion that could survive modern science and be useful for the progress of democracy. This means, however, that religion is answerable, and therefore somehow subject, to science. The conflict between religion and science, Dewey claims, is the result of the fact that religions of the past have held doctrines concerning "matters of fact" in such areas as cosmology, history, and politics. But "with the advances of science in these fields [religion] has in consequence found itself involved in a series of conflicts, compromises, adjustments, and retreats" (1929, 303). The conflict between religion and science will be removed as religion "extricates itself from these unnecessary intellectual commitments" (303). The conflict can be removed, in other words, if religion surrenders wholly to science on "matters of fact," including existence (304). Dewey's terms of surrender are uncompromising: the "religious attitude would surrender once for all commitment to beliefs about matters of fact, whether physical, social or metaphysical. Nor would it substitute in their place fixed beliefs about values, save the one value of the worth of discovering the possibilities of the actual and striving to realize them" (304).

Thus religion must surrender moral supremacy as well to science. Dewey asserts that "the course of religion in its entire sweep [is] marked by practices that are shameful in their cruelty and lustfulness, and by beliefs that are degrading and intellectually incredible" (1934, 5–6). The cause of religion's shameful record is mankind's lack of practical science: "What else than what we find could be expected, in the case of people having little knowledge and no secure method of knowing; with primitive institutions, and so little control of natural forces that they lived in a constant state of fear?" (6). The rise of science, however, means an ever greater familiarity with natural regularities, and therewith an ever greater power to secure our safety and (all) other objects of our desires. Technology removes the need for such fantastic and desperate faiths as those exhibited in the unscientific religions. Dewey proposes the "disposal of outgrown traits of past religions." Above all this means that "there is nothing left worth preserving in the notions of unseen powers controlling human destiny to which obedience, reverence, and worship are due" (7).

It may seem that Dewey empties religion of all content. What is to be preserved in religion, however, is by no means trivial, from Dewey's point of view: "the union of ideal and actual," which is "operative in thought and action" (1934, 52). This union points, as we indicated above, to the one human value Dewey is willing to call fixed: the "value of the worth of discovering the possibilities of the actual and striving to realize them" (1929, 304). It points, in other words, to the most effective means of realizing human ideals: science. Dewey, however, is much more committed to the scientific character of the highest human activities than to their religious character: "Whether one gives the name 'God' to this union . . . is a matter for individual choice" (1934, 52). But whatever one's choice of names, there should be no mistake: there is "nothing mystical about [this union]; it is natural and moral." In fact, Dewey warns, "there is . . . a danger that resort to mystical experiences will be an escape, and that its result will be the passive feeling that the union of actual and ideal is already accomplished"; and Dewey appears sure that "the union of the actual and the ideal" is not accomplished in "mystical experience" (52). Dewey is concerned that "the associations of the term with the supernatural are so numerous and close that any use of the word 'God' is sure to give rise to misconception and be taken as a concession to traditional ideas" (51). Yet "use of the words 'God' or 'divine' may protect man from a sense of isolation and from consequent despair or defiance" (53).[5]

By Dewey's own account, however, there may be reasonable cause for modern human beings to despair. He certainly cannot be said to have put to rest all reasonable doubts about the capacity of social science to fulfill the deepest human longings or to solve the other enormous problems facing modern society. Dewey thus may easily fail to put us at ease respecting the continued advance of modernity. Dewey's contention, however, is that our *only* hope for satisfying our longings lies with science — not just any science, but specifically social scientific technology — "social engineering." How could Dewey reach this conclusion? Because the success of Deweyan science lies in its capacity to bring about future results, the ultimate goodness of science must be said to rest in faith, but it is a faith chosen with open eyes, based on the preponderant evidence. Recall Dewey's definition of pragmatism as "the formation of a faith in intelligence, as the one and indispensable belief necessary to moral and social life" ([1931] 1963, 35). As a result of the undeniable successes of modern natural science, scientific method had demonstrated itself to be the only sure way to knowledge in *all* areas. Any proposition not arrived at scientifically must be viewed with profound skepticism. The "new methods of inquiry and reflection have become for the educated man today the final arbiter of all questions of fact, existence, and intellectual assent" (1934, 31).

Evidence of the intellectual dominance of scientific method can be found in the fact that even many "religionists are moved by the rise of scientific method in other fields," and try to "affirm that they are as good empiricists as anybody else — indeed, as good as the scientists themselves" (1934, 11). Since "scientists rely upon certain kinds of experience of certain kinds of objects, so the religionists rely upon a certain kind of experience to prove the existence of the object of religion, especially the supreme object, God."[6] This means, however, that "the educated man today" may not agree that religion has been refuted by science concerning God's being and God's interaction with human beings; nor may he agree, therefore, with Dewey's scientific program. Having been deeply impressed by scientific method does not preclude continued belief in what Dewey calls the supernatural. Dewey himself does not deny the reality of "mystical experiences." Indeed, he admits that among human beings such experiences "occur so frequently that they may be regarded as normal manifestations that take place at certain rhythmic points in the movement of experience" (37).

Dewey refrains from calling mystical experiences natural: as we saw above, he distinguishes the mystical from the natural and moral. He does not mean thereby to suggest that their cause is supernatural. On the contrary, when mystical experiences are considered in terms of the natural versus the supernatural, Dewey shows no openness to the possibility that their true cause is anything other than natural. Indeed, he appears to admit the remarkable possibility that the scientist, or unbeliever, may have mystical experiences. Conversion to the scientific attitude does not, in Dewey's view, remove the disposition to mystical experience. This admission allows Dewey to state that "the assumption that denial of a particular interpretation of th[e] objective content [of mystical experiences] proves that those who make the denial do not have the experience in question, so that if they had it they would be equally persuaded of its objective source in the presence of God, has no foundation in fact" (1934, 37). If the scientist were to have a mystical experience, he would not rush to attribute it to some supernatural source. He would, we are led to believe, calmly and curiously set out to analyze it. "As with every empirical phenomenon, the occurrence of the state called mystical is simply an occasion for inquiry into its mode of causation" (37). Dewey thus denies that mystical experience ("revelation") itself proves anything. The mystic may suppose he hears the voice of a god. But this is the mystic's own dubious interpretation imposed on a more basic, nebulous experience. His experience in itself is only a "complex of conditions." Dewey asserts: "The particular interpretation given to this complex of conditions is not inherent in the experience itself. It is derived from the culture with which a particular person has been imbued. A fatalist will give one name to it; a Christian Scientist another, and the one who rejects all supernatural being still another" (1934, 13). We might add that the one who asserts that every interpretation is a product of culture, i.e. of merely human origin, is among those who reject all supernatural being. Does this mean that the scientific interpretation of "mystical experience" is the product of a prior assumption?

Science, however, would appear to distinguish itself precisely in the fact that it does not rush to explanations of phenomena but instead examines them methodically, or at any rate attentively, open to what truly is. In Dewey's view, the scientist is distinguished from the unscientific mystic by the fact that the latter's "interpretations have not grown from the experience itself with the aid of such scientific resources as may be available. They have been imported by borrowing without criticism from ideas that are current in the surrounding culture" (36). But how has Dewey distinguished "the experience itself" from the mystic's interpretation of it? Is not excluding all specific content from the experience, reducing it to a vaguely mystical experience, already to exercise an interpretation? It seems that the mystical experience as Dewey describes it is not the experience itself prior to interpretation, but the product of an interpretation.

Is the scientific interpretation the correct interpretation? Dewey admits that the true cause of mystical experiences has not yet been scientifically laid bare. Yet given all that science has shown us about geology, astronomy, and chemistry, and given that modern psychology is in its infancy, "he is bold to the point of rashness who asserts that intimate personal experience will never come within the ken of natural knowledge" (1934, 35).[7] By admitting in this way that the matter is unsettled, however, Dewey thus runs the risk of abandoning science's principle of attentiveness to things as they are and of turning science into a dogmatic naturalism, or at any rate a faith in the scientific progress of future generations. The true cause of "mystical experience" remains a loose end for science. But this is not just any loose end — the very possibility of science and, more importantly, the supremacy of a life guided by reason depend upon our understanding of it. In short, the validity of pragmatism as Dewey understands it depends upon its capacity to understand, and not simply dismiss as Dewey comes too close to doing, "mystical experiences." James's treatment of religion in *The Varieties of Religious Experience* reveals the extent to which religion remains a unsettled question for pragmatism.[8]

Dewey himself seems to admit that the matter is *radically* unsettled in a comment on James's "theory of the will to believe," or the "right to believe," which Dewey describes as "a new advance in Pragmatism" ([1931] 1963, 21). Dewey writes that James "maintained the thesis that the greater part of philosophic problems and especially those which touch on religious fields are of such a nature that they are not susceptible of decisive evidence one way or the other. Consequently he claimed the right of a man to choose his beliefs not only in the presence of proofs or conclusive facts, but also in the absence of all such proof" (21–22). Dewey denies that this means that we may believe in the face of proof to the contrary. Rather, James means that "it may be that, in order to discover the proofs which will ultimately be the intellectual justification of certain beliefs — the belief in freedom, for example, or the belief in God — it is necessary to begin to act in accordance with this belief" (22). What course of action, then, does pragmatism demand? Might it not demand obedience, and thus the abandonment of science and the perhaps hubristic attempt to master creation?

Rather than attempt to tackle pragmatism's difficulty with religion head on, Dewey dodged it. Indeed, Dewey's reconception of rationalism seems to demand that he do so. As we have already seen, Dewey means to turn the attention of philosophy from the fixed to the changing. This means, according to Dewey, a turn away from concern with first or final causes and toward concern with "secondary" causes, away from the "unknowable absolute" and toward the "specific values of particular truth" ([1910] 1965, 16, 14). He states that "the displacing of this wholesale type of philosophy [of first and final causes] will doubtless not arrive by sheer logical disproof, but rather by growing recognition of its futility" (16). Pragmatism is not a different approach to the old questions (metaphysics/theology), in the manner of Socrates' famous "second sailing" (see *Phaedo* 99c–d and context). "Old questions are solved by disappearing, evaporating"; which is to say that "we do not solve them: we get over them" (19). Pragmatism turns our attention away from the eternal and toward the future.

But can the truth concerning "first causes" (indifference to which Rorty will radicalize) be thought of no practical importance unless the competing possibilities have somehow been limited? Must not even a pragmatic indifference to first causes depend upon some confidence that the difference between possible first causes makes no practical difference for human life? Even from the perspective of pragmatism — from the moral and pragmatic concern for practical consequences — the eternal remains important. Dewey states that James sought to show that philosophic questions can "have a real importance for mankind, because the beliefs which they bring into play lead to very different modes of conduct" ([1931] 1963, 19). For the pragmatist, "God . . . has the meaning of a power concerned with assuring the triumph of ideal and spiritual values."

This, however, is precisely what Dewey wants to avoid: leaving our future well-being to invisible powers. To do so would mean that human intelligence relinquishes control: "As long as mankind suffered from this impotency [a confession of the inability to master the course of things that specifically concern us], it naturally shifted a burden of responsibility that it could not carry over to the more competent shoulders of the transcendent cause" ([1910] 1965, 17).[9] The cause of science is ultimately the cause of human responsibility. This suggests, however, that Dewey's attachment to science is at bottom moral rather than scientific. Be that as it may, this message of ultimate human responsibility appears to be central to the "right mental attitude" represented by scientific method and toward which liberal public education should be directed. Democratic self-governance and liberty mean that citizens at large self-consciously guide their own lives by the light of their own reason. Thus, while Deweyan science is neutral, in the sense that it yields the same results to persons with different purposes and moral intentions, it is not neutral to the question of human versus divine authority. Human beings must become keenly aware of the limitations of human knowledge (no eternal truths or revelation); nevertheless, the human intellect alone is or must be authoritative for guiding human life.

That, ultimately, is the meaning for Dewey of liberty and thus of liberalism. As we saw above, the *laissez-faire* state that leaves its citizens as they are may well be leaving them to their mental or economic enslavement. What, then, becomes of religious liberty in Deweyan liberalism? Might not leaving religions to themselves mean leaving the minds of citizens enslaved to tradition, dogma, or priests? Does not the spread of the scientific attitude throughout society require breaking the hold of the various religions in society? Although this does seem to be Dewey's ultimate intention or hope, the means by which science spreads through the culture must be consistent with the scientific attitude itself. This means that "the open air of public discussion and communication is an indispensable condition of the birth of ideas and knowledge and of the growth of health and vigor" ([1931] 1963, 297). Religious freedom thus appears to remain intact; but religion cannot be said to be cherished, as Stephen Carter would have it, by Deweyan liberalism. However that may be, Dewey's suspicions concerning religion are with a view to the "possibility of freedom [that] is grounded in our very beings" (297). Notwithstanding Dewey's doubts concerning the permanence of human nature, liberal democracy appears to remain *the* perfection of human political society for all time. For according to Dewey liberal democracy represents "ideal aims and values to be realized — aims which, although ideal, are not located in the clouds but are backed by something deep and indestructible in the needs and demands of humankind" (1939, 156).

### Rorty's Critique of Dewey

In the Introduction to *Objectivity, Relativism, and Truth,* Rorty states: "As I have repeatedly suggested, I view the position developed in these essays as continuous with Dewey's — the figure who, in the decade since I wrote *Philosophy and the Mirror of Nature,* has, in my imagination, gradually eclipsed Wittgenstein and Heidegger" (1991a, 16). He notes Dewey's "somewhat different account of the relation of natural science to the rest of culture" but comments that he does not see this difference "as very great." Elsewhere, he states that "Dewey overdid the attempt to make the natural scientist a model for the rest of culture" (1986, xviii). In *Contingency, Irony, and Solidarity,* he goes further, suggesting that the "ideally liberal polity would be one whose culture hero is [Harold] Bloom's 'strong poet' rather than the warrior, the priest, the sage, or the truth-seeking, 'logical,' 'objective' scientist" (1989, 53). In "Pragmatism without Method," he goes so far as to refer to his own brand of pragmatism as "anti-scientific" (1991a, 66).

On the surface, the difference between Rorty's and Dewey's pragmatisms is enormous. There is perhaps no more important concept for Dewey than scientific method. Sidney Hook states that "the heart of Dewey's social philosophy is the proposal to substitute for the existing modes of social authority the authority of scientific method" ([1939] 1995, 151). David Fott goes so far as to say that faith in scientific method was "Dewey's fundamental conviction" (1991, 39). It was on scientific method that Dewey pinned his hopes for the future of democracy. Moreover, for Dewey scientific method may be said to be the perfection of human experience, combining the most effective practice with the most authentic manner of knowing. Science was both the supreme means for bringing into being the moral ideal and somehow a central part of that ideal itself. As Gary Bullert puts it, "Dewey maintained an unyielding commitment to scientific intelligence as an instrument that could remedy humankind's material insecurity and its spiritual homelessness" (1983, 9). Rorty rejects nearly all of this while claiming to continue Dewey's work in its essentials. But yet, if one takes scientific method away from Dewey, what is left?

In Rorty's view, the "constant exaltation" of scientific method by Dewey represents one of two conflicting tendencies in his thought and in early pragmatism generally (1991a, 63–64). One tendency is toward a "fuzzy" experimentalism, where the governing concern is not with finding the theoretically objective truth for all time but only with finding what works practically in the situation at hand. The other tendency, the one represented by scientific method, is toward securing rigorous and objective theory. "From a theoretical angle," Rorty explains, "this tension can be viewed as a special case of the tension between pragmatism's conception of inquiry (in any sphere, not just in philosophy) as a response to particular historical circumstances, and the traditional conception of inquiry as the discovery of eternal 'objective' truths" (1986, x). According to Rorty, however, it is "the pragmatist claim that beliefs are rules for action, to be judged in terms of their effectiveness in resolving problems" (x). Rorty means here practical, not theoretical, problems. There are, at bottom, no theoretical problems. (Rorty thus is speaking loosely when he speaks of approaching the tension in Dewey's thought "from a theoretical angle," and of "a theoretical solution to [Dewey's] theoretical problem.")

Sometimes Dewey presents himself as a social reformer who was simply responding to concrete situations with concrete solutions. "At other times, however," Rorty observes, "Dewey writes as if there were some neutral, more or less professional, ground which he occupies in his capacity as philosopher or psychologist, rather than as social critic" (1986, xii). But, while Dewey did argue against the distinction between, or at any rate the radical separation of, theory and social action, he frequently slipped back into imagining that he was uncovering timeless universal truths. The principal example of this backsliding is "his constant exaltation of something called 'the scientific method'" (1991a, 17). According to Rorty, Dewey starts down the right track, the track that will lead Rorty away from science and toward esthetics, away from "critical inquiry" and toward "creative redescription." Rorty asserts, however, that Dewey's commitment to scientific method is the product of the continuing intellectual dominance of the idea of objective theory in Dewey's day. Dewey's "scientism" lies in a blind spot from the point of view of the innovative heart of pragmatism: the analysis of thought in terms of its practical results rather than in terms of its theoretical propositions. Dewey used this insight to criticize many errors of his day, but he failed to apply it comprehensively, even to his own thinking. Rorty grants, however, that Dewey, "like all of us, . . . could not question all his beliefs at once" (1986, xvii–xviii).

The potential tension in Dewey's thought that Rorty identifies is between pragmatism as (1) what works here and now and as (2) objective theory. We can approach the matter in a Platonic, and therefore un-Rortian, way by asking if a lie might not at times prove useful. Plato teaches that all political societies, even the best, depend on a lie. What "works" morally and politically is not necessarily what is true. Rorty asks, if something "works" morally and politically for us here and now, why should we care if it is true in some ahistorical or objective sense? Why should we not be content to call true what "works"? Thus, Rorty believes, pragmatism can retain its most distinctive characteristic of defining "truth" in terms of what "works," while abandoning Dewey's concern for objective science.

Rorty's critique of Dewey indicates a loss of faith in the capacity of science, or reason, to satisfy humankind's deepest needs. Rorty appears to suggest that Dewey's faith in science was indeed naive. Liberalism cannot meet the deepest human needs, which differ profoundly from society to society and age to age. What liberals call "tyranny" is only tyranny from a culturally biased perspective. One people's tyranny is another people's liberty. Moreover "science," both natural and social, is not the powerful tool Dewey thought it was. Rorty admits that there is in the United States a spirit of "unease." That unease, however, is

> just the result of running up against some unpleasant, stubborn, merely material facts. For example: that this has not turned out to be the American Century, that the "American moment in world history" may have passed, that democracy may not spread around the world, [and] that we do not know how to mitigate the misery and hopelessness in which half of our fellow humans (including a fifth of our fellow citizens) live. (1988, 33)

Rorty tries to play down the significance of giving up on liberalism's rationality and universality by claiming that it need not lead to "the 'deep spiritual malaise' of which we have been hearing so much lately." Amazingly, he identifies his nonchalance regarding the failure of liberalism's promise as Deweyan: "Deweyans suspect that we Americans are not suffering from anything deeper or more spiritual than having bitten off more than we turned out to be able to chew" (33).[10]

Biting off more than we can chew, however, means for Rorty not just failing to enlighten the rest of the world but failing to enlighten ourselves, as well as failing even to make sense of what "enlightenment" means. Thus, in Rorty's view, Dewey's insistence on the fundamental difference between, on the one hand, governing one's own life in full awareness of one's needs and capacities and, on the other hand, blindly following tradition, dogma, or the specious rhetoric of a demagogue, cannot be maintained. There is no "guarantee against wholesale misleading by propaganda" (Dewey 1939, 149), for there is no difference between rational or wise counsel and propaganda. Liberals, according to Rorty, cannot enlighten (or be enlightened); they can only make liberalism look good. Ultimately "one cannot confirm or disconfirm, argue for or against" a "truth-value candidate"; "one can only savor it or spit it out" (1989, 18). It is hard to imagine Dewey finding this a salutary doctrine for a self-governing people. Must not the people be taught the value of rigorous, critical analysis if they are to avoid falling under the spell of those who would usurp their sovereignty? Must not the people insist on seeing the facts for themselves, facts that only the scientific attitude can guarantee will not be obscured?

Rorty disputes that there are "facts" as Dewey thought of them. Dewey, as we observed above, defended science as neutral, as offering the same facts to persons with profoundly different concerns. Rorty seeks to subordinate theory to practice more radically than Dewey had done, by denying that such neutral knowledge is possible. Human concerns, Rorty argues, fundamentally shape what the "facts" are. Scientific "facts" are not objective discoveries but the products of the essentially prescientific, or moral, concerns of the scientist. Persons with different morals or concerns will find different "facts."

Rorty is not convincing, however, in his portrayal of Dewey as one who simply lost sight of the problem of knowledge of eternal truths when he promoted scientific method. For Rorty does not do justice to the fact that method was intended by Dewey to solve scientifically the problem posed by the mutability of nature, i.e. the fact that there are no scientifically discernible eternal truths. Science for Dewey meant *method,* over any possible conclusions that might result from that method or any particular subject-matter. Scientific method was not concerned with identifying immutable truth but rather with gathering data to use experimentally for some purpose. Method was the only means to approach objective knowledge. But, for Dewey, truth need not be eternal in order to be objective. At no point were scientific conclusions to be accepted as finally authoritative. Only the claims of modern science deserve trust, but even they are not to be "hypostatized." To hypostatize even scientific conclusions is contrary to the permanent and principled openness of scientific method. Thus only scientific method scrupulously avoids any manner of supernaturalism, which would lift some "facts" above the radical flux of nature. In the end, what is true remains for Dewey, as for Rorty, what works. But we can only be confident of what works through careful, methodical, and repeated experimentation. (Dewey may well have been wary of Rorty's "fuzzy" experimentalism.) Scientific method is intended to avoid hypostatization while anchoring human action to nature, which, though fluid, is sufficiently sure relative to the wild fancies of the unscientific.[11]

But while Rorty ignores this fundamental aspect of Deweyan method, Dewey remains vulnerable to the main thrust of Rorty's critique: the difficulty science has in establishing itself as the correct interpreter of reality, or as the true perception of what is, or of the "facts." To return to the example of "mystical experience," how could the scientist ever show that the scientific interpretation of such experiences is the correct one, except to those already predisposed to accept the scientific interpretation? Rorty contends that Dewey has recourse to no demonstration that is not circular, that does not presuppose a natural cause and exclude the alternative interpretation of the "mystic." Straying from Rorty's line of critique, one may ask how the scientist can know that he is not blind to what the "mystic" sees clearly. Rorty, who has given up on objective knowledge, may be willing to say that "there are . . . cases in which the other person's, or culture's, explanation of what it's up to is so primitive, or so nutty, that we brush it aside" (1982, 200). But can Dewey as a man of science — indeed, as a human being — so easily brush aside the possible significance for human life of what he admits is an extremely common human phenomenon?

This, however, is just the sort of question Rorty wants to get away from. Rorty does receive encouragement in his indifference, it must be admitted, from Dewey's hope that our concern for the eternal will disappear.[12] Rorty supposes that it is only those who have not sufficiently outgrown religion who are drawn to insist that science be objective, rigorous, and methodical, lest we become tempted to return to the old authorities. Recall Rorty's comment that "the scientistic, method-worshiping side of Dewey, his constant exaltation of something called 'the scientific method,' was an unfortunate legacy of Dewey's youth, a youth spent worrying about the warfare between science and theology" (1991a, 17). If we are no longer haunted by the old authorities, if we can simply no longer take them seriously, then we need no longer cling to and be entrapped by "scientific method." If we can truly liberate ourselves from theology, we need no longer cling to science. Moreover, we need not be so overawed as Dewey was by science's success. Rorty contends that "science doesn't have a reason of success . . . there is no metaphysical or epistemological or transcendental explanation of why Galileo's vocabulary has worked well so far, any more than there is an explanation of why the vocabulary of liberal democracy has worked so well so far. . . . [Galileo] just lucked out" (1982, 192, 193).

According to Rorty, there is no point in trying to describe "method" — how we should proceed in future, unpredictable circumstances — in precise terms. One's attention should be not on getting the method right but on the problem at hand. This, according to Rorty, is the guiding idea of pragmatism. A variety of problems will call for a variety of "methods," which need not be scientific. Dewey himself, Rorty claims, was partially aware of this situation. Rorty points out that, alongside his praise of scientific method, Dewey sometimes warned against the "overconscious formulation of methods of procedure" (quoted in Rorty 1986, xiv, n. 8). Such comments reveal Dewey's own tendency toward what Rorty calls "anti-method." Rorty describes Dewey's predicament thus: "Dewey wants to praise certain ways of thinking which he thinks have become more common since the seventeenth century, but he cannot specify these ways too narrowly, for fear of erecting an abstract formalism as constrictive as any of those erected by his more 'rationalistic' predecessors" (xiv).[13]

Rorty's route out of this impasse is "science without method," or "pragmatism without method." "Method" will take care of itself as people grapple with sticky practical problems. The best anyone can do is to muddle through. But this means that people need not, and indeed ought not, think of "method" at all. Avoiding defining "epistemic principles" too narrowly is what Rorty means above all when he calls for "pragmatism without method." "It may be helpful," Rorty writes, "and sometimes has been helpful, to formulate such principles. It is often, however — as in the cases of Descartes' *Discourse* and Mill's 'inductive methods' — a waste of time" (1991a, 67). Rorty promotes a view of the epistemic principles of science that he calls (using a term coined by a critic) "the new fuzziness." There is no reason to devote oneself to a specific method if that method is of little or no use in a particular circumstance. The same reason that led Dewey to value experimental thinking itself over any possible set of conclusions resulting from that thinking leads Rorty to reject the supremacy of scientific thinking. Experimental thinking will not permit itself to be reified into method, since "method" is one of the chief things that must be subject to experimentation.[14] But what of Dewey's basic contrast of the methodical, empirical, reflective thinking of the scientist with thinking dependent on "tradition, instruction, imitation," or, in a word, "prejudice" (Rorty 1986, xvi)? Rorty is not impressed with that distinction, which may reveal how much of rationalism he takes for granted. Everyone's thinking is shaped by tradition, instruction, and imitation, Rorty argues. As for scientists, "they use the same banal and obvious methods all of us use in every human activity" (1982, 193).

### Rorty, Hook, and the Quarrel over the Legacy of Pragmatism

The "new fuzziness" is not, then, simply a correction of how science should proceed, one that nevertheless seeks to preserve science's epistemic supremacy. Rorty denies that science enjoys any epistemic supremacy whatever. Rorty's most radical break from Dewey comes with this denial. Rorty points toward what is at stake here in a criticism of the pragmatism of Sidney Hook. Hook continued to insist that the supremacy of science, especially vis-à-vis theology, is crucial to the true legacy of pragmatism. Rorty quotes Hook:

> Science and theology represent two different attitudes toward the mysterious: one tries to solve mysteries, the other worships them. The first believes mysteries may be made less mysterious even though they are not cleared up, and admits there will always be mysteries. The second believes that some mysteries are final. (quoted at 1991a, 66)

Science, Hook claims, weighs evidence and therefore can offer truths, whereas religion can only offer comforts.

Rorty counters by arguing that "anything can, by suitably reweaving the web of belief, be fitted either into an anti-naturalistic worldview in which Divine Providence is a central element *or* into a naturalistic worldview in which people are on their own" (1991a, 66).[15] To say this, he continues, is to side with William James in claiming that "'evidence' is not a very useful notion when trying to decide what one thinks of the world as a whole." Contrary to the hopes of Dewey and Hook, science is not uniquely anchored to what is real.

Moreover, pragmatism is in no position to look down its nose at those who seek comfort rather than objective truth. For once one has conceded that what works is true, we must ask: works for what? If Rorty's answer is that what comforts is what works, then he will conclude that what comforts is true. We can thus see, on Rorty's own terms, the possibility of an apology for belief in divine providence. Rorty contends that we should proceed "without much reference to" the distinction "between 'truth' and 'comfort'" (1991a, 76).

One is forced to note that in the context of Rorty's critique of Hook, the conclusion that all we have to go by is what comforts, or promises comfort, though we can never know if what promises comfort is true, may itself seem a harsh, discomforting truth. Rorty concludes his essay on Hook by claiming to be discouraging us from "falling back" into the "hope" of getting "right down to the things themselves, stripping away opinion and convention and the contingencies of history," while encouraging us to turn to "detailed, particular dangers" (1991a, 77). Rorty appears to be exhorting us to resist the false comfort promised by objective knowledge and to steel ourselves for facing our true problems. But what sense could Rorty give to a *false* comfort? And why should Rorty the pragmatist seek to turn away from or suppress the desire underlying the hope of transcending mere opinion and convention?

For his own part, Rorty does not appear to see any relation between religion and detailed, particular dangers. But this does not prevent him from adopting a "laissez-faire attitude that sees religion and science as alternative ways of solving life's problems, to be distinguished by success or failure, rather than rationality or irrationality" (1991a, 66). (Rorty does not explain what rational failure and irrational success might mean.) One of life's problems, however, is death — what it is, what follows it, and how to live in light of the possible answers to the first two questions. How could a "laissez-faire attitude" determine the "success" of a religion in addressing the particular dangers and comforts associated with death? If comfort is our only guide, does not divine providence or the promise of a resolution after death offer more comfort than "a naturalistic worldview in which people are on their own" (66)? Can we judge such "success" on the basis of what is evident in the world around us? Despite Rorty's attempt to redefine "truth," it is still meaningful to say that belief in divine providence may comfort without being true. The comfort of such a belief depends on the hope that it is true, not merely comforting. As we will see below, Rorty in fact does not adopt a laissez-faire attitude toward religion but is a committed partisan of a "culture of liberalism [that] would be enlightened, secular, through and through," one in which "no trace of divinity remained" (1989, 45). Rorty's critique of scientistic pragmatism, however, leads one to wonder how such a thoroughly secular program can be maintained.

Hook, in the name of scientistic secularism, had criticized Heidegger for "really asking theological questions" and promoting "a mystical doctrine" (quoted at Rorty 1991a, 72), and Paul Tillich for his explicitly theological treatment of Heideggerian themes. Rorty points out that Hook also wishes to promote pragmatism's fuzzy experimentalism with respect to morals and politics. Yet he wishes to do so while drawing a sharp line so as to exclude anything resembling theology. Rorty demurs:

> I doubt that this can be done. If we stretch [this fuzziness] as far as morals and politics, then we shall have to cover cases in which we are not choosing between alternative hypotheses about what will get us what we want, but between descriptions of what we want, of what the problem is, of what the materials to hand are. (68)

Rorty's broadmindedness extends as far as a somewhat patronizing toleration of the need of Tillich and Dewey to continue to speak of God "even after they had given up on supernaturalism" (70). Rorty sees their theological language, however, as "a rhetorical blemish, a misleading way of getting one's point across" (71). Theological language is misleading, it seems, because it connotes supernaturalism; and Rorty's new fuzziness cannot go so far as to blur the line between the secular and the supernatural.

But Rorty seems to be faced with precisely the same difficulty with which he confronted Hook. If what we want, what the problem is, and what the materials to hand are, all remain up in the air, how can Rorty open the door to Tillich but not to Calvin, Maimonides, and Muhammad?

Rorty, it must be underscored, wishes to avoid supernaturalism no less than Hook and Dewey. But Rorty's radicalization of pragmatism into a variety of postmodernism only exacerbates the difficulties faced by Dewey and Hook. Rorty's critique of science makes his own stand against supernaturalism deeply problematic. Dewey can still speak of our "knowledge about nature" (1929, 44). Nature for Rorty, on the other hand, is almost entirely eclipsed. Nature is replaced by "naturalism," or "physicalism," which is only a useful interpretation for some purposes. For that reason, the role of naturalism in Rorty's thought becomes as marginal as the role of science. The centrality of scientific inquiry into nature for Dewey is replaced in Rorty by the "web of belief" — that is, by man — which refers not to nature but only, or almost only, to itself. But Rorty's web of belief is even less capable than Dewey's scientism of establishing its own true secularism and of confirming that such a secularism is truly pragmatic and not the greatest folly.

# 3

## RORTY'S
## REPUDIATION OF
## EPISTEMOLOGY

Near the beginning of Plato's *Theaetetus*, Socrates shows the young Theaetetus that he is ignorant of just what knowledge (*epistēmē*, science) is. Socrates admits that he himself is unwise in this matter (150c–d). In the fashion typical of the Platonic dialogues, the puzzles multiply as the dialogue progresses, and we never find the answer to the question "what is knowledge?" The dialogue ends with Socrates suggesting that they all return the next day to continue the investigation. The perplexity about what it is to know aroused by Rorty's critique of epistemology is not altogether different from that aroused by the *Theaetetus*. But whereas the Platonic dialogue "problematizes" knowledge with a view to awakening us to our need to inquire further (our ignorance is a lack), Rorty "problematizes" knowledge with a view to denying that such a need exists. Rorty does not invite us to return the next day to inquire further; he invites us only to hear again about the futility of such inquiry. But how do we know that the *conclusion* Rorty draws from his problematization of knowledge is warranted and not simply the testimony of a frustrated misologist of the sort Socrates describes in the *Phaedo* (90b–d)? If warranted, would that conclusion itself not signal a theoretical discovery of enormous magnitude?

Epistemology is indeed a dark and difficult subject. My purpose in this chapter is not to solve the puzzles that Rorty raises but rather to argue that Rorty does not show that epistemology addresses "pseudo-problems." Indeed, Rorty at his best awakens us to some important problems facing epistemology. I would argue, however, that Rorty's questions are not radical enough. He does his best to make sure that the consequences of the failure of epistemology (a failure, assuming Rorty's conclusion is correct) are "safe" ones — safe from any serious challenge to his easygoing neopragmatist moralism. But the trajectory of his own critique, I will argue, threatens that "safety."

Specifically, Rorty concludes from the critique of science (epistemology) that science and religion (i.e., all religions) are "epistemologically on a par." It seems that Rorty hopes that the critique of science is made "safe" from a renewed challenge from religion by the fact that the believer too, as a human being, is subject to the same radical limitations respecting knowledge. Such an argument, however, would itself depend on an epistemology, i.e., on a clear understanding of just what knowledge is for human beings as such. Rorty denies that he is offering such an epistemology, or that one is possible. Moreover, not all alleged religious knowledge purports to be *epistēmē*. Rorty's conclusion that science and religion are on a par with respect to knowledge of "ultimate reality" is not warranted unless *epistēmē* is the only valid form of human knowledge, which is certainly not a Rortian thesis.

Rorty hopes that his critique of epistemology will bring to an end the very raising of the questions over which the struggle between science and theology takes place. That critique instead helps to reveal that the assumption on the part of modern human beings like Dewey that science has all but won that struggle is questionable. Rorty believes that in obscuring this question, he helps direct our attention toward more concrete human concerns. But if the struggle between science and religion is truly radically unsettled, that would be a matter of enormous human concern — and not simply our concern to know and be aware of our place in the universe but, as I suggested in the previous chapter, our concern with how we should live as well. It is a "pragmatic" concern.

Rorty may respond that he is not interested in directing us to the world of concern to human beings as such, but to us late-twentieth-century liberal democrats. The world of human concern is always the world of concern to particular, historically situated human beings. *We* are secular humanists. *We* are not interested in theology. Such questions have died for us at the hands of History. Rorty's "we" are themselves heirs or products of the Enlightenment, though they themselves no longer believe in enlightenment, in rationally guided liberation. Yet, according to Rorty, giving up on enlightenment is actually a sign of the maturity of the Enlightenment's project. Enlightenment rationalism felt the need to justify itself as transcending historical peculiarities, justifying itself as if before some eternal judge. Rorty states that positing a "limit-concept of ideal truth," as all forms of rationalism do, "seems merely a way of telling ourselves that a nonexistent God would, if he did exist, be pleased with us" (1991a, 27). The Enlightenment's need to refute religion's claims to absolute truth with its own claims to absolute truth betrays a merely partial liberation from religion. The rationalist, like the religious believer, has in his head a picture of some nonhuman reality that is somehow more real and permanent than the ephemeral human things around us. Rorty "crudely sum[s] up" his account of the development of modernity thus:

> Once upon a time we felt a need to worship something which lay beyond the visible world. Beginning in the seventeenth century we tried to substitute a love of truth for a love of God, treating the world described by science as a quasi divinity. Beginning at the end of the eighteenth century we tried to substitute a love of ourselves for a love of scientific truth, a worship of our own deep spiritual or poetic nature, treated as one more quasi divinity. (1989, 22)

Each stage served its purpose in helping to sever our attachments to the old authorities. Rorty's neopragmatism "is antithetical to Enlightenment rationalism, although it was itself made possible (in good dialectical fashion) only by that rationalism. It can serve as the vocabulary of a mature (de-scientized, de-philosophized) Enlightenment liberalism" (57). This means above all that everything has been "de-divinized." Rorty "suggests that we try to get to the point where we no longer worship *anything,* where we treat *nothing* as a quasi divinity" (22). This means, according to Rorty, that we "treat *everything . . .* as a product of time and chance," or "sheer contingency."

The core of the Enlightenment then, at least for us looking back on it, was not reason's authority but freedom from authority. Rorty encourages us not to concern ourselves with whether those authorities have actually been refuted. The rationalist's need to refute — his concern that he may be fatally wrong — is another sign of immaturity. It seems, however, that Rortian maturity remains to be realized. The figure who for Rorty is freest of the need for "metaphysical comfort," the "ironist," is not yet completely free from the weakness for the absolute that plagued earlier human beings. That weakness manifests itself in the ironist intellectual as "the metaphysical urge, the urge to theorize," or the attempt "to see everything steadily and see it whole" (1989, 96–97). Ironism is defined by its opposition to metaphysics, which is not the same as freedom from metaphysics or from concern with the questions of metaphysics: "The topic of ironist theory is metaphysical theory"

(96).[1] Rorty evidences this in the fact that he writes of little else than the subjects from which he wishes to turn our attention: objectivity, relativism, truth, etc. The ironist looks upon the need to know the whole as an unhealthy one, as a sickness. Thus ironist theory may also be called therapeutic: "Just as the [psychiatric] patient needs to relive his past to answer his questions, so philosophy needs to relive its past in order to *answer* its questions" (1979, 33, my emphasis). It seems that a healthy freedom from the need to know the whole remains, for the ironist, an unfulfilled goal: "The goal of ironist theory is to understand the metaphysical urge . . . so well that one becomes entirely free of it. Ironist theory is a ladder which is to be thrown away as soon as one has figured out what it was that drove one's predecessors to theorize" (1989, 96–97).

This passage recalls two other famous passages. One occurs at the end of Wittgenstein's *Tractatus Logico-Philosophicus*. Rorty claims Wittgenstein as an important influence, yet the contrast between their ladder metaphors is striking. According to Wittgenstein, to follow his propositions to the end means to transcend the limitations of language and of logic. At the peak is not a Rortian denial of or indifference to the highest things, but a sort of enlightenment: "anyone who understands me . . . must, so to speak, throw away the ladder after he has climbed up it. . . . He must transcend these propositions, and then he will see the world aright" ([1921] 1961, 151). Wittgensteinian enlightenment, moreover, is explicitly mystical: "There are, indeed, things that cannot be put into words. They make themselves manifest. They are what is mystical" (151). But whereas Wittgenstein implies that enlightenment is attainable, we cannot be so sure from Rorty's account whether the overcoming of metaphysics does not remain an unattainable goal.

Rorty's metaphor of the ladder also recalls Nietzsche's statement on the "great ladder of religious cruelty." The final rung of that ladder is "to sacrifice God himself and, from cruelty to oneself, worship the stone, stupidity, gravity, fate, the nothing" (*Beyond Good and Evil*, aph. 55). Following Nietzsche's account, Rorty's urge to be free from his need to theorize — his goal of worshiping nothing — appears to be itself a variety of religious asceticism, of cruel self-denial or suppression of his own desires. The ironist's torn soul, his battle against himself, could thus be thought a sign of ill health. One might wonder whether the Rortian ironist is not rather numb to the pain Nietzsche speaks of. Be that as it may, is not the ironist one who cannot satisfy his own apparently deep need, his "metaphysical urge"? Is irony not therefore a sign of a "pragmatist" failing? Can the ironist, or indeed any human being, avoid holding opinions about the whole? And is it not only natural to desire those opinions to be as sound as possible and therefore to reflect upon them when one comes to question their soundness?

### Ironism, Metaphysics, and Common Sense

Rorty, however, is convinced that "metaphysical" concerns are idle. He claims that they are futile and therefore uninteresting and, moreover, distracting from questions of more immediate human concern. Problems of truth and knowledge are in fact pseudo-problems. Philosophers imagine that they have uncovered the perennial and fundamental questions of the human condition as such. Modern philosophy especially, Rorty claims, has supposed that the single most fundamental question for human beings concerns human knowledge — not simply, or even primarily, of the whole, but rather of anything whatever. Must not the grounds of human knowledge as such be demonstrated before any further problem, whether theoretical or practical, can be adequately addressed? Rorty responds that human beings managed to cope with their environments before philosophy was ever dreamt of, and they continue to cope despite the countless revolutions of philosophic "solutions" to the allegedly deepest human questions. People are happy enough. At any rate, human beings do not have a problem of knowledge, such that their every action and thought is suspect without a clear demonstration of epistemological foundations. There are undoubtedly occasions when human beings feel some inadequacy in their knowledge. But these occasions arise in concrete practical situations, and people generally manage to muddle through with concrete practical solutions. This is so despite the fact that human beings may differ profoundly across societies in what they consider the highest or most fundamental truth, the one thing needful.

The allegedly universal epistemological questions addressed by philosophers are in fact, according to Rorty, only historical peculiarities. Their real significance should be understood not theoretically but practically. The idea of valid scientific knowledge served a practical function in the past, but our own situation today calls for something quite different. Rather than concerning ourselves with universal knowledge, let alone the grounds of universal knowledge, we should be trying to broaden the sympathies of our fellow citizens and ourselves for the sake of democratic toleration. The search for final and universally valid knowledge is a distraction from the "detailed, particular dangers of [our] times" (1991a, 77). Philosophers are debating, as it were, how many angels can dance on the head of a pin.

Rorty's critique of modern philosophy thus recalls the Enlightenment's critique of scholasticism. In this respect, Rorty seeks to recover modernity rather than repudiate it. But Rorty's critique of metaphysics must be distinguished from the Enlightenment's. (The starting point for the Enlightenment, it must be remembered, was a certain critique of metaphysics, especially Aristotelian metaphysics.) Modern philosophy, Rorty contends, followed Descartes's musings about the abstracted human subject and his radical concern for certainty about reality rather than Bacon's emphasis on judging thought according to its practical benefits (1991b, 172). However much modern philosophy may have wanted to move away from medieval abstraction and preoccupation with another, nonhuman world, it has fallen into its own version of scholasticism's vices. For the moderns, the "other world" is not heaven, *esse*, or utopia, but the "true world," the world in itself, apart from any human shaping. At best, philosophy's speculations about the "true world" have been a harmless and useless distraction. But at their worst, they encourage or accompany or manifest a spirit of absolutism that lends itself easily to intolerance and even cruelty, the opposition to which almost entirely defines liberalism (good politics and morals) for Rorty. Philosophy best serves democracy today by the relentless critique of the very possibility of universal knowledge. Today, epistemology and metaphysics are antidemocratic.

What distinguishes Rorty's rejection of metaphysics most sharply from the Enlightenment's rejection of it is that Rorty ceases to aspire to being scientific. Rorty does not claim to offer universally valid insights into what human beings can know, what they want, or how they can secure what they want, as had the early modern critics of scholasticism. The early modern return to the world of human concern featured most prominently the concern for comfortable self-preservation, secured by science made useful in the form of technology. While Rorty is no critic of bourgeois comforts, he does not think that there are any scientific means for determining what people want or how they should get it. Science and technology should no longer be the focal point of democratic culture if they no longer grip the imagination of the people (as, he claims, they in fact no longer do [1989, 52]). Rorty's turn away from science is therefore for the sake of human purposes as human beings themselves determine them. Rorty thus continues, we may say, in the spirit of technology, precisely by calling into question the supremacy of science and technology narrowly defined.

Rorty's democratic attack on metaphysics and epistemology also needs to be distinguished from the commonsensical debunking on the part of the man on the street, who knows what he knows, does not see what all the philosophic fuss is about, and has more pressing and real concerns in any case. In places, Rorty's presentation resembles and appeals to such sentiments. He states: "The pragmatist theory about truth . . . says that truth is not the sort of thing one should expect to have a philosophically interesting theory about" (1982, xiii). Indeed, pragmatist philosophy "will have no more to offer than common sense (supplemented by biology, history, etc.) about knowledge and truth" (1979, 176). But in fact Rorty's theory about truth and knowledge — ironism, or anti-representationalism — is extremely elaborate, sophisticated, and very far from commonsensical. Rorty might have attempted to recover the primacy of concrete human concerns with a return to taking seriously common sense, or human concerns as they appear naively. He does not take this approach, perhaps owing to the unnamed supplements by natural science, history, etc. So far, indeed, is Rorty from returning to take common sense seriously that he states that "the opposite of irony is common sense" (1989, 74). This is so because the person of common sense accepts without question that the opinions inherited from his society are simply true and authoritative. Common sense is too "metaphysical." [2] All opinions, Rorty suggests, have become problematic for the ironist as a result of his sympathetic encounters with the opinions of other groups (73–75). Because the ironist has been impressed with a variety of conflicting worldviews, he finds it hard to believe that any one of them could be the sole true one. We must say, then, that knowledge does begin as a problem for Rorty; it is not simply a "pseudo-problem." Indeed, the problem of knowledge is *the* reason that the ironist is ironic.

Rorty acknowledges that recognition of this problem played a central role in the birth of the philosophic concerns about knowledge and truth (1991a, 21). That is, far from beginning as a justification, let alone an expression, of received opinion (of Greek culture), philosophy originated in profound doubts respecting the soundness of received opinion. [3] Moreover, being impressed with the opinions of others regarding the most important things by no means leads necessarily to Rortian irony. It may well lead to an inquiry into which, if any, of the competing opinions is right. Such, indeed, is the position this book as a whole is meant to defend. In light of philosophy understood as such an inquiry, the ironist contention that no human opinion is ultimately true comes to light as another positive assertion regarding the human situation, an assertion that is not self-evident and must be duly evaluated.

Rorty insists, however, that philosophers have wasted their time trying to solve this problem. There is, we can be sure, no solution, no objective knowledge. The problem is permanent. But it is precisely for this reason, Rorty believes, that the problem of knowledge ceases to be a problem. That is, the affirmation of the permanence of the problem of knowledge relieves one of concern for a solution to that problem and frees one to consider radically new ways of conceiving the human situation. In particular, it frees one to adopt a devil-may-care attitude regarding the rightness of all worldviews, including one's own. The insolubility of the problem of knowledge frees one, moreover, to do away with the very notion of objective knowledge. The problem of knowledge is universally human only if a certain kind of solution is sought, only if the expectation that knowledge be objective is universally human, only if the human need for objective knowledge — the need to see for oneself — is universal, or natural. But, in Rorty's view, knowledge is only a problem according to the standards of disillusioned common sense.

Rorty moves furthest from common sense, however, not so much in denying objective knowledge but in concluding from our lack of objective knowledge that the idea of objective reality carries no human significance. Objective reality is not, or need not be, of human concern. This is certainly not what the person of common sense would have in mind were he to affirm, as he well might, the need for faith, i.e., the lack of certainty concerning the highest things. Faith in that case means faith in the objective reality of what is not objectively known. Faith in God does not mean indifference to the reality of God and God's sanctions. On the contrary, faith is necessary precisely because what is not objectively known continues to be of human concern and to demand our response or judgment.

Rorty thus undertakes a paradoxical project. He seeks to restore the dignity of the world of primary human concern without returning to the naiveté of the commonsensical belief in "objective reality." He understands the restoration of the world of human concern to require the relentless attack on the specific human concern that one's beliefs about the world are true and that what one is concerned with is or will become real. He therefore runs the risk of intensifying just the difficulty he wishes to set aside, viz. the flight to "another world." Rorty runs the risk, in other words, of turning away from the primary world of human concern by turning to the highly artificial "web of belief." We turn now to consider in greater detail Rorty's theoretical critique of the human attempt to obtain knowledge of the whole, the attempt that Rorty labels simply "foundationalism."

### The Critique of Foundationalism

Rorty denies that his critique of foundationalism rests on or culminates in an alternative epistemology. He is instead making the case that we need no epistemology at all. Rorty does not mean to promote a radical subjectivism or skepticism. Subjectivism and skepticism are merely the other side of the objectivist coin. So long as the unrealizable goal of objective knowledge is retained, skepticism is sure to follow. Moreover, insofar as they still wish to explain the final truth regarding human knowledge (or the lack of it), subjectivism and skepticism reveal themselves to be in agreement that the questions of objectivist philosophy are truly fundamental ones, which as such demand some final judgment (1979, 112–13; 1991a, 2ff.).

Rorty, however, wishes to "change the subject" of philosophy altogether. The question is not what the truth of the human situation is, but what it is useful for us to believe. If we concern ourselves only with what is useful for us to believe, then we will not care if our beliefs are true, as that word is generally understood. If we find that our beliefs help us get what we want, then we will call our beliefs true. This avenue, Rorty contends, has the added benefit of stimulating dialogue. Rival conceptions of "final knowledge" inevitably run into inexorable disagreements, precisely because they aim at finality. The very point, or at any rate the would-be consequence, of the pursuit of final knowledge is to bring conversation to an end. Rorty proposes that philosophy see itself as "keeping the conversation going" rather than seeking to end the conversation in the form of final knowledge (1979, 389–94). In one respect, then, despite his disclaimers, Rorty represents yet a further radicalization of modern skepticism, at least insofar as his thought is guided largely by the desire to get as far away from anything resembling a concern for objective truth as he can. But the final break with skepticism as he sees it comes with "changing the subject" altogether, the subject with which even the most radical skeptic as such is concerned. Thus Rorty can claim not to represent simply a variety of a perennial strand of serious philosophic thought but to have transcended the plane of the great philosophic debates altogether.[4]

The concern with foundations is replaced in part with the concern with foundationalism. What is foundationalism? As Rorty presents it, foundationalism is the attempt to move beyond the world of inherited opinion and mere appearance to the "true world." Opinions and appearances, which constitute the world that is primary for us human beings, may contradict one another and change over time; but, the foundationalist asserts, the true world, the fundamental reality, or Being, is one and eternal. Thus the foundationalist asserts a dualism, separating the world of mere appearance from the true world. The true world exists as a substratum, somehow beyond the world of our primary experience.[5] That world is the foundation of all true opinion, or knowledge. Knowledge, according to the foundationalist, is the same for all persons at all times, in all contexts, because of the permanence and universality of the objects of knowledge. The task of the foundationalist in transcending opinion toward knowledge is to link his opinions somehow with that foundation, or somehow to get beyond or behind mere appearance and perceive the true world directly, or to sort the true appearances from the false. The overwhelming thrust of Rorty's critique is directed against the foundationalist theory of "correspondence," or "representationalism" — the doctrine that true beliefs or statements are true because they somehow correspond to or represent reality as it is in itself.[6] John Caputo puts Rorty's understanding of representationalism thus: "language is here, on the subjective side, and the world is there, on the objective side, and the task of philosophy is to build a bridge between them" (1985, 256–57).

Rorty reports, however, that no one has ever been able to make sense of how it is that true beliefs are supposed to link up with or be made true by reality. Typically, what was thought of as objective inquiry "was a matter of putting everything into a single, widely available, familiar context — translating everything into the vocabulary provided by a set of sentences which any rational inquirer would agree to be truth-value candidates" (1991a, 95). What Rorty seems to mean is that any given inquiry appears to depend upon certain basic assumptions that are taken for granted (at least for the time being). Those background assumptions, however, vary historically as well as across societies. How can those background assumptions be inquired into?

It could not, Rorty argues, be done piecemeal, for the reason already stated. Inquiry into any particular belief, however basic it is thought to be, takes for granted the validity of other beliefs not then in question. Our entire set of beliefs, what Rorty calls a "web of belief" or "vocabulary as a whole," is like a dictionary in this respect: No word can be defined in itself, without reference to other words. No word will find a place unless a more or less comprehensive vocabulary is already in place. So it is with a "web of belief."

Nor could one examine one's entire "web of belief" at once, as a whole. For if we could cast all of our beliefs into doubt, we would have nothing to appeal to in evaluating them. All questioning, indeed all thought, according to Rorty, requires background assumptions. Rorty contends that our experience of the world is shaped from the outset by our vocabularies, which we have, for the most part, inherited from our society's chance history. In focusing on "vocabularies," Rorty follows most immediately what he calls philosophy's "linguistic turn," but also Hobbes's doctrine according to which "true and false are attributes of speech, not of things. And where speech is not, there is neither truth nor falsehood" (*Leviathan* 4.11). We cannot, Rorty argues, get behind or suspend our linguistically shaped experience of the world in order to experience it "directly." There is no "pre-linguistic awareness" (1989, 21; 1979, 182–92). It therefore makes no sense to speak of the foundations of our beliefs, because there is no behind or underneath of our beliefs that we can approach. There is no "neutral, noncircular" reasoning (1989, 197, 73).

Rorty's critique of Kant is particularly helpful at this juncture. Kant, Rorty explains, never questioned "the assumption that manifoldness is 'given' and unity is made" (1979, 153). That is, Kant assumed that the objects of our understanding are the products of a synthesis by the mind of a "sensible manifold," presented to the mind unsynthesized. But why, Rorty asks, should we think that there ever was a stage of unsynthesized "givenness" prior to an act of synthesis? For we never experience this prior stage. "We are," he states, "never conscious of unsynthesized intuitions, nor of concepts apart from their application to intuitions. . . . If we are going to argue that we can only be conscious of synthesized intuitions, how do we get our information about intuitions prior to synthesis?" (154).

Instead, however, of saying as he might have done that the world is "given" to us as whole "objects," Rorty suggests that we abandon the idea of "givenness" altogether. For the idea of "givenness" maintains implicitly a distinction between things as they are represented in our ideas and things out there apart from our ideas — the things prior to being "given" and the things as they are received, or spoken of. The result is the tendency or attempt to peer past the world of primary human concern, which is intelligible and indeed exists only on the plane of appearances, or rather of beliefs and opinions. (Talk of appearances too would presumably be problematic, following Rorty's reasoning, since the notion of appearance requires that there be something that appears, something that is not reducible to the appearance itself.) Rorty thinks that the quagmire of foundationalism can be escaped only if we abandon the dualism it presupposes.

### The Neopragmatist Solution

We may freely admit that Rorty has identified a number of puzzles regarding human knowledge. No theory of knowledge, it seems, can be surer than the "naive knowledge" it would demonstrate the grounds for. As Rorty suggests, regarding the vast majority of things this fact poses no real problem, since there is virtually universal agreement concerning them — such as that snow is white, childbirth is painful, and human beings are mortal (see 1982, 12–14). The fact that we are talking about the same world is almost always confirmed, if it is indeed ever drawn into question. But "naive knowledge" is not universal regarding a number of things most important to human beings — such as what death is, what justice is, and what the gods are. When this fact is confronted squarely, these things become puzzles. And the failure of foundationalism as Rorty has described it only deepens the puzzle by exposing profound difficulties facing one important avenue of response.

But yet Rorty tells us that we should not be puzzled. We will cease to be puzzled when we cease to think of beliefs as referring to "nonbeliefs" rather than simply to other beliefs. Rorty proposes that when we speak of what a belief is about, "we use the term 'about' as a way of directing attention to the beliefs which are relevant to the justification of other beliefs, not as a way of directing attention to nonbeliefs" (1991a, 97). Put otherwise, we can avoid the problem of knowledge by "taking knowledge to be of propositions rather than of objects" (1979, 154). Truth and knowledge reside not in a correct relation between our opinions of things and things as they really are. Truth and knowledge reside wholly on "this side" of that divide. Our beliefs refer not to "objects" but only to other beliefs. The world remains "out there," but not as the object of "belief." Rorty thus appears to retain the foundationalist dualism (and so, I will argue, he does). Rorty, however, calls this view "holistic"

as opposed to dualistic. For a belief, according to Rorty, has meaning by virtue of holding a place in a whole system of beliefs rather than by referring
across a divide between belief and world.

Human language and beliefs are created, Rorty contends, by human beings, not for the sake of "cut[ting] reality at the joints" (1991a, 80) but for the
sake of coping with it (1). Language is not a medium that expresses or reveals
the truth about the world or about oneself. Language is better thought of as
a set of tools. If we so conceive of language, Rorty argues, we will not be
forced to choose which "vocabulary" is the absolutely right one. The fact that
different "vocabularies" may not lie well together (such as "self-creation and
justice, private perfection and human solidarity" [1989, xiv; cf. 1993b, 36–43])
ceases to pose a problem. We need not try to synthesize them or choose one
over the other, any more than we need do so with paintbrushes and crowbars
(1989, xiv).

Truth, moreover, is something made, not discovered, by human beings.
Rorty's argument appears to take the form of the following syllogism. Truth
is an attribute only of sentences, propositions, or other linguistic constructions. Human beings make language. Therefore, human beings make truth.[7]
Truth is determined by linguistic rules, forming what Rorty, following Wittgenstein, calls language games. The rules of language games are chosen by
human beings, and they are as conventional as the rules of checkers. But the
rules of a language game are infinitely more complex and ever in the process
of being amended and, periodically, radically transformed.

Rorty makes clear that multiple language games, multiple worldviews, do
not mean multiple worlds (1991a, 49–51). Thus contradictory truths may exist
simultaneously in the same world, though not in the same language game.
This is possible because truth is not determined by the world "out there." The
truth is extra-worldly.

Rorty's epistemological doctrine is difficult to understand and easy to mis-
understand. Rorty denies that he is advocating "antirealism": "the realism-
vs.-antirealism . . . issue arises only for representationalists" (1991a, 2). Rorty
claims to give "realism" its due by affirming that "there are objects which
are *causally* independent of human beliefs and desires" (101). He continues:
"that is all that is required to satisfy our realist intuitions. We are not required
to say that our descriptions *represent* objects." There are no formal or final
causes. Our "realist intuition" does not tell us that when we speak of rain we

are speaking, not just of other of our beliefs, but of some *thing* that is not itself a belief — a "nonbelief." Our realist intuition is satisfied simply by acknowledging that when we speak of rain, there is indeed out there some "brute physical resistance," which is not itself rain. Such brute physical impingements in themselves are not anything we can fit into a worldview. They are not yet things, and certainly not facts. The Rortian pragmatist "agrees that there is such a thing as brute physical resistance — the pressure of light waves on Galileo's eyeball, or of the stone on Dr. Johnson's boot. But he sees no way of transferring this nonlinguistic brutality to *facts*" (1991a, 81).[8] There is brute physical resistance, but there are no brute facts. A "fact" has already been given some shape by finding a description among our concepts. The same brute physical impingement can therefore become manifest to human beings as a variety of different facts.

Perhaps what is most puzzling about this suggestion is Rorty's insistence that his doctrine does not mean that we are "more 'cut off from the world' than we had thought" (1979, 178). For has Rorty not accomplished his "holism" by severing the link between the truth, and our beliefs generally, on the one hand and the world external to those beliefs on the other? If our beliefs are only about other beliefs, are we not more cut off from the world than we had thought?

We can begin to understand Rorty's response to such questions by thinking of the external world as simple matter, formless stuff. We can never experience or say anything meaningful about that world. Our experience is always of this and that form, the variety of forms being determined by our pre-existing vocabulary or opinions. It is not the case that we are "cut off" from the world. But our beliefs qua beliefs cannot be *about* the world. Now, Rorty would hesitate to give the external world even as much a description as "formless stuff," because as soon as we begin to speak of it even in this way, we give it a shape (see 1982, 14–15). He insists, to repeat, that we have no prelinguistic awareness.

Nevertheless, Rorty is willing to allow that the external world can, in a narrow sense, cause us to hold certain beliefs. He states that "we often let the world decide the competition between alternative sentences (e.g., between 'Red wins' and 'Black wins' or between 'The butler did it' and 'The doctor did it')" (1989, 5). The claim that we have no prelinguistic awareness, then, cannot mean that our experience is purely linguistic. Nor can Rorty mean that we have the power to make something so (i.e., true) merely by saying that it is so. There is a power that transcends human power, a power that human beings must respect. We are aware of an external world beyond our making, but we are only so aware once a vocabulary is in place to give our experience some shape. And the world cannot, Rorty insists, help us decide among vocabularies. In a sense, the world may be said to decide whether Red or Black wins, but it does not decide that Red and Black are in competition or what it means to win. Thus, the world does not decide the truth. The world, then, can only decide that Red wins after what the world cannot decide — what it would mean for Red to win — is already in place.

Rorty clarifies his doctrine in the following way:

> We need to make a distinction between the claim that the world is out there and the claim that the truth is out there. To say that the world is out there, that it is not our creation, is to say, with common sense, that most things in time and space are the effects of causes which do not include human mental states. To say that truth is not out there is simply to say that where there are no sentences there is no truth, that sentences are elements of human languages, and that human languages are human creations.
>
> Truth cannot be out there — cannot exist independently of the human mind — because sentences cannot so exist, or be out there. The world is out there, but descriptions of the world are not. Only descriptions of the world can be true or false. The world on its own — unaided by the describing activities of human beings — cannot. (1989, 4–5)

The world in itself is mindless and mute. It has no self-understanding, no self-description. It has, therefore, no truth to be discovered by human beings. To ask what the world is apart from its interaction with human beings is a pointless question. We have no way to conceptualize it. As soon as we begin to think about such a question, we impose pre-existing human concepts — imposed, because our concepts are shaped by human interests. We cannot for a moment step outside of our interests or our concepts — our language, or vocabulary — in order to encounter the world immediately and purely. Nor can we pretend that any one description of the world belongs to the world in itself, apart from human beings. Unless the word "truth" is so vague and vacuous (like "thing in itself") as to be worthless, it must be made sense of within our pre-existing concepts. It is the truth of those concepts that the foundationalist is concerned with. But those concepts must be prior to all "truth." Truth, then, exists on the plane of concepts, and not on some prior or underlying plane.

It seems that we can say little about the world that is "out there," apart from our "descriptions" of it, except simply that it is "out there," since anything we say constitutes a human description. The world "out there" — the world apart from human description of it — is what Rorty calls the "world well lost." Rorty states:

> The notion of "the world" as used in a phrase like "different conceptual schemes carve up the world differently" must be the notion of something *completely* unspecified and unspecifiable — the thing-in-itself, in fact. As soon as we start thinking of "the world" as atoms and the void, or sense data and awareness of them, or "stimuli" of a certain sort brought to bear upon organs of a certain sort [brute physical resistance?], we have changed the name of the game. For we are now well within some particular theory about how the world is. (1982, 14)

Rorty wishes to end all discussion of such a world, since a *discussion* of that world can never be a discussion of *that world*. He does wish to retain as meaningful the notion of the world as "just whatever the vast majority of our beliefs not currently in question are currently thought to be about." He wishes to retain the "human world" and jettison the "world in itself."

But has Rorty succeeded in jettisoning the "world in itself"? Has he really transcended the plane of foundationalist epistemological disputes? It seems that Rorty's strategy for overcoming the dualism between the "human world" and the "true world" does not culminate in the thesis that the human world *is* the true world. This possible solution remains unexplored by Rorty. In some sense Rorty wishes to make such an equation, but his historicism prevents him from doing so. Rorty's historicism points to the conclusion that there are many human worlds, i.e., many worlds — as many as there are worldviews. But this conclusion, as we noted above, Rorty explicitly denies. His "realist intuition" forbids it. He insists that there is one world. Rorty could only conclude that the human world is the true world, if he could claim there is something like a natural (as opposed to both neutral and conventional or historical) human worldview, if he could abandon his historicism. As a consequence, Rorty cannot fully jettison the "true world," and therewith the foundationalist dualism, as he wishes to do.

Rorty's strategy for overcoming the dualism between the human world(s) and the "true world" is to radicalize that dualism, to the extent that the true world, the world in itself, becomes so ineffable and inscrutable as to disappear from our purview. Rorty does not deny the existence of a world in itself. He says instead that he "can find no use for the notion" (1991a, 101). Rorty's "holism" represents the attempt to turn our attention away from the world as it is apart from human making, except as brute material forces that must be coped with. *What* is being coped with is so radically inscrutable that it can, or must, no longer be of interest, or even a source of wonder.[9]

Thus Rorty continues to operate within the dualism he seeks to transcend. Rorty admits that "the world," and indeed "most things in time and space," are "out there," apart from "the describing activities of human beings." He argues that he can concede this much to the realists without having to say that we have any substantial awareness of that world. The foundationalist wants to link his beliefs to the world; Rorty denies that this is possible. But Rorty accepts the basic foundationalist dualism; he simply believes that the foundationalist project is futile.[10]

We arrive at the following question. What is the status for Rorty of the indifferent or value-free X out there with which we must cope? According to the positivists, value-free nature is knowable through value-free science. But after Rorty's critique of value-free science, on what basis does Rorty retain his equivalent of value-free nature — the world devoid of purpose? Is the world "out there" objectively indifferent to our descriptions of it? Or is that indifference the product of Rorty's choice of language game? If it is the latter (a possibility I will pursue below), then perhaps the "world" is *not* indifferent to our descriptions of it and our actions within it.

Rorty gives the strong impression — one is tempted to say that it is simply evident — that he believes his claims about the indifference of the world to our descriptions have an objective status. As Alasdair MacIntyre points out, Rorty's work would take on a very different appearance if he were entirely to avoid that impression (1990, 709). Does Rorty not try to *demonstrate* the failure of foundationalism? Does he not everywhere imply that the antifoundationalist *understands* something about the human situation to which the foundationalist is blind? It is hard to answer these questions otherwise than affirmatively.

But Rorty is forced to deny objective status to his teaching for the simple reason that his teaching denies objective status to all human beliefs. Thus, three pages after asserting that "truth cannot be out there," he states:

To say that we should drop the idea of truth as out there waiting to be discovered is not to say that we have discovered that, out there, there is no truth. It is to say that our purposes would be served best by ceasing to see truth as a deep matter, as a topic of philosophical interest, or "true" as a term which repays "analysis." (1989, 8)

To claim that his teaching is true would reproduce what Rorty calls the "self-referential fallacy," a self-contradiction, which is a "confusion" into which even Nietzsche and Derrida have fallen. Rorty does not make clear why a self-contradiction should pose a problem if beliefs are like alternative tools (at what point does consistency become a Rortian virtue?). Still, Rorty appears to believe that denying objective status to his teaching gets him out of a bind. The belief that the world is indifferent to human concerns is not objectively true but only what it is useful for us to believe at this point in our history.

I will argue below that Rorty does not, as he supposes, escape a bind by confessing that his own interpretation is mere redescription and not "true," but only moves from one horn of a dilemma to the other. The more clearly the lack of objective status of Rorty's interpretation is seen, the more we are in a position to face the possibility that Rorty is objectively wrong. Before we consider this possibility, however, we should consider in more detail what use the world devoid of purpose serves in Rorty's scheme.

### Rorty's Use of a Purposeless World

Rorty never acknowledges how closely the "world well lost" resembles the world of his minimal realism, the world "out there," devoid of purpose. More than this, he does not acknowledge the role that the "world well lost" plays in establishing the doctrine that the truth is of human making. That world is not altogether lost but rather is ever present in Rorty's arguments. He makes use of the positive claim that the world in itself is indifferent and purposeless in the cause of human freedom. He wishes at once to remove the world in itself from the realm of human concerns and to keep it squarely in view precisely for the sake of human concerns. In Rorty's account, the recognition of the purposelessness of the world in itself is, in fact, crucial to human liberation. The purposelessness of the world is revealed in its materialistic determination, or "mechanization." Mechanization — above all, the mechanization of man — is for Rorty the pre-eminent achievement of modern science because of its role in human liberation.

At first glance, this contention is paradoxical. In what sense may a machine be free? Would not a completely mechanistic account of the human soul, an account that showed the operations of the soul to be determined by a natural necessity, reveal that human freedom and creativity (and indeed the soul itself) are illusory and false? Does not man's freedom, as Dostoyevsky's underground man felt so profoundly, depend upon his *not* being naturally determined? How is it that Rorty can maintain both that man is governed by the order of external causes (and in this case, the electrical and chemical motions of the brain are external) and that he imposes order on the world?[11] This difficulty becomes apparent again when we consider that the purpose of science and human thought generally, according to Rorty, is not simply to predict, but to predict and control. If every operation of the human soul were to be subject to prediction, where would the seat of human control lie? Is the human will the effect of natural causation, with the consequence that its freedom is merely illusory, or is the will free, capable of mastering nature, and thus transcendent of the natural order of causation?

Rorty presents his doctrine on the relationship between mechanization and human freedom in the essay "Freud and Moral Reflection" (1991b, 143–63). There Rorty begins by setting mechanization in contradistinction to Aristotelian teleology — the science of natural purposes, or ends. Teleology, Rorty explains, offered an account of the world's division into "natural kinds." Beings were said to be distinguishable according to their ends; ends determine essences; and particular beings can be understood as members of a species, according to a common end. As Rorty makes clear elsewhere, he takes for granted that teleology is essentially related to the belief that "the world is a divine creation, the work of someone who had something in mind, who Himself spoke some language in which He described his own project" (1989, 21). The division of the world into "natural kinds" is possible only if there are intrinsic ends or purposes that define those kinds. And intrinsic purposes are possible only if beings were created by an intelligent Being for those purposes.[12]

Modern natural science replaced this body of doctrines by ushering in the "mechanization of the world picture." This made it impossible to believe that the world is governed by reason or divine will, or to believe that the world truly consists of natural kinds. Rorty instructs us to "think of the claim that 'man is a natural kind' not as saying that human beings are the center of something, but that they *have* a center, in a way that a machine does not"

(1991b, 143). A natural kind has a "built-in purpose," whereas "the same machine . . . may be used for many different purposes. A machine's purpose is not built in." Mechanization thus does not do away with purpose in the world altogether. Rather, beings are freed for multiple purposes, which admit of no natural hierarchy.

But since the division of the world into distinct species depends upon the existence of distinct purposes, the mechanization of the world picture meant that there were no longer distinct beings by nature. Modern natural science "predicted events on the basis of a universal homogeneous microstructure, rather than revealing the different natures of the various natural kinds" (1991b, 144n.). There are no irreducible differences among beings but a radical homogeneity to all Being. Radical heterogeneity (irreducible difference) depends on or is identical to permanent essential difference, the difference between natural kinds. ("Essentialism" is not opposed to "difference" but presupposes it.) The division of the world into distinct kinds, which continued to be humanly necessary, came to light as the product of nothing "more than a practical convenience." Thus the various "beings" do not in fact have multiple purposes. Rather they themselves have no purposes at all. Indeed, they are not, in themselves, at all. They are human artifacts, "machines," present only because we human beings somehow have purposes amidst the naturally undifferentiated motions of the world.

Mechanization, in Rorty's account, thus ultimately means that all purpose is the product of *human* making. And since human beings too are part of that motion of homogeneous particles, human beings have no intrinsic purposes. "Mechanization meant that the world in which human beings live no longer taught them anything about how they should live" (1991b, 145). The more radically mechanized the world is, the more radically free human beings are. Rorty acknowledges that modern mechanization is often thought to mean that "we have discovered, humiliatingly, that humanity is less important than we had thought" (143). But that conclusion "is not perspicuous," since "it is not clear what 'importance' can mean in this context." Rorty suggests: "Copernicus and Darwin might claim that by making God and the angels less plausible, they have left human beings on top of the heap" (143). Being does, Rorty seems to suggest, admit of a hierarchy, with man on top; a hierarchy that is, if perhaps not quite natural, at any rate permitted and in some sense even made necessary by nature's purposelessness. Man does stand out, is on top, somehow by nature — nature is not simply a homogeneous flux. Be that as it may, if there are no natural kinds and no human nature, then mechanization can have no natural human significance. It is what we make of it. Because nature is plastic and completely indifferent, human beings may call the shots. All is permitted. And should we not make of it what best suits us? Modern mechanization should not be rued. It should be celebrated.

It appears, then, that for Rorty the demise of science, as well as of political rationalism, is the outcome of science. Science seems to have led us to *see* the futility of coming to an awareness of nature or Being. Could it have done so otherwise than by leading us to see nature, not as we had anthropomorphically supposed it to be, but as it truly is in itself — an eternal flux, devoid of purpose? But would that not mean that science has *succeeded* in arriving at an awareness of nature or Being? Rorty sees that the claim that nature in itself is a purposeless flux would contradict too starkly the conclusion of the futility of metaphysics to which science has led us. Yet must we not conclude that, for Rorty as for Dewey, the recognition of the futility of metaphysics is the product or byproduct of the advance of science, that is, has been rationally determined? That recognition would appear to depend on modern natural science's somehow carrying objective validity, at least to the extent that the metaphysical failure of modern natural science itself is decisive for metaphysics as such.

The objection could be raised to Rorty's cosmology that the world in which human beings live — the human world — is not one of universal, homogeneous, purposeless particles. Do we not live in a world of friends, enemies, trees, cats, health, shame, and so forth? We might at this point reiterate Rorty's own objection to Kant discussed above. Do we ever experience a world devoid of purpose? If not, whence the supposition that the world "out there," the world apart from human imposition, the true world, is one devoid of purpose? Newton himself, after all, claimed (albeit in a scholium) that his mechanistic physics was fully compatible with the notion that the world was the design of a purposeful Creator.[13] A machine, after all, is a tool, something whose being is *defined* by its purpose. Even Rorty admits that "teleological thinking is inevitable" (1995, 13). Rorty's response, as we have already indicated, must be that the mechanized world is not the "true world" but a human fiction, though a useful one. Mechanization and the world devoid of purpose are free human creations.

At this point, however, it is unclear how we are to understand the order of the argument. On the one hand, because the world is devoid of purpose, human beings are free to create their own purposes and their own truth. Absolute human creativity depends on mechanization. Yet on the other hand, absolute human creativity means that the world devoid of purpose cannot have been a human discovery but must be a human creation. Mechanization depends on absolute creativity. Which, then, is prior: mechanization or creativity?

As before, Rorty's answer must be creativity. Rorty propounds what he calls "non-reductive physicalism." By non-reductive, Rorty means that his is not a metaphysical materialism (just as his is not a metaphysical atheism). He does not reduce reality to matter in motion. He merely claims that it is sometimes useful for us to think about the world in materialist terms. I asserted above that in making this move, Rorty moves from one horn of a dilemma to the other. The horn he avoids is the self-contradictory claim that it is objectively true that there is no objective truth. Let us turn to the other horn of Rorty's dilemma — a challenge of which Rorty is almost wholly oblivious.

### Non-reductive Physicalism and the Struggle between Science and Religion

In the essay "Non-reductive Physicalism" (1991a, 113–25), Rorty argues that it is an error to conclude from natural science's ability to describe the world in terms of microstructures and microprocesses, that the real stuff of the world is those microstructures and microprocesses. A chair is not really elements, atoms, or subatomic particles. Nor is it really an artifact to be sat upon. It in itself is not really anything. Rather, Rorty argues, we may speak of it as atoms or as something to sit upon according to our purposes in a given circumstance. Alternative ways of describing the chair are not alternative descriptions of the reality of the chair but are rather different tools put to some use. The chair (or tree, or cow) has no being apart from the uses we have for it. Human concerns pervade every interaction with it; so at no point can we see it as it is in itself. More precisely, at no point is it ever in itself. The same reasoning applies to the operations of the soul. A thought is not really neurons firing, even if thought could be predicted strictly in terms of the firing of neurons.[14]

Rorty's "physicalism" therefore claims to be non-reductive owing to its "ontological neutrality" (1991a, 121). Such a physicalism "is no longer in any way scientific" (113). Rorty presents his non-reductive physicalism as a way of reconciling the typical materialism of American philosophy with the typical disdain for natural science of Continental philosophy. One can embrace "materialism," provided it is nonmetaphysical, and still do full justice to the power of human imagination and creativity. Rorty states:

> It is often thought that a proper acknowledgment of the cultural role of imaginative literature (and, more generally, of art, myth, and religion — all the "higher" things) is incompatible with a naturalistic philosophy. But this is because naturalism has been identified with reductionism, with the attempt to find a single language sufficient to state all the truths there are to state. (124)

Rorty's contention is that his alternative is not a reduction, but that it permits a countless variety of what had appeared to be incompatible worldviews to flourish in their rich and complex significance.

Rorty nevertheless has already signaled that he does in fact engage in a reduction of his own. For now when art, myth, and religion are called "higher," the merely alleged character of that elevation must be indicated with quotation marks. Just as art, myth, and religion are not *really* just neurons firing, they also are not *really* high. They are, it appears, *really* products of the imagination. The Bible is not the revealed word of the one true God, but imaginative literature, or myth. Whether imagination can be reduced to neurons firing is infinitely less important than whether revelation can be reduced to imagination. If that reduction were not possible, the denial of the existence of a "privileged description" would be radically questionable.

The peculiar, not to say ludicrous, character of what Rorty considers "nonreductive" is clear in the following passage of *Contingency, Irony, and Solidarity:*

> For all we know, or should care, Aristotle's metaphorical use of *ousia,* Saint Paul's metaphorical use of *agape,* and Newton's metaphorical use of *gravitas,* were the results of cosmic rays scrambling the fine structure of some crucial neurons in their respective brains. Or, more plausibly, they were the result of some odd episodes in infancy — some obsessional kinks left in these brains by idiosyncratic traumata. It hardly matters how the trick was done. (1989, 17)

It hardly matters how the "trick" was done, only after certain possibilities, the most serious possibilities, the possibilities claimed by Aristotle, Paul, and Newton (reasoning based on what is evident to human beings as such or

divine inspiration), have been discounted. But if we are to take Rorty's ontological neutrality seriously, how could these possibilities be discounted?
Rorty's ontological "neutrality," like Dewey's indifference to the first cause,
in fact applies only after substantial ontological possibilities have been discounted, or, in other words, after a positive and important ontological claim
has been staked. Rorty restricts the ontological possibilities to severely limited, even trivial, turf. That is to say, Rorty is not ontologically neutral at all.
But how has this ontological ground been taken from Paul, Aristotle, Newton
and all the other "foundationalists"?

Rorty claims that the work of rendering unbelievable, if not refuting, all
premodern (teleological) metaphysics and theology was done by modern science's mechanization. But just how has it done so? Perhaps Rorty could argue
that science demonstrated in case after case that things do lend themselves
to prediction. Events reveal themselves to be governed by a natural necessity.
For example, at one time, human beings believed that eclipses were signs of a
divine will responding to human deeds. Once it was shown that eclipses occur
regularly and can be predicted, it became harder to believe that eclipses were
omens, even without a metaphysics. Even Rorty's "non-reductive physicalism" allows for the "hope that physiology may sometime trace a pathway
from the distribution of electrical charges in my brain to nerve-muscle inter-
faces in my throat, and thereby enable us to predict utterances on the basis
of brain-states" (1991a, 114).[15] That is, Rorty seems to take for granted that
"physicalism" (material determinism) works. However limited our knowledge of Being may be, we have every reason to believe that everything occurs
as the necessary effect of some proximate cause. Rorty seems to share Dewey's
(and Bacon's) faith that science will one day give an account of the (natural)
necessities underlying "mystical experience." Rorty seems still to retain faith
in the objective validity of science to this extent: There are no miracles,
no nonhuman support for justice, no "mystical experience," or supernatural
revelation.

Rorty, however, cannot allow himself to make any such argument, since he
denies science any claim to objective validity. He glibly announces that science
and religion are "epistemologically on a par." But if modern science becomes questionable, does not its power to render traditional religious claims,
as well as other premodern "metaphysics," unbelievable, become questionable as well?

We must go further. If science lacks objective validity, then it cannot even be shown that science is "epistemologically on a par" with religion and not rather "epistemologically" *inferior.* Rorty's claim that all parties are equally remote from the truth is presented as a modest, "contritely fallibalist" position (1991a, 67). It is instead a positive claim of enormous significance regarding the universal limitations of human knowledge. Yet Rorty, of course, has forsworn any such epistemology. If Rorty forswears epistemology altogether, he must leave open the question of whether all parties, including those who claim supernatural knowledge, are "epistemologically on a par." Rorty's glibness in proclaiming "epistemological" parity leads one to suspect that he has not recognized the radical implications opened up by his critique of science, or the extent to which he continues to take science's objective validity for granted.

## Conclusion

At the end of the previous chapter, I raised the following question: How does Rorty suppose that his critique of science's ability to discover objective truth does not reveal the questionableness of the modern secularism it supports, but instead settles the quarrel between science and theology with a more thoroughgoing secularism? No simple answer can be gleaned from Rorty's writings.

Rorty's critique of foundationalism is first and foremost a critique of rationalism — in particular, that form of rationalism that Rorty calls "correspondence theory" or "representationalism." Rorty seems to maintain that the critique of correspondence theory cuts to the heart of rationalism as such. Setting aside for the moment the adequacy of that assumption and the critique it is based on, we are left to wonder just how that critique is relevant to the claims of revealed theology. Rorty seems to view his critique of foundationalism as an extension of the Enlightenment's critique of the "other worldliness" of both biblical theology and Platonic-Aristotelian metaphysics. All claims to universal and transhistorical knowledge are metaphysical; and metaphysics is merely surrogate theology, faith, or piety. Rorty aims at utter this-worldliness, which requires an attack on metaphysics (theology) in all its forms.

Although science, in Rorty's view, cannot claim to offer objective knowledge of the true world, the same limitations faced by the scientist are faced by all other human beings. The prophet too cannot claim awareness of the highest or most fundamental truths. Scientific "knowledge" is the product of human interpretation, but so too is religious "knowledge." The world in itself is indifferent to all human descriptions. This is not to say that Rorty does not intend to knock science down a notch and breathe new life into nonscientific "areas of culture." But Rorty has in mind for reinvigoration primarily art (especially poetry) and politics or solidarity. The same train of thought can be seen in one of Rorty's fellow neopragmatists, J. Wesley Robbins: "People who happen to hit on the internal structure of the atom, for example, are no more firmly in touch with reality than people who dream great dreams of social justice or people who come up with new forms of art. . . . We are self-reliant human beings in any event, not the mouthpieces for higher powers, whether talking about the motions of the atoms in the void or about the artistic merits of French Impressionism" (1993, 342). Because the world in itself is, so to speak, nothing in itself (or, perhaps, nothing more than material causal forces), we are free, Rorty insists, to make of it what we will. He suggests that we think "of language as a way of grabbing hold of causal forces and making them do what we want, altering ourselves and our environment to suit our aspirations" (1991a, 81). The doctrine of the world's inscrutability thus serves the goal of absolute human mastery of the world, including of "ourselves" (and "ourselves" includes other human beings).

Yet to say with Rorty that the world is indifferent to how it is described is in fact to say something quite substantial about the world as it is in itself. It is to lay a profound mystery bare. The Rortian pragmatist, it seems, has plumbed the mystery of Being to its core and has returned to tell us there is nothing to see or fear there, that we may feel free to do just as we list. Rorty, of course, could never make such a claim. He feels that in order to avoid a self-contradiction, he must refrain from the claim that his doctrine is true and claim only that it is useful for us in our present historical circumstances. Rorty professes to be an atheist (1991a, 202); but like his materialism, his atheism cannot be metaphysical atheism. Perhaps Rorty's ironism will someday lead him to cast that part of his upbringing (see 1993, 33f.) into doubt. However that may be, as it stands Rorty's atheism can only reveal something about his own purposes; it can say nothing about God. Strangely, in Rorty's scheme, to deny God's existence would be to "divinize." It is therefore less theistic (more a-theistic) not to deny God's existence.

Now perhaps the world is such a place that it is impossible for us to speak of it without contradiction. Yet Rorty believes that claiming objective status for his doctrine would be "self-refuting." As I argued above, however, by avoiding that difficulty, he opens himself up to a more radical difficulty to which he appears almost wholly insensitive. To repeat: if Rorty's doctrine is merely his own interpretation, arising from his own prejudices and interests, then the claim that all human beings are subject to the same epistemological limitations becomes questionable. Rorty states:

> Conforming to my own precepts, I am not going to offer arguments against the vocabulary I want to replace. Instead, I am going to try to make the vocabulary I favor look attractive. (1989, 9)

We thus seem to have been misled in speaking of Rorty's "critique." Rorty supposes that the ironist is too mature a human being to concern himself with arguments or refutations. He answers to no one. My simple objection is this: Rorty's opponents thus stand unrefuted. Rorty's "critiques" are in truth "creative redescriptions" based on "strong misreadings." As such, they do not tell us about any inadequacy in the opinions of his opponents. They tell us only about Rorty and his agenda. At best, Rorty's "critique" of epistemology could represent a confession of his own ignorance.

Because Rorty opts for "creative redescription," his discussion of epistemology remains profoundly unsatisfying.[16] As I noted above, Rorty is trying to close down this line of investigation, not deepen it. If pragmatism identifies truth with what "works," we have the right to wonder if Rorty's critique of epistemology, indeed his pragmatism, works. Whether it does would depend, of course, on what we mean by "work," on what our purpose is, on what we want from raising these questions. If what we want is understanding, Rorty's usefulness as a guide is limited. If Rorty inspires us to pursue the matter more attentively, we may be grateful; but we must then turn elsewhere.

In fairness, Rorty does not hide the fact that his intention is not to pursue these puzzles wherever they may lead but rather to effect a moral change. We may justly say that he is not a philosopher but a moralist. His discussion of epistemology is limited by, or rather is a strategy of, his moral-political agenda. That agenda, by his own account, is the true ground of Rorty's "theoretical" doctrine. That is where we must turn, then, for an adequate treatment of Rorty's posture to religion.

# 4

## RORTIAN IRONY AND
## THE ``DE-DIVINIZATION''
## OF LIBERALISM

Richard Rorty's vision of the fate of religion in his "liberal utopia" is made clear in the following statement: "In its ideal form, the culture of liberalism would be one which was enlightened, secular, through and through. It would be one in which no trace of divinity remained" (1989, 45). How Rorty does or can understand liberalism's ideal enlightenment in this passage is unclear. It is clear that Rorty understands liberalism as such to be essentially secular, and indeed deeply suspicious of religion and religious "inclinations." Antifoundationalism, in Rorty's view, does not jar this confidence in secularism; on the contrary, it is animated by it. To Rorty's mind, religion and the worship or reverence it entails represent the surrender of human freedom. Rorty's critique of rationalism — the once proud attempt of human beings to know the truth for themselves — culminates in the suggestion "that we get to the point where we no longer worship *anything*, where we treat *nothing* as a quasi divinity, where we treat *everything*— our language, our conscience, our community — as a product of time and chance" (22). In the previous chapter, we examined how Rorty is able to suppose that claiming chance (and the mechanization Rorty supposes follows) as the first cause of the whole, and of human affairs in particular, liberates human beings. We now confront the political question of whether the religious freedom liberalism has guaranteed is threatened or erased in Rorty's "liberal utopia." Rorty's official answer must be no. Nevertheless, liberal toleration of religion comes under severe strain in the Rortian dispensation.

*The Opening or Closing of Liberalism?*

Rorty's essay, "The Priority of Democracy to Philosophy," was written for a conference at the University of Virginia "to celebrate the two-hundredth

67

anniversary of the Virginia Statute of Religious Freedom" (1991a, x). He begins that essay with a certain version of the query that began this book: is any
justification available for the liberal solution to the theologico-political problem after the demise of liberal rationalism? Rorty's presentation of the liberal
posture to religion is peculiar. He describes religious freedom not as a right
but as the product of a "compromise" between Enlightenment rationalists
and believers. We will return to this peculiarity later. For now we will limit
ourselves to a superficial observation. Rorty recognizes that central to the
liberal political doctrine concerning religion was a certain understanding of
the primacy of human reason: it is reason that "gives the human individual
dignity and rights" (175). Liberalism's original justification was rationalist.
That is, liberalism sought to establish itself, not above all through appeals to
tradition or authority or the will, but through theorizing, through arguments
intended to be intelligible to unassisted human reason. Rorty recognizes,
moreover, that it is possible to question whether liberalism can legitimately
survive the loss of the beliefs constituting its original justification. After all,
as Rorty himself argues, the justification for a belief is constitutive of that
belief. Would not a fundamental change in justification signal a fundamental
change in belief? Rorty cannot take for granted that liberalism can survive
the demise of its original justification. And since, as Rorty states elsewhere,
"the secularization of public life [is] the Enlightenment's central achievement" (1994, 1), it is the survival of that achievement that is, above all, at
stake.

Rorty's affirmation of the demise of liberal rationalism is unqualified. So
too is his affirmation of liberalism's legitimate survival. Rorty is able to affirm
both because he disputes the notion that rationalism lies at the heart of liberalism. Or rather, he argues that what lies at the heart of liberalism may
change over time as circumstances change. According to Rorty, for us liberals
today the heart of liberalism is indicated in its name: liberty. "The ideal liberal
society is one which has no purpose except freedom" (1989, 60). Enlightenment liberals would not, of course, dispute that liberalism is fundamentally
about liberty. But they would claim (and Dewey would join them) that only
the life lived rationally, the life guided in full self-consciousness of one's needs
and capacities, is truly free. Rorty, however, believes that rationalism is too
constraining. As Steven Kautz puts it, "the formerly liberating language of
reason and nature" now stifles "those self-creative impulses that enable human beings to liberate themselves from inherited, tired, used, ways of life"

(1995, 78). Our own scientism has become just such a tired way of life; so it must go the way of epic heroism, serene contemplation, and Christian asceticism — into the trash bin of history. Insofar as rationalism has become an impediment to human liberty, its demise should be welcomed and trumpeted. Yet since there is nothing intrinsically human to be liberated, the meaning of liberty must also change with the times. Liberty can no longer mean self-governance. In Rorty's "utopia," liberty means the unimpeded pursuit of nonrational, private, "idiosyncratic fantasies" (1989, 53). Rorty's liberalism is, as Thomas Pangle puts it, "peculiarly apolitical and uncivic" (1992, 58).[1]

In this chapter we will explore the transformation Rorty envisions for liberalism, with a view to the question of how the liberal principles of religious freedom and the separation of church and state would fare in the course of that transformation. Rorty's official position must be that they will remain perfectly intact. He surely does not envision a liberal regime that will forcibly shut down houses of worship, deny rights (or what Rorty calls "rights") to believers, or establish atheism as official liberal doctrine. If anything, he envisions a liberalism where such things are increasingly less likely to occur. Yet his characterization of religious freedom as a "compromise" indicates that a fundamental transformation has taken place in Rortian liberalism, the consequences of which are ambiguous for the fate of religion.

In coming to the defense of liberalism against Stephen Carter's charge that liberalism trivializes religion, Rorty seems to reaffirm the respect that liberalism claims to afford religion. He denies that liberalism necessarily trivializes religion. He says that "Carter's inference from privatization to trivialization is invalid unless supplemented with the premise that the nonpolitical is always trivial" (1994, 2). But serious activities may occur in private. Rorty states: "The poems we atheists write, like the prayers our religious friends raise, are private, nonpolitical, and nontrivial" (2). As for Carter's charge that liberalism is characterized by disbelief in and even hostility to religion, Rorty responds that in liberal society "political arguments are best thought of as neither religious nor nonreligious" (3). It is true, Rorty concedes, that liberalism discourages the believer from justifying policy by appealing to the divine will. But, he claims, no greater burden is placed on the atheist, who ought not appeal to the authority of Darwinism, behaviorism, or any other rationalistic justification. Rorty even gives some indication that the status of religion may be enhanced in a post-rational liberalism:

The best parts of [Carter's] very thoughtful, and often persuasive, book are those in which he points up the inconsistency of our behavior, and the hypocrisy involved in saying that believers somehow have no right to base their political views on their religious faith, whereas we atheists have every right to base ours on Enlightenment philosophy. The claim that in doing so we are appealing to reason, whereas the religious are being irrational, is hokum. Carter is quite right to debunk it. (4)

Could it be that Rortian liberalism, while preserving the separation of church and state, will be somehow more respectful of expressly religious faith than a strictly rationalistic liberalism?

Despite the occasional indication to that effect, the overwhelming current of Rorty's thought flows in the opposite direction. Rorty proves to have little patience with religious beliefs and concerns like Carter's. Rorty states:

Carter frequently speaks of religion as a "source of moral knowledge" rather than as a "source of moral beliefs." Of course, if we knew that religion were a source of moral knowledge, we should be foolish to shove it to the outskirts of the [political] square. But part of the moral of Rawls's and Habermas's work . . . is that we should be suspicious of the very idea of a "source of moral knowledge." (1994, 4)

Rorty's precise meaning is far from clear. What is clear, however, is that the suspicion of the very idea of a source of moral knowledge entails the suspicion of revelation, of *God* as the source of moral knowledge. And when Rorty says "we should be suspicious," he does not mean that we should proceed carefully; he means it, rather, as a dismissal. Carter will not find Rorty's "post-metaphysical" mode of justification any more respectful of his Christian convictions than the liberal rationalism both he and Rorty criticize. Rorty asks Carter to accept consensus as the sole "epistemology suitable for a democracy" (5). If Carter could only accept that premise, he would no longer care whether his beliefs came from God or not: "The more consensus becomes the test of a belief, the less important is the belief's source." Thus Rorty does indeed encourage the trivialization of religious conviction. As we will see below, trivialization — of God and reason or nature alike — is precisely what Rorty has in mind for liberal society.

If Rorty had hoped to allay Carter's concerns about liberalism's hostility to religion, we may suppose that he failed (unless he caused Carter to realize that things could be worse). For if Carter had hoped that a "postmodern liberalism" might be less vehemently secularist because it is less dogmatically rationalistic, he will find no comfort from Rorty: "the claims of religion need, if anything, to be pushed back still further, and religious believers have no business asking for more public respect than they now receive" (1994, 2). Rorty does not intend for the critique of liberal rationalism to usher in what Frederick Gedicks calls a "post-secular" society. Instead, Rorty envisions a more radically secular society than humanity has ever known (more so even than Communist Europe), one in which "no trace of divinity remain[s]" (1989, 45).

Rorty's reply to Carter reveals a tension that runs throughout his teaching on liberalism. Will what Rorty calls "postmetaphysical liberalism" be more tolerant, open, and neutral than liberalism has ever been before — remaining, therefore, at least as tolerant of religion as liberalism has been in the past? Or will postmetaphysical liberalism have a clear conscience about, and therefore feel free to be dogmatic and heavy-handed in, its exclusion of all those who are not one of Rorty's "we"?[2] If Rorty tends toward the former, does he not run the risk of forgetting the antifoundationalist critique of neutrality, or the pretense of transcending partisan commitment? If he tends toward the latter, does he not emerge with a distinctly illiberal teaching?

In the section that follows, I will attempt to do justice to that side of Rorty's thought which seeks to describe a postmodern liberalism that is more radically open and tolerant than liberalism has ever been. Surely the impression of that openness is a significant part of Rorty's appeal. In the remainder of the chapter, I will trace Rorty's struggle to wed liberal openness with the lesson he believes he has learned from postmodernism, viz. that liberalism is inescapably ethnocentric, or closed. Rorty never fully resolves this tension. Insofar as he embraces closedness, however, he does so to the exclusion of religion. And insofar as he rejects the idea of justification of moral and political agendas, his exclusion of religion proves to be nakedly dogmatic and therefore of dubious liberality.

### Liberty and the Demise of Liberal Rationalism

Reason, according to Rorty, became the Enlightenment's replacement for God. Accordingly, the demise of the Enlightenment's political rationalism

represents for Rorty merely the extension or deepening of the demise of political religion. As Eugene Goodheart puts it, "Rorty, it would seem, is fulfill-
ing the uncompleted anti-religious projects of the Enlightenment" (1996,
225). In making his case for a postrational liberalism, Rorty appeals to the
recent work of John Rawls, seizing hold of Rawls's claim that his theory of
justice is "political not metaphysical." Rawls contends that he is not offering
a comprehensive doctrine about the universe and human life or even a distinctly political doctrine that is universally valid, but only a political doctrine
for a modern pluralistic democracy. He wishes "to avoid . . . claims to universal truth, or claims about the essential nature and identity of persons"
(Rawls 1985, 223). Rawlsian liberalism is only concerned that there be an
"overlapping consensus" among citizens regarding fundamental political issues. Citizens may respect fundamental rights believing them ordained by
God, or inherent in rational subjects, or part of some other comprehensive
doctrine. It does not matter to Rawlsian liberalism why citizens respect fundamental rights, as long as they do so.

Rorty makes capital out of "Rawls's effort to, in his words, 'stay on the
surface, philosophically speaking'" (1991a, 181). Rorty interprets Rawls's "political not metaphysical" turn thus:

> We can think of Rawls as saying that just as the principle of religious tol-
> eration and the social thought of the Enlightenment proposed to bracket
> many standard theological topics when deliberating about public policy
> and constructing political institutions, so we need to bracket many stan-
> dard topics of philosophical inquiry. (180)

Rawls "can be seen as taking Jefferson's avoidance of theology one step further" (181). That step means "bracketing" off the topic of liberalism's grounding, its justification and deepest self-understanding. Thus Rorty and Rorty's
Rawls seem to initiate a more open, more tolerant, more *liberal* liberalism.
Far from signaling a fundamental change in liberalism, let alone its corrup-
tion or death, the demise of liberal rationalism represents for Rorty a radicalization of liberalism along its fundamental trajectory.

Because rationalism is intent on understanding the goal of deliberation
and investigation to be the determination of some "one right answer," it is
essentially directed away from the plural and novel and toward the unitary
and permanent. Thus Rorty will not be satisfied with Jefferson's justification

of religious freedom: "Reason and free enquiry are the only effectual agents against error. Give a loose to them, they will support the true religion, by bringing every false one to their tribunal" (Jefferson [1787] 1954, 159). Rortian liberty is not the liberty to seek the one truth. Rorty states: "I want to replace this with a story of increasing willingness to live with plurality and to *stop asking* for universal validity" (1989, 67, my emphasis).

Rorty understands his insistence that we stop asking for universal valid-ity — whether through philosophy, science, or religion — as serving to keep the cultural "conversation" going. In politics, religion tends to shut down moral discourse, blocking the path to consensus. Rorty states that "the main reason religion needs to be privatized is that, in conversation with those outside the relevant religious community, it is a conversation-stopper" (1994, 3). If, when discussing some matter of public concern, someone ap-peals to his deep religious convictions in front of others who do not share those convictions, the conversation is unlikely to progress, especially if the believer's interlocutors doubt, as Rorty does, "that we'll get anywhere arguing theism vs. atheism" (3). In the context of political discourse, Rorty's response to appeals to religious convictions is to say, "So what? We weren't discussing your private life; . . . let's see if we have some shared premises on the basis of which we can continue our argument . . ." (3). Philosophical speculation is to be "privatized" for the same reason. Absolutism — not just taking an absolute stand, it seems, but seeking an absolute answer as well — is a conversation-stopper. Because foundational questions are inherently contro-versial, they must be bracketed for the sake of keeping the conversation going (cf. 1989, 51).

The aspect of Rortian liberalism under discussion here does not seek to homogenize society but only to keep the plurality of viewpoints as private as possible. In the private spheres, Rorty hopes to find "a radical diversity of . . . purposes" (1989, 67). A "postmetaphysical" liberalism will welcome ever more types into its fold. Rorty invokes an image of a Kuwaiti bazaar, which he imagines to be characterized by people who would prefer "to die rather than share the beliefs of many of those with whom they are haggling," and yet they haggle "profitably nevertheless" (1991a, 209). They wrangle over money, but never over their deepest beliefs, which they are content to share with their "moral equals" back in their "exclusive private club." Radical di-versity — including, it seems, religious diversity — is retained.

Thus, insofar as rationalism is hostile to at least certain varieties of religion, postmodern liberalism might be supposed more tolerant theologically than the old liberalism. Locke had insisted that toleration, respect for the natural rights of others, is "the principal criterion of the true church" (Locke 1963, 6; my translation). Postmodern liberalism, in contrast, says nothing about the truth, with a view to making the slightest demands of citizens it can. "All you need" for citizenship in a postmodernist liberalism "is the ability to control your feelings when people who strike you as irredeemably different from you show up at City Hall, or the greengrocers, or the bazaar" (1991a, 209). Rorty's liberalism makes no pretensions of enlightenment.

Openness to pluralism is, of course, nothing new to liberalism. Indeed, radical pluralism, as Rorty observes, was just the sort of social condition liberalism was intended to deal with (1991a, 209). Postmodern liberalism, however, unlike the liberalism of the Enlightenment, will not appeal to Nature or Nature's God, "universally shared human ends, human rights, the nature of rationality, the Good for Man, nor anything else" (1989, 84). The less said about such things, the more types of people may be eligible and willing to sign up for liberal citizenship. "Postmetaphysical" does not mean skeptical, let alone atheistic. It means not taking any position whatever on "matters of ultimate importance." The aim of Rortian liberalism appears to be the most radical openness possible, based on the most radical political and theoretical neutrality possible.

Notice that the radical openness of Rortian liberalism, as it has been described to this point, has culminated in an account of the radical closedness of those groups or individuals within liberal society. Precisely because the diversity within postmodern liberal society is understood to be radical, the diverse groups taken separately appear to be deeply exclusionary, or closed. Their differences are not superficial compared to a common humanity that they all recognize. Indeed, it is what they have in common, their haggling, that is superficial compared to their private beliefs and purposes, which they would rather die than abandon. By this account, Rortian liberalism will ask them to abandon nothing of their private beliefs and purposes (but this is not Rorty's final word). Rorty observes that "such a bazaar is, obviously, not a community, in the strong approbative sense of 'community' used by critics of liberalism like Alasdair MacIntyre and Robert Bellah" (1991a, 209).

But what, we must ask, happened to Rorty's famous solidarity, which he assures us will "remain intact" (1989, 190) or perhaps even be "renewed"

(1982, 166) as a result of embracing antifoundationalism? The question concerning the solidarity of postmodern liberalism is deepened when we consider the remarkable way in which Rorty completes his account of the various sects at the bazaar:

> Wet liberals will be repelled by this suggestion that the exclusivity of the private club might be a *crucial* feature of an ideal world order. It will seem a betrayal of the Enlightenment to imagine us as winding up with a world of moral narcissists, congratulating themselves on neither knowing nor caring what the people in the club on the other side of the bazaar are like. But if we forget about the Enlightenment ideal of the self-realization of humanity as such, we can dissociate liberty and equality from fraternity . . . we will not try for a society which makes assent to beliefs about the meaning of human life or certain moral ideals a requirement for citizenship. (1991a, 210)

Is Rorty to propose solidarity without fraternity? Solidarity among narcissists? Solidarity among those who are proud not to care about one another?

A partial explanation for this most bizarre proposal for liberal society may be found in the fact that Rorty is here applying his own principles of liberalism (he also attributes them to Rawls!) primarily to the question of the "international community." Rorty may understandably have less reason to hope for a substantial solidarity on a global scale than within a single country. But this observation, upon reflection, explains little. For these do remain, after all, the principles of Rortian liberalism at work amidst a presumably genuine cultural diversity, and Rorty is willing to speak of a "radical diversity of private purposes" in the context of a domestic liberalism (1989, 67). Moreover, it is part of the liberal West's ethnocentric ambition to "attempt to build a cosmopolitan world society," and Rorty sees "no reason why either recent social and political developments or recent philosophical thought should deter us from" that attempt (1991a, 213). In sum, the political principles are the same on the international and domestic levels, and the "private" diversity is expected to be in both cases "radical."

According to Rorty, "procedural justice" is the liberal "ideal" (1991a, 209). One might find it amazing that the marriage of postmodernism with liberalism would culminate in a merely procedural liberalism, since Rorty repeatedly inveighs against any pretense of neutrality (for Rorty, neutrality is always a pretense). Liberal rationalism, at least as Rorty criticizes it, claims a position that transcends the many competing, partisan agendas. Rorty's postmodern procedural liberalism, however, appears to be little more than an exaggerated form of neutral liberal rationalism, which is already exaggerated enough in Rorty's hands. Is it not precisely the intention of procedural liberalism to remain nonpartisan, neutral, above the fray? Perhaps Rorty is a bit qualmish about the possibility that liberalism may turn out to be narrow and exclusionary, suppressing radical differences rather than tolerating and encouraging them.

But yet if we return to the surface of Rorty's project for political theory, we are immediately reminded that it is precisely the idea that liberalism is inescapably narrow and exclusionary that Rorty wishes to embrace. Indeed, his account of the procedural justice of the multicultural bazaar occurs in the essay "On Ethnocentrism" — a defense of liberalism's ethnocentrism, or (again perhaps with a bit of qualmishness) its "anti-anti-ethnocentrism" (1991a, 207). Liberalism is not above the partisan fray; it is fully within it. Liberalism is not, as Dewey had believed, distinct from merely inherited prejudices. It is our merely inherited prejudice. The embrace of "liberal ethnocentrism" is Rorty's solution to the demise of liberal rationalism.

### Liberal Ethnocentrism

There are times in Rorty's account of postmodern liberalism when it appears that liberalism will in fact continue on much as before. It is in part for this reason that Rorty has recently distanced himself from the label "postmodern." He excludes himself from "those who think that something new and important called 'the postmodern' is happening," aligning himself instead with those who "think we are (or should be) still plugging away at the familiar tasks set for us by the Enlightenment" (1994, 1). The only significance of postmodern liberalism, it may seem, is that liberals carry on without concerning themselves with liberalism's foundations, without giving a thought to its justification.

Such a presentation of Rorty's thought, however, is misleading. Rorty in fact proposes, as Steven Kautz points out, "an altogether novel liberalism" (Kautz 1995, 87). Rorty cannot simply accept liberalism as our cultural inheritance, since, as Thomas McCarthy puts it, he issues "a radical critique of received [liberal] notions of reason, truth, and justice" (McCarthy 1990, 367). Would not a liberalism that took its foundations for granted take rationalism for granted? Or, since a rationalism taken for granted cannot be rationalism, must we not say that the reasoned recognition of universal human rights and the belief in the possibility of transcending our ethnocentrism are at the core of "the way we do things around here," or at least of the way we aspire to do things?[3] Must not a liberalism that affirms and embraces its own ethnocentrism be an altogether novel liberalism? How, in fact, can the embrace of ethnocentrism signal anything other than the repudiation of liberalism? How is ethnocentrism compatible with a regime dedicated to human rights?

Rorty's answer to the last question is that human rights must be dramatically reconceived. We will turn to Rorty's reconception of human rights in a moment. First we must make clear the moral motivation that lies behind Rorty's embrace of ethnocentrism. In a word, Rorty understands ethnocentrism to be the necessary basis for any political and moral solidarity. In his short chapter "Solidarity" in *Contingency, Irony, and Solidarity*, Rorty contends that a common humanity is too thin a basis for genuine solidarity. He states that

> our sense of solidarity is strongest when those with whom solidarity is expressed are thought of as "one of us," where "us" means something smaller and more local than the human race. That is why "because she is a human being" is a weak, unconvincing explanation of a generous action. (1989, 191)

We feel the most powerful bond to those around us, above all to those who are like us, those with whom we identify.

This is part of the reason that the demise of liberal rationalism — the recognition that liberalism does not rest on universal principles, that liberalism is not uniquely enlightened — may conceivably strengthen liberalism. For if liberals own up to their true situation, they may embrace liberalism as precious simply because it is their own. Moreover, they may feel a certain tribal kinship for their fellow liberals. According to Rorty, liberalism's basis

> can *only* be something relatively local and ethnocentric — the tradition of a particular culture. According to this view, what counts as rational or as fanatical is relative to the group to which we think it necessary to justify ourselves — to the body of shared belief that determines the reference to the word "we." (1991a, 177, my emphasis)

Liberalism is simply the name for the way we conduct our social and political life in modern Western societies. We do so not thanks to Nature or God, but thanks simply to the sort of people we happen to be. This, Rorty believes, makes for a relatively more secure liberalism.

Liberalism, then, is ethnocentric — a fundamentally closed society. Yet if liberalism too is ethnocentric, what sets it apart from and above those other closed societies on which liberals used to look down as unenlightened or immoral precisely because they were narrow and ethnocentric? According to Rorty, liberalism is set apart by the fact that "this culture is an *ethnos* which prides itself on its suspicion of ethnocentrism,"[4] "on constantly . . . expanding its sympathies" (1991a, 2, 204). Rortian liberals "keep trying to expand our sense of 'us' as far as we can" (1989, 196). But if Rorty has brought us to see that solidarity depends on exclusiveness, why should liberals thus pride themselves? Is not Rorty encouraging liberals to abandon their suspicion of ethnocentrism? If solidarity depends on local exclusivity, does not liberalism's tendency to expand its sympathies reveal an inherent weakness? Does not liberal expansiveness (the tendency toward universalism) tend to weaken or undermine the basis of liberal solidarity?

Rorty's answer is finally incoherent: the liberal "suspicion" of ethnocentrism (which he wishes to praise) is strengthened by the affirmation of liberalism's own ethnocentrism. Insofar as the question posed to Rorty can be reduced to why anyone should be liberal, Rorty can always respond that such questions "should not be answered but evaded," since our most important moral "choices are not made by reference to criteria" (1989, 54). There is no answer to the question why liberals *should be* liberals. If Rorty offers any "justification" at all, it is that liberals *are* liberals simply by chance. Due to an infinite number of historical contingencies, a people with our moral and political outlook just happened to come into being. Another way of stating Rorty's "justification" for our liberalism is that this is the sort of society we happened to be born into. We are liberals for reasons no more profound than the reason that the typical Saudi is Muslim or the typical Italian is Catholic: chance or sheer contingency. Liberalism is not something we came to accept, or can come to accept, rationally.

This means also that liberalism is not rooted in individual consent, nor, to repeat, is it fundamentally a regime of self-governance. Rather, liberalism is our cultural inheritance, our common tradition. Rorty seems able to abandon these components of liberal self-understanding with relative ease. He has a more difficult time letting go of the notion of human rights (although human rights are admittedly connected with consent and self-government).

Rorty fudges the issue by speaking "ethnocentrically" of "our human rights culture"; yet he thereby reveals that the notion of human rights retains moral significance for him.

Be that as it may, Rorty is forced to a radical reconception of rights. The notion of human rights such as liberals have conceived of it till now depends upon respect for something intrinsically human. Rorty denies that there is anything intrinsically human: "To abjure the notion of the 'truly human' is to abjure the attempt to divinize the self as a replacement for a divinized world" (1989, 35). This includes, not merely one's own self, but the "selves" of others as well. Rorty believes that nothing is intrinsically deserving of respect and encourages us to "treat *nothing* as a quasi divinity" (22). What this means for Rorty is that we may feel free to manipulate the world around us for our own needs and desires. Rorty leaves no doubt that he does not exempt human beings from being viewed as means, not ends. Not even the mind has intrinsic dignity. He coolly states:

> To say that a given organism — or, for that matter, a given machine — has a mind is just to say that, for some purposes, it will pay to think of it as having beliefs and desires. To say that it is a language user is just to say that pairing off the marks and noises it makes with those we make will prove useful in predicting and controlling its future behavior. (15)

Hobbes presents a similarly mechanized account of human beings. But Hobbes's account is part of a science of man that showed man as such to be in possession of *jus naturale* (see *Leviathan* 14.1). For Rorty, no science of man is possible; and this means that Rorty denies the existence of *jus naturale*. There are, it seems in Rorty's account, no natural limits (none revealed by right reason) to how we may manipulate one another. How can human rights emerge from such an account of human association?

According to Rorty, what we want — the uses to which we put our fellow human beings — has been shaped by our community and its history. Human beings are not simply self-interested monads, manipulating other monads, but social beings. Human beings not only have selfish intentions as individuals; they also share intentions with certain other human beings with which they happen to feel some bond. Rorty says, "I start off from . . . Wilfred Sellars's analysis of moral obligation in terms of 'we-intentions'" (1989, 190). Rorty quotes Sellars: "people constitute a community, a *we*, by virtue of thinking of each other as *one of us,* and by willing the common good *not* under the species of benevolence — but by willing it as one of us, or from a moral point of view" (quoted at 190, n. 1). Apparently altruistic, benevolent, or dutiful actions are in fact, by this account, an exercise in, to speak loosely, group self-interest. As for those not in our group or our present "we-intentions": "we are under no obligations other than the 'we-intentions' of the communities with which we identify" (190). It obviously follows, as Rorty acknowledges, that there are no universal human rights. Others have no rights, so far as "we" are concerned. Moreover, insofar as we fail to identify with even our fellow citizens at a given moment, they would appear to have no claim on us and therefore no "rights": "our responsibilities to others constitute *only* the public side of our lives, a side which competes with our private affections and our private attempts at self-creation, and which has no *automatic* priority over such private motives" (194). We feel the tug of our "responsibilities" to others; yet "we may have a responsibility to ourselves" (a healthy dose of selfishness) as well (xiv).

What Rorty calls "rights," as he makes clear in "Human Rights, Rationality, and Sentimentality" (1993a), depend on compassion or pity, on the capacity to imagine what it would feel like to suffer as those who claim some "right" are suffering. "Rights" are claimed by the weak and dependent. This dependence is not merely practical but reveals what a "right" is. To claim a right is in truth to seek "condescension" from "the powerful" (16). It is not to seek the dignity one deserves; it is to supplicate the mighty by assuming a piteous posture. This, Rorty contends, is the best way to get "the strong to turn their piggy little eyes, slowly open their dried-up little hearts, to the suffering of the weak" (16). The weak must not let their resentment of their dependency prevent them from making shameless appeals to sentiment.

By this account, Rortian liberalism is rooted in sentiment, or the "mere niceness" of the powerful (1993a, 16). By Rorty's account the powerful, like the rest of us, are under no obligation to others beyond what they *feel* like doing, i.e., they are under no obligation at all. Rorty, in fact, wants to get away from talk of moral obligation, since "the distinction between morality and prudence, and the term 'moral' itself, are no longer very useful" (1989, 58; cf. 44). (Rorty does, in fact, use the word "moral" frequently.) Thanks to the Enlightenment, and above all to Christianity, modern human beings are more likely than human beings of old to feel like being "nice" to the weak. The most effective means of encouraging "niceness" on the part of the powerful are novels, films, and newspaper articles sympathetically describing the plight of the oppressed. Philosophical treatises are just so much wasted effort.

And while the expansion of our group identity comes as close to being a moral imperative as anything does for Rorty, there are real limits to liberal sympathy:

> We heirs of the Enlightenment think of enemies of liberal democracy like Nietzsche or Loyola as, to use Rawls's word, "mad." We do so because there is no way to see them as fellow citizens of our constitutional democracy, people whose life plans might, given ingenuity and good will, be fitted with those of other citizens. They are not crazy because they have mistaken the ahistorical nature of human beings. They are crazy because the limits to sanity are set by what *we* can take seriously. This, in turn, is determined by our upbringing, our historical situation. (1991a, 187–88)

Rorty would like to be able to identify "our moral community" with "our biological species — defined not in any essentialistic way, but simply as consisting of any organism with which any of us can interbreed" (1996, 8). Yet at the end of the day, there are likely to remain many outside the liberal pale; and it may happen that we do not "think their lives worth living" (15). Rorty uses the analogy of triage: Those who cannot be saved in a medical emergency "are, as we say, 'dead to us.' Life, we say, is for the living" (13). Put less dramatically, if someone "repeatedly" does "the sort of thing *we* don't do," "that person ceases to be one of us. She becomes an outcast, someone who doesn't speak our language, even though she may once have appeared to do so" (1989, 59–60).

What is the fate of religious freedom in Rortian liberalism? If no trace of divinity remains, if all conform to Rortian atheism, then there would, of course, be no religion at all, and so the question of religious freedom need not arise. Yet given that the transformation to postmetaphysical liberal "utopia" could not take place overnight, supposing it were feasible at all (one supposes "utopia" for Rorty the pragmatist and nonmetaphysician is believed feasible), how would Rorty's "we" see religion treated? Will the religious (and perhaps many others besides) be seen as "mad," "outcasts," lacking "rights"? However convinced we may be that Rorty himself is a "nice" man, it cannot be denied that he invites such questions. Something dark and indefinite seems to lurk in the background of Rorty's hopes for liberal society.

The hard, cold edge of Rorty's moralism may seem to be blunted by the single moral rule to which he reduces all liberal sentiment and which he invokes repeatedly: "don't be cruel." It is usually clear enough what Rorty has in mind — most often something like, live and let live. Yet the meaning of this lodestar of Rorty's moral universe (which, contradicting himself, he calls "an overriding obligation" [1989, 88]) becomes harder and harder to make out when it is considered in light of his overall doctrine. As Richard Bernstein points out, Rorty claims "that what we take to be cruelty and humiliation in one vocabulary may not be described and perceived as such in another vocabulary" (1990, 51). As Rorty might put it, "cruelty" is such a thin, flexible term, that it is of little use in itself. Rorty's "mere niceness" may seem cruel to Nietzsche or Loyola.[5] The prohibition against cruelty in itself does not point clearly in the direction of liberalism, Rortian or other.

This leads us to a related difficulty. Rorty leaves no doubt that his promotion of irony is intended to be a promotion of liberal moral sentiment. He states: "the citizens of my liberal utopia would be people who had a sense of the contingency of their language of moral deliberation, and thus of their consciences, and thus of their community. They would be liberal ironists" (1989, 61). But why should "irony" tend toward liberalism? In order to see the moral vision that drives Rorty's entire project, we must turn to the "liberal ironist."

### The Liberal Ironist as Citizen

The ironist, according to Rorty, has renounced "the attempt to formulate criteria of choice between final vocabularies" (1989, 73). The very notion of a "final vocabulary," it appears, precludes such an attempt. Rorty defines a "final vocabulary" as "a set of words" used to justify one's actions, beliefs, and life. "It is final," he states, "in the sense that if doubt is cast on the worth of these words, their user has no noncircular argumentative recourse" (73). According to Rorty, whatever characteristics are universally human, or universal to human justification, are so "thin" and "flexible" that they are really of little use. Christian, Muslim, communist, scientist, nationalist, liberal, all may appeal to "truth," "justice," and "goodness," without making much progress in justifying themselves before the others. A more substantive justification will need to appeal to things about which there is ultimate disagreement, the things that are most in need of justification. Justification is possible only before those who are ultimately one's friends, before those who least demand it. But a justification that is acceptable only to one's friends is a dubious justification. Rorty's definition of "final vocabulary" is effectively a denial of the possibility of justification.

The ironist is one who accepts this denial as final. Rorty "define[s] an 'ironist' as someone who fulfills three conditions":

> (1) She has radical and continuing doubts about the final vocabulary she currently uses, because she has been impressed by other vocabularies, vocabularies taken as final by people or books she has encountered; (2) she realizes that arguments phrased in her present vocabulary can neither underwrite nor dissolve these doubts; (3) insofar as she philosophizes about her situation, she does not think that her vocabulary is closer to reality than others, that it is in touch with a power not herself. (1989, 73)

The renunciation of attempts to formulate criteria of judgment or justification results in the first place from having been deeply "impressed by other vocabularies." This leads to profound doubts that the ironist qua ironist can never quiet. The ironist, one notices, is able to cast a critical eye on the final vocabulary into which he was socialized. The ironist thus *has* somehow transcended his socialization, without simply adopting another of the competing final vocabularies. He is not enthralled by any final vocabulary — they all seem equally remote from the truth. One is tempted to say that the ironist partakes of the "god's eye view," detached from or somehow beyond all final vocabularies.

Be that as it may, the ironist does not feel liberated:

> The ironist spends her time worrying about the possibility that she has been initiated into the wrong tribe, taught to play the wrong language game. She worries that the process of socialization which turned her into a human being by giving her a language may have given her the wrong language, and so turned her into the wrong kind of human being. (1989, 75)

No "final vocabulary" seems to deserve to be *the* final vocabulary, *the* final standard of human life — or, at any rate, the ironist feels no right to judge the matter. Thus the ironist finds his own standards to be ever shifting. Ironists "are always aware that the terms in which they describe themselves are subject to change, always aware of the contingency and fragility of their final vocabularies and thus of their selves" (73–74). Rortian irony lacks the self-confidence of Socratic irony. Socratic irony means not fully believing what one says to others; Rortian irony means not fully believing what one thinks to oneself. For this reason, Rortian ironists are "never quite able to take themselves seriously" (73).

Given this description of the ironist, one has a right to wonder how irony could be good for liberal democracy (or for the ironist) and how the ironist could be a good, let alone the ideal, liberal democratic citizen. Although he does not always keep the fact before the reader, Rorty admits that the ironist need not be a liberal. Rorty is well aware that a good number of the most important thinkers whom he considers ironists were far from being liberal democrats. The group of nonliberal ironists includes such considerable figures as Nietzsche, Heidegger, Foucault, and Lyotard.[6] (If these are ironists, as Rorty would allow, then one must question Rorty's claim that an ironist does not take himself seriously.) Nothing in Rorty's definition of irony indicates that the ironist is especially likely to be liberal. Rorty does assert, however, that most ironists keep their pursuits a private matter and that politically they are liberals (65).

Even setting aside for the moment these illiberal ironists, why should irony make one who is already liberal a better rather than worse liberal? Amending Rorty's definition of the ironist, we find the liberal ironist to be one who "has *radical* and continuing doubts about" liberalism, who is "always aware of the contingency and *fragility*" of his attachment to liberalism, who "spends [his] time worrying about the possibility that [he] has been initiated into the wrong tribe" (75), who "has been impressed by other [illiberal?] vocabularies," one who cannot take liberalism seriously. The liberal ironist does not sound like an ardent and solid liberal citizen. He sounds rather more like someone a good liberal citizen should keep a close eye on.

But of course the liberal ironist *does* take liberalism seriously. Rorty does his best to give a believable account of the ironist as one who "naturally" inclines toward liberalism. The failing of illiberal ironists, it may seem, is their insufficient irony, their continued attachment to metaphysics (see esp. 1989, xiii, 63ff., 99ff.). Rorty accuses Nietzsche, for example, of supposing that there is a true, deep self, underneath the historically conditioned (by modern democracy) and therefore superficial attributes of the self. Thus Nietzsche failed to be deeply ironic about himself; he failed to hold consistently to the ironic dictum that the self is a product of socialization "all the way down." So it is with any ironist who longs for some radical liberation from the liberal bourgeois worldview into which he or she was born. Why should a historicist born and reared in bourgeois society be ashamed of being bourgeois?

Unless one believes that there is recourse to some higher truth, why not the last man?[7] Now it seems that having *really* deep doubts about one's "final vocabulary" — doubts about modern democratic life — turns one back into a metaphysician.

Yet Rorty's case for the marriage between liberalism and irony goes well beyond an appeal to historical dispensation, or to a "why not?" Rorty gives the impression that irony, consistently thought through, tends toward liberalism. I have already indicated the basic thrust of the argument Rorty seems to have in mind: The more we come to see that our "final vocabulary" — whatever it may be — is not universally valid, the less we are likely to wish to impose what we now recognize to be our "idiosyncratic" values on others. The less absolutist we become, the more tolerant we become — even, it seems, if the absolute in question is liberal toleration. It is not a part of this argument that the imposition of an invalid "vocabulary" on others is simply unjust (although one wonders whether the argument would have the same force if this were not felt to be the case). Recall that Rortian liberals are "moral narcissists, congratulating themselves on neither knowing nor caring what people in the club on the other side of the bazaar are like" (1991a, 210). The Rortian liberal is tolerant, not because of a moral obligation, but because he lacks sufficient incentive to be intolerant. Tolerance, says Richard Bernstein, "for Rorty is close to indifference" (Bernstein 1987, 544; cf. Lutz 1997, 28).

This argument, however, is insufficient, and it is not Rorty's last word. For it does not yet indicate any positive bond among citizens. Not caring about others enough to oppress them does not deserve, even for Rorty, to be called solidarity. In the same paragraph that Rorty speaks of the "moral narcissists" "neither knowing nor caring" what their fellow but dissimilar liberal citizens are like, he speaks of them as "connoisseurs of diversity." Rorty indicates an attraction to and curiosity about the great variety of one's fellow citizens. By "connoisseurs of diversity" Rorty does not seem to mean those who are highly discriminating but rather those who enjoy diversity for its own sake, and the more the better. They have perhaps more of the glutton than of the connoisseur in them. Be that as it may, their taste for diversity as such makes them, according to Rorty, instinctively liberal (tolerant).

The taste for diversity is possessed preeminently by the liberal ironists and is animated, it seems, partly by the recognition that neither they themselves nor anyone else have ways that are finally right, true, or natural. All human ways of life and beliefs are "merely cultural artifacts" (1989, 53). Rorty states that his ideal liberal culture would be one "which, precisely by appreciating that *all* touchstones are such artifacts, would take as its goal the creation of ever more various and multicolored artifacts" (53–54). Recall that the ironist has "renunciat[ed] . . . the attempt to formulate criteria of choice between final vocabularies" (73). The ironist has been reduced to, if not complete indiscrimination, a simple picking up on the basis of "diversification and novelty" alone. But does this not serve merely to reveal how thin and trivial the diversity Rorty has in mind is — what Fish calls "boutique multiculturalism"[8] — as well as how thin and fragile is the solidarity, as well as the *toleration*, Rorty builds upon? Do Rorty's "connoisseurs of diversity" seek out ever more various and multicolored artifacts like flea marketers exchanging baubles and gewgaws? After all, what is easily picked up is easily discarded.

The ironists, however, do not look upon the diverse beliefs and ways of life of their fellow citizens as only so many shiny trinkets. These artifacts are, or might prove to be, valuable. But pursuing the question "valuable to what end?" only leads us to more troubling waters. The question of the strength, indeed the very character, of the attachment the ironist feels for his fellow citizens becomes even more urgent when we see that Rorty traces it to a quasi Nietzschean will to power. The ironist recognizes that he is a product of chance historical influences. He finds that he is the product of his predecessors' creative acts — redescriptions of the world that have come to appear in his own world as common sense. The ironist does not, it seems, simply embrace this fact ironically (as Rorty blames Nietzsche for failing to do in the case of modern democracy). Realizing that these redescriptions are not natural but the product of someone else's creativity, the ironist feels what Harold Bloom describes as the "horror of finding himself to be only a copy or replica" (Bloom 1997, 80). He rebels, "doing the same thing all ironists do — attempting autonomy" (Rorty 1989, 97). The ironist cannot, of course, go back in time and change the forces that made him what he is. But he can redescribe them in such as way as to remake them as *he* would have it:

> To see one's life, or the life of one's community, as a dramatic narrative is to see it as a process of Nietzschean self-overcoming. The paradigm of such a narrative is the life of the genius who can say of the relevant portion of the past, "Thus I willed it," because she found a way to describe that past which the past never knew, and thereby found a self to be which her precursors never knew was possible. (1989, 29)

The ironist engages in creative "redescription," seeking to leave his mark on the world through that redescription. Since he recognizes that reality is nothing other than such redescriptions, we may say that he seeks to reshape reality. But he wishes to do so in a special sense, a sense that seems to limit his will to power. The ironist "is not interested in invoking a reality-appearance distinction, in saying that something is 'merely' or 'really' something quite different. He just wants to give us one more redescription of things to be filed alongside all the others, one more vocabulary, one more set of metaphors which he thinks have a chance of being used and therefore literalized" (39).

To return to the question of the "value" of the "multicolored artifacts" (i.e., the beliefs and ways of life of our fellow human beings), we see that the ironist "values" them as grist for his mill. They are not respected, but "objects for manipulation" (1995, 10). If we ask what the purpose of these manipulative redescriptions is, "the only available answer . . . seems to be the one Nietzsche gave: It increases our power" (1989, 115). Perhaps the ironist's fellow citizens would be better off if he did think of them merely as colorful artifacts. Hobbes too had understood human activity in terms of the accumulation of power. But Hobbes's understanding of human nature and its needs led him to claim that the desire for power leads rationally to the mutual recognition of natural rights. Rorty follows Nietzsche in rejecting the notion that human beings have a nature. For Nietzsche, the exercise of power could not be rationally limited by the equal rights of others, since equal rights depend upon a common human nature. Such considerations led Nietzsche to a severe rejection of liberal democracy as an arbitrary and small-souled limitation on the will to power of the greatest, the most powerful. How or why does Rorty avoid following Nietzsche's reasoning?[9]

For reasons beyond what we saw above, Rorty is aware that he cannot simply invoke the prohibition against cruelty. He states:

Ironism, as I have defined it, results from awareness of the power of redescription. But most people do not want to be redescribed. They want to be taken on their own terms — taken seriously just as they are and just as they talk. The ironist tells them that the language they speak is up for grabs by her and her kind. There is something potentially very cruel about that claim. For the best way to cause people long-lasting pain is to humiliate them by making the things that seemed most important to them look futile, obsolete, and powerless. (1989, 89)

This seems to be the Rortian equivalent of Nietzsche's dictum that the "truth is deadly." The ironist, by Rorty's understanding, is potentially the cruelest of human beings. How can the Rortian liberal — who knows no moral principle other than "don't be cruel" — also be an ironist? Indeed, to return to our earlier question, how can an ironist be the ideal liberal?

Rorty is aware of this difficulty and responds to it by invoking a public/private distinction. Rorty insists that "we need to distinguish between private and public purposes" (1989, 91). The liberal ironist, it seems, keeps his redescriptions of others — the sort of redescription that would humiliate others if they felt its sting — to himself, or perhaps shares them only with those fellow ironists who may be interested in the poetic novelties he invents. Keeping his potentially cruel and destructive irony private is the liberal ironist's public service, as it were. The desire to avoid humiliating others, however, demands something further:

> As I am a liberal, the part of my final vocabulary which is relevant to [my public] actions requires me to become aware of all the various ways in which other human beings whom I might act upon can be humiliated. So the liberal ironist needs as much imaginative identification with alternative vocabularies as possible, not just for her own edification, but in order to understand the actual and possible humiliation of the people who use these alternative final vocabularies. (91–92)

What Rorty means is difficult to discern. Rorty surely does not mean that the ironist will attempt to keep as far from the public eye as possible the fact that belief in God, science, human rights, and so forth, have no foundations. Rorty does, it is true, concede that "as *public* philosophers [ironists] are at best useless and at worst dangerous" (68). But Rortian irony, to repeat, does not dissemble as Socratic irony does. Certainly Rorty has shown no restraint in broadcasting and even encouraging the loss of faith in all foundations.

Rorty's main point seems to be this: "I want to insist on the role [ironist philosophers] can play in accommodating the ironist's *private* sense of identity to her liberal hopes" (1989, 68). The public/private distinction is necessary for one who has been dipped in the acid bath of Nietzsche, Heidegger, Derrida, and Foucault, and yet continues, in spite of it all, to feel the strong hold of liberal democratic morality. Rorty accepts that "there is no practicable way to silence doubt" (54), but he quarantines that doubt to a private sphere. Ironism does not merely permit such isolation; it helps make it intellectually bearable by repudiating the notion that man is or can ever be a harmonious whole. The profound tension that irony addresses is an age-old, even timeless, one: "The attempt to fuse the public and the private lies behind both Plato's attempt to answer the question 'Why is it in one's interest to be just?' and Christianity's claim that perfect self-realization can be attained through service to others" (xiii). Rorty can side neither with those who give up on human society nor with those who focus exclusively on justice and community. Ironism tells us that no "comprehensive philosophical outlook would let us hold self-creation and justice, private perfection and human solidarity, in a single vision" (xiv). Man can have both (and thus in some sense be whole) if only he can accept his radical incongruity.[10]

And yet, Rorty does not want his private ironism to alienate him from liberal *culture.* A new dimension of the problem posed by Rorty's public/private divide appears when one considers the ambiguous role "culture" plays in his thought. He states: "My 'poeticized' culture is one which has given up the attempt to unite one's private ways of dealing with one's finitude and one's sense of obligation to other human beings" (1989, 83). He thus appears discontented with keeping his ironism fully private. He claims that his entire moral and political doctrine "turns on making a firm distinction between the private and the public" (83). Yet "culture" seems to operate for Rorty somewhere in between the private and public. At any rate he does not clearly identify its place next to his allegedly firm distinction between private and public. Thus he can say "I cannot . . . claim that there could or ought to be a culture whose public rhetoric is ironist," only a few pages prior to approving of "our increasingly ironist culture" (87, 94). Rorty's lack of clarity here serves to draw our attention back from the trees to the forest. Rorty *does* seek to disseminate irony through liberal culture, with a view to the *public* good. Rorty claims that "the prevalence of ironist notions among the public at large" would not "weaken and dissolve liberal societies," but strengthen them, by analogy of the "decline of religious faith" which "has indeed strengthened them" (85).

This returns us to the question of whether the spread of Rortian irony would be good for liberal society. Rorty appeals to what he takes to be a manifest truth, viz. that liberal society has been strengthened by a decline in religious faith. Earlier liberals anticipated something like what Rorty calls the "decline of religious faith" that has resulted in our "postreligious culture" (1989, 85, xvi). But they, unlike Rorty, aimed at political moderation. Liberal society produces fewer religious zealots who threaten the civil order; that religious tendency has indeed been moderated. Rorty's appreciation of this accomplishment of liberalism, on the other hand, lacks all moderation. He would radicalize it in a scorched earth crusade against all "foundational-ism," losing sight, in the meanwhile, of the benefits to liberal society of some kinds of "foundationalism," including religious faith. (Rorty would do well to elaborate his anomalous admission that as a public philosophy, ironism may be dangerous.)

In his *Notes on the State of Virginia,* Jefferson asks rhetorically, "can the liberties of a nation be thought secure when we have removed their only firm basis, a conviction in the minds of the people that these liberties are the gift of God? That they are not to be violated but with his wrath?" ([1787] 1954, 163).[11] Tocqueville went further, insisting on the ways in which liberalism benefits from religion and would be impoverished and indeed endangered without those benefits. The benefit of religion to liberal democracy is evident, as Tocqueville puts it, even if the matter is considered "in a purely human point of view" ([1835] 1945, 2:24). Tocqueville claims (in contrast to Rorty) that "fixed ideas about God and human nature are indispensable to the daily practice of men's lives; but the practice of their lives prevents them from ac-quiring such ideas" (22). The situation is all the worse in a free country, where "in the midst of the continual movement that agitates a democratic commu-nity, the tie that unites one generation to another is relaxed or broken" (4). The result, which Tocqueville assumes his reader will recognize as debased, could easily be a description of the Rortian ironist:

> When the religion of a people is destroyed, doubt gets hold of the higher powers of the intellect and half paralyzes all the others. Every man accus-toms himself to having only confused and changing notions on the sub-jects most interesting to his fellow creatures and himself. His opinions are ill-defended and easily abandoned; and, in despair of ever solving by him-self the hard problems respecting the destiny of man, he ignobly submits to think no more about them. (23).

Rorty supposes that only a "communitarian" would be concerned about the sort of person a society tends to produce. He rebuts such a concern by saying that even if liberal society does tend to produce ignoble human beings, "the prevalence of such people may be a reasonable price to pay for political free-dom" (1991a, 190). But Tocqueville's concern is not simply with such debase-ment in itself. He is also concerned that "such a condition cannot but enervate the soul, relax the springs of the will, *and prepare a people for servitude*" ([1835] 1945, 2:23, my emphasis). A free society must concern itself with the sort of people it produces, lest it produce those who do not vigilantly guard their liberty.

Tocqueville states that he is "inclined to think that if faith be wanting in [man], he must be subject; and if he be free, he must believe" ([1835] 1945, 2:23). For religion alone is capable of drawing the attention of the vast majority away from their narrowest and pettiest individual concerns, and of enabling them to overcome their isolation from one another. For all Rorty's talk of solidarity, in the end it amounts to merely a consensus among individuals to leave one another to that isolation and narrow self-concern, to their own "idiosyncratic fantasies" (1989, 53). Rorty expresses his confidence near the end of *Contingency, Irony, and Solidarity* that his liberal ironists will still find liberty "worth dying for," despite believing that their attachment to liberty is "caused by nothing deeper than contingent historical circumstance" (189). Yet, despite the fact that this is "the fundamental premise of the book" (189), Rorty does not begin to make clear how those who see their beliefs as fragile and constantly changing, who "are never quite able to take themselves seriously" (73), and who merely want to be left alone to their fantasies, would die (and kill?) for a liberal regime. Rorty's assertion that the decline of religious faith in liberal society has strengthened liberalism is highly questionable; even Rorty admits that there is a growing "unease" about the health of liberal society (1988, 33). Rorty is untouched or unfazed by that unease and wishes, as Ronald Beiner puts it, to "spin the dials all the more" (Beiner 1993, 25). Perhaps it is only in Rorty's own idiosyncratic fantasy that more agitation, fragmentation, and isolation — all qualities that make up Rortian irony — and less stability and transcendence, could be imagined to strengthen the spirit of a free people.

But even if irony and liberalism *can* go together in one person, if that person is willing or able to make a firm distinction between his public and private purposes, Rorty does not show that ironism points to or lends any obvious support to such a distinction. Indeed, insofar as Rorty traces the motivation of the ironist to the will to power, must we not suspect that ironism tends to threaten that distinction? What sense can be made of an essentially *private* will to power? If the ironist is self-conscious about his need to leave his mark on the world, must he not turn outward and, at the very least, "reconsider cruelty" (*Beyond Good and Evil*, aph. 229)? Rorty admits that

Heidegger took "the sort of humanism and pragmatism advocated in this book . . . to be the most degraded versions of nihilism in which metaphysics culminates" (1989, 116). What finally can be said to Nietzsche or Heidegger by Rorty the liberal ironist?

> The best one can do with the sort of challenges offered by Nietzsche and Heidegger is . . . [to] ask these men to *privatize* their projects, their attempts at sublimity — to view them as irrelevant to politics and therefore compatible with the sense of human solidarity which the development of democratic institutions has facilitated. . . . In my view, there is nothing to back up such a request, nor need there be. (1989, 197)

Is that really all the thoughtful liberal can say against the "sublime" politics of Nietzsche and Heidegger? Rorty's is the flaccid reply, not of a man who keeps his most radical doubts for a private hour, but of a man who has given up trying to answer those doubts. Rorty replies to the profoundest challenges to liberalism with smug complacency. Rorty's ironism indicates that such challenges continue to nag him. Yet such a reply does justice neither to the power of the challenges to liberalism nor to the serious, thoughtful, and reasoned replies of which liberalism at its best is capable.

One burden of Rorty's argument is that he is trying to turn something into a support for liberalism that originated out of what meant to be a death blow to liberalism. Not Dewey but Nietzsche is the ultimate source of Rorty's anti-enlightenment. Perhaps the fact that Rorty makes as plausible an appropriation as he does of the Nietzsche-inspired critique of reason while turning Nietzsche's intention on its head only indicates Nietzsche's failure, or unconscious dependence on liberal thought. Be that as it may, one must doubt that Rorty can fully dispel the destructive force for liberalism of Nietzsche's attack on liberal rationalism, however much the substance of that attack he may strip away.

### The Liberal "Compromise" with Religion

What is true of Rorty's unwillingness to engage the challenges of Nietzsche and Heidegger in their full breadth is all the more true with respect to the challenges of religion. Rorty believes that there remain vital lessons to be learned from Nietzsche and Heidegger, but he seems to have thoroughly insulated his opinions from any challenge from religion. The place of believers among Rorty's "we" seems to be tenuous at best. If Rortian liberals find themselves incapable of sympathizing with believers, incapable of thinking of believers within their "we-intentions," then believers may find themselves "outcasts," labeled crazy, and beyond any feeling of liberal obligation — in short, without rights.

Rorty does not have an oppressive intention. On the contrary, as we noted near the beginning of the chapter, Rorty envisions the progressive alleviation of oppression through the "postmodernization" of liberalism. So much, in fact, is Rorty concerned with protecting toleration as the core of liberalism that it can be said to be the principal motivation behind his "going postmodern." Rorty wishes to "change the subject" away from fundamental questions in order to protect liberalism from fundamental challenge. Richard Bernstein states:

> There is no evidence that Rorty ever really doubts his commitment to liberal democracy. He never really questions it and asks himself whether there are alternatives that should be considered. He has, in effect, insulated his liberal convictions from any doubts. (1990, 58)

Bernstein goes too far in asserting that Rorty has never doubted liberalism. Yet he is correct in claiming that Rorty has attempted to insulate his cherished liberal beliefs from doubt by shutting down all fundamental questioning.

Rorty hides from himself what he does not wish to see, given license to do so by the epistemological premise that if you ignore something it really does go away. This appears to go both for God and for religion as a socio-political force. Rorty is guilty of what Leo Strauss called "fanatical obscurantism" (Strauss 1953, 5–6).[12] Jean Bethke Elshtain comments on a disquieting aspect of Rorty's obscurantism in his appeal to the French Revolution in the opening paragraph of the first chapter of Contingency, Irony, and Solidarity. The utopian aspirations of the French Revolution, it seems, are to set the tone for the book's own "liberal utopianism." But, as Elshtain points out, this is the French Revolution "redescribed." The French Revolution represents for Rorty the power of human imagination and creativity: "The French Revolution had shown that the whole vocabulary of social relations, and the whole spectrum of social institutions, could be replaced almost overnight" (Rorty 1989, 3). Elshtain objects:

> [Rorty's] bland description wipes the blood off the pages. Utopian politics becomes the stuff of intellectual politics. The French Revolution takes on

a quasi-foundational status as the mother of all political redescriptions. The modern utopian ironist moves away from the guillotine, to be sure, under the 'don't be cruel' rule, but the French Revolution continues to edify, to lie at the heart of the project of political hope. (1992, 205)

Rorty, of course, despite his praise of the French Revolution (and Jefferson), stresses that "liberal society is one whose ideals can be fulfilled by persuasion rather than force, by reform rather than revolution" (1989, 60). Yet less than twenty lines earlier, he had identified the "heroes of liberal society" as "the strong poet and *the utopian revolutionary*" (60, my emphasis).

My principal objection here is not that Rorty hides from himself the possibility of a new terror on the part of those who no longer distinguish between morality and prudence or who no longer feel obligations beyond ethnocentric sympathies. My main objection is rather that Rorty has abandoned all hope of a vital and humane political rationalism, one that does not shrink from the fundamental questions, sober reflection on which would point to the superiority of liberalism in our time. When Rorty fears the "absolutist" spirit of political rationalism in every form — from Aristotle to Jefferson, Madison, Lincoln, and Wilson — what precisely are his fears? Rorty, who calls us to turn away from rationalistic abstraction and toward concrete and particular dangers, never himself makes clear what the concrete and particular dangers of liberal rationalism are. How can Rorty ignore the possibility that his own rejection of political rationalism — his headlong rejection of all "absolute truths," such as "that all men are created equal, that they are endowed by their Creator with certain unalienable rights" — could prove (as earlier cases have in fact proved) more dangerous?

Even given his own liberal attachments, Rorty's "post-rational" (irrationalized) liberalism runs the risk of ceasing to be liberal at all. In order to assess that risk, it would be necessary first for Rorty to clarify what he means by describing religious freedom as a "compromise." Jefferson, Rorty contends, distinguished distinctly liberal politics from its more radical Enlightenment alternatives, which sought, explicitly and forcefully, to expunge religion from society altogether. Jefferson refused to go that far: "Citizens of a Jeffersonian democracy can be as religious or irreligious as they please as long as they are not 'fanatical'" (1991a, 175). All that is required for a religious believer not to be "fanatical" is keeping his religion a private matter. This is the Jeffersonian compromise, or the terms of the compromise. The believer "must abandon or modify opinions on matters of ultimate importance, the opinions that may hitherto have given sense and point to their lives, if these opinions entail actions that cannot be justified to most of their fellow citizens"; the believer "must sacrifice her conscience" (1991a, 175).

But just what is being compromised, from Rorty's point of view? Must it not be the "liberal utopia," the liberal polity in its "ideal form," whose "culture" would be "secular, through and through," where "no trace of divinity remained"? What once was the bedrock of liberal constitutionalism — freedom of religion — now remains, not as a matter of principle or unalienable right, but as a compromise. That bedrock is in truth the product of sheer contingency, not essential to liberalism, and as vulnerable to the vagaries of history as anything else. And this, we are told, should hearten liberals. Perhaps the liberal ironist will wait patiently for the tide of history to sweep the last vestiges of religion away from liberal society. But can the same be said of Rorty's liberal hero: the utopian revolutionary? Mustn't religious freedom be seen as a mere practical expedient, of temporary and strategic value only?

Already, Rorty is more willing than Jefferson to make explicit the demand that the believer "abandon or modify opinions on matters of ultimate importance" and "sacrifice her conscience." How Rortian liberalism would express or enforce that demand is kept obscure. But it is worth contrasting Rorty's account of the Jeffersonian "compromise" (Rorty's "strong misreading") with Jefferson's own words in his "Act for Establishing Religious Freedom," which Rorty's account is meant to commemorate. Jefferson states in the Act that "no man shall . . . suffer on account of his religious opinion or belief; but . . . all men shall be free to profess, and by argument maintain, their opinion in matters of religion, and the same shall in no wise diminish, enlarge, or affect their civil capacities" (Jefferson [1787] 1954, 224). Moreover, Jefferson does not understand the polity to be capable of demanding, as Rortian liberalism would, a sacrifice of the conscience. In his *Notes on the State of Virginia*, Jefferson states: "The rights of conscience we never submitted, we could not submit" (159).

But it must be admitted, and indeed emphasized, that Jefferson did anticipate a profound transformation of the character of religious opinion and the demands of private conscience among citizens of the American regime, as a product of the American regime. It is not the case that Jefferson naively supposed that any religious belief whatever was compatible with citizenship in a liberal regime. He, like Rorty, pays lip service to the great value of difference of opinion ([1787] 1954, 160). But he, like Rorty, also looks forward to a future conformity to a bland theological and metaphysical indifferentism. Jefferson, no more than Rorty, expected that liberal political society should or could be neutral with respect to religion. Liberal politics does place certain demands on religious opinion and conscience. Rorty's "misreading" of Jefferson is not altogether without basis.

Yet the differences between Rorty and Jefferson remain crucial. Jefferson at his best recognizes the necessity of justifying liberal politics, owing to, if nothing else, "a decent respect to the opinions of mankind." Rortian liberalism, in contrast, will *not* justify itself, but rather will "assert itself without bothering to ground itself" (1991b, 176). What moderates Rortian ethnocentric self-assertion, or protects minorities, including religious minorities? Rorty's indifferentism is not to be confused with moderation. It certainly cannot be said that the liberal protection of religious freedom looks more rather than less secure under Rorty's "redescription," where it remains, not as a matter of principle, but as a compromise with or of "liberal utopia." Jefferson, in contrast, concluded the "Act for Establishing Religious Freedom" in this way:

> And though we well know that this Assembly, elected by the people for the ordinary purposes of legislation only, have no power to restrain the acts of succeeding Assemblies, constituted with powers equal to our own, and that therefore to declare this act irrevocable, would be of no effect in law, yet we are free to declare, and do declare, that the rights hereby asserted are of the natural rights of mankind, and that if any act shall be hereafter passed to repeal the present, or to narrow its operation, such act will be an infringement of natural right. ([1787] 1954, 224–25)

# 5 RELIGION AND RAWLS'S FREESTANDING LIBERALISM

We move from Richard Rorty to Stanley Fish — two theorists with unimpeachable antifoundationalist credentials — via the recent work of John Rawls, whom few would list as an antifoundationalist. Rawls is at the center of a school of political theory known as "political liberalism" which has a set of concerns that seem to be distinct from those of antifoundationalism. Yet central to both antifoundationalism and political liberalism is the rejection of any "metaphysical" aspect or aspiration of political theory. As we saw in the previous chapter, Rorty claims to share Rawls's "political not metaphysical" approach to liberalism. Rorty understands Rawls to have learned the lesson of liberal rationalism's demise. Rawls attempts to make no "metaphysical" claims; he attempts to remain "metaphysically" neutral — neutral, in particular, to religious truth. According to Fish, however, such neutrality is the most characteristic mark of liberal rationalism. However much Rorty may wish to enlist Rawls in his antirationalist crusade, at the heart of Rawls's political liberalism stands the notion of "public reason." Rawls seems to remain some kind of rationalist. Indeed, to Fish's mind Rawlsian liberalism is the most extreme manifestation of liberal rationalism. As such, the pitfalls to which liberal rationalism is inherently prone, according to Fish, may perhaps be most easily discerned in Rawlsian liberal theory.

If we take up Rawls's own beginning point as he presents it in the introduction to *Political Liberalism*, Rorty's account of Rawls seems closer to the truth. Rawls does not purport to present a rationalist doctrine of liberalism. Indeed, what distinguishes "political liberalism" from the earlier liberalisms of Locke, Mill, Kant, Dewey, and others (including the liberalism of Rawls's own *A Theory of Justice*) is precisely the fact that political liberalism self-consciously seeks to avoid basing itself in a rationalist, or any other sort, of "comprehensive doctrine" (where rationalism is understood as a doctrine). Rawls sees the question of the authority of reason in human affairs to be one of many fundamental questions about which "reasonable" people may disagree. Political liberalism attempts to bracket this and all such contentious issues and to construct a political order that transcends or ignores them. Liberal theorists have no more succeeded in building a consensus around a single comprehensive philosophic (rationalist) doctrine than have divines around a single religious doctrine. Following from this contention, Rawls's political liberalism seeks, as Rorty points out, a sort of extension of the posture liberalism already adopts to religion. But this would be no simple extension, since political liberalism by that very extension changes the liberal posture to religion. Political liberalism no longer purports to represent a rational or enlightened political order or to allow for a uniquely rational and enlightened way of life. "Political liberalism is not," Rawls states, " a form of Enlightenment liberalism" (1996, xl). It does not look down on benighted nonliberals. It will not try to educate them or make them more rational. There is even room at the outset to wonder if it will try to make them liberal.

Thus Rawls deserves, as much as the more full-fledged antifoundationalists Rorty and Fish, serious attention in an account of the demise of liberal rationalism. Moreover, he deserves a place in the present study since it is particularly his concern about the place of religion in a liberal political order that has led him away from the comprehensive claims of *A Theory of Justice* to the more narrowly political scope claimed by *Political Liberalism*. So it may appear, at any rate, from the introduction to *Political Liberalism* and the introduction to the paperback edition. In the latter, Rawls states that the "the philosophical question [political liberalism] primarily addresses" "should be . . . sharply put this way: How is it possible for those affirming a religious doctrine that is based on religious authority, for example, the Church or the Bible, also to hold a reasonable political conception that supports a just democratic regime?" (1996, xxxix). And the religious doctrines in question may be, Rawls makes clear, nonliberal (xl).

In claiming to have answered this question, Rawlsian liberalism would appear to be far friendlier to religion than Enlightenment liberalism. Nonliberal religious believers are not to be looked down on or even merely tolerated. They are rather to be respected as equals, respected indeed as equally reasonable. That is, their sub-political comprehensive doctrines, whatever they may be, are to be seen as equally reasonable; or, at any rate, believers themselves are to be seen as no less reasonable for holding the doctrines they do. Rawlsian liberalism will respect and embrace to an unprecedented degree a radical plurality of metaphysical/theological doctrines and, it would appear to follow, ways of life. Rawls fears that any liberal project that hopes to eliminate this radical pluralism is destined to fail and may well turn illiberal in the attempt to fulfill its hopes. Rawls will accept radical metaphysical/theological pluralism as a basic fact of modern liberal society without trying to "liberalize" the parties' core or comprehensive beliefs. Rawls hopes to lay out a liberalism that not only accepts the fact of this pluralism but that also provides the grounds for the mutual respect of the parties as morally and politically reasonable equals. This means, it is true, that Rawls must limit himself to considering not pluralism as such but "reasonable" pluralism, that is, the pluralism of fundamentally "reasonable" parties; and we will return to this distinction below. Nevertheless, Rawls leaves no doubt that he understands the pluralism which political liberalism will embrace to be, for liberalism, unprecedentedly radical in depth and broad in scope.

Rawls's abandonment of the Enlightenment project thus reveals what is in some ways an even more ambitious project. For the challenge of transforming the members of diverse parties into rational individuals is replaced by the challenge of finding a way to encompass or comprehend politically the greatest possible number of these diverse parties without fundamentally transforming them. What political liberalism claims to have done or to do is in a way more remarkable than what the Enlightenment hoped to do. Enlightenment liberalism in its various shapes would have handled the problem of deep "metaphysical/theological" disputes by fostering an enlightened and rational (as it understood enlightened and rational) indifference to such disputes. Rorty, in this respect, shadows the Enlightenment by seeking to promote an easygoing postmodernist indifference.[1] In both cases, a certain basic conformity seems to be required. According to Rawls, the project to produce such a basic conformity has failed, as will any attempt to produce conformity in the context of free political institutions. Free political institutions necessarily lead to radical pluralism, so this is where any liberal theory must begin.

The difficulty we are left with, however, is this. If this pluralism is so deep with respect to "comprehensive doctrines" — what Rorty calls "matters of ultimate importance," such as religion, the good life, and morality — how can we expect such a people (or peoples) to agree on this most important matter: the common organizing principles of political life? Is not precisely this question *the* contentious question of political life? Is not disagreement about how and for the sake of what we should live together the essence of the political problem? Is the political really so narrow a sphere that Rawls can reasonably hope that those who disagree so profoundly on so much can agree here, on the question of justice? Is the question of justice, which is the question of the political, not *the* comprehensive question? Rawls in fact does not go so far as to say that he will embrace a pluralism with respect to justice.[2] On the contrary, building a consensus concerning justice is the express goal of political liberalism.

We might therefore reasonably suspect at the outset that the pluralism that political liberalism will comprehend is not so very deep. In fact, the boundaries of that pluralism, the boundaries of the "reasonable," I will argue, are defined by the willingness to embrace Rawls's solution. The solution is present in the very terms of the "problem." But this only means that political liberalism faces more serious problems, which it fails to address squarely. In order to identify those problems with precision, we must go through Rawls's argument on behalf of political liberalism more carefully, seeing in the first place if our suspicion about the dubious character of its problem and solution is correct.

### From "A Theory of Justice" to "Political Liberalism"

This chapter will focus on Rawls's doctrine of political liberalism rather than on the doctrine presented in *A Theory of Justice*. If some theoretical alignment between Rawls and the antifoundationalists is plausible, it would appear to be the product of a shift in Rawls's thinking sometime between the publication of *A Theory of Justice* (1971) and the publication of *Political Liberalism* (1993). Certainly Rorty could not endorse the "metaphysical" assumptions underlying the opening pages of *A Theory of Justice*: "Justice is the first virtue of social institutions, as truth is of systems of thought. A theory however elegant and economical must be rejected or revised if it is untrue; likewise laws and institutions no matter how efficient and well-arranged must be reformed or abolished if they are unjust. . . . Being first virtues of human activities, truth and justice are uncompromising" (1971, 3, 4). Rawls appears not to share Rorty's easygoing moral and intellectual "flexibility." He must be concerned that his theory of justice, as a theory, is true.

Michael Sandel, in his famous critique of *A Theory of Justice*, claims that Rawls's theory belongs to what Sandel calls "deontological liberalism" (1982,

15). A deontological liberal, by Sandel's account, holds a peculiar doctrine of the nature of the self. The self according to deontological liberalism is without natural ends. It is indeed directed toward ends, but only ends that it freely chooses for itself. A human being, according to Rawls, is not defined by his or her ends or way of life, by what he holds dear, by his family, country, religion, vocation, and so forth. More important than these things is one's capacity *to choose* one's ends or way of life, which appears to presuppose a certain radical detachment from these things. Rawls seeks to lay out a theory of justice that will be independent of any substantive notion of the good for human beings, one without any notion of what human ends are or should be. According to Rawls's theory, the substantive character of human ends, actual or potential, is irrelevant to how political society should be organized. Moreover, political society can and should be organized in a way that is neutral to views of the good and ways of life. No particular way of life or view of the good belongs to liberalism. Justice involves the inviolable freedom of the individual to choose and change his way of life as he will. Thus liberalism alone is just.

By Sandel's account (1982, 15–24), Rawls's doctrine of the self is the theoretical basis of his theory of justice and, from Rawls's point of view, of liberalism itself. Rawls states that "a moral person is a subject with ends he has chosen, and his fundamental preference is for conditions that enable him to frame a mode of life that expresses his nature as a free and equal rational being as fully as circumstances permit" (1971, 560). Only this doctrine of the self can make sense of human beings as both moral and free. Rawls's doctrine of the self, moreover, is part of a doctrine concerning human nature: "It is not our aims that primarily reveal our nature but rather the principles that we would acknowledge to govern the background conditions under which these aims are to be formed and the manner in which they are to be pursued. For the self is prior to the ends which are affirmed by it; even a dominant end must be chosen from among numerous possibilities" (560). The right to choose, and the political protection of that right, must be absolute in order to do justice to our nature as free, moral beings. If some end or claim takes precedence over the right of ourselves and others to choose some other end, we have sacrificed our freedom and betrayed our natures. Thus Rawls speaks of the priority of the right to the good. This, of course, makes right itself an end. Right, moreover, is not simply one end that we are allowed to choose from among other possible political ends. Right is *the* determinative political end. For the only alternative to the absolute priority of the right to choose one's ends is enslavement to chance: "What we cannot do is express our nature by following a plan that views the sense of justice [that is, the right of choice] as but one desire to be weighed against others. For this sentiment reveals what the person is, and to compromise it is not to achieve for the self free reign but to give way to the contingencies and accidents of the world" (575).

Sandel objects on a mixture of theoretical and moral grounds. Rawls's account of the self is theoretically implausible, and this implausibility can be seen in our moral experience. When we feel the pull of moral obligation, we feel it not as something we have freely chosen but rather as something that grips us. We are born with certain powerful bonds — bonds of family, religion, country. These bonds would not be binding in the way we experience them as binding, unless they were somehow prior to us, superior to our "choice" for or against them. We may, indeed, turn our backs on our obligations, but this does not mean that the obligatoriness of our obligations is the product of our choice. It means that we have failed to live up to our obligations.[3]

Sandel's critique of Rawls is part of what emerged in the 1980s as a debate over communitarianism and liberalism. *Political Liberalism* and the work leading up to it do not address directly the communitarian critiques of *A Theory of Justice*. Indeed, in *Political Liberalism*, Rawls denies, albeit obliquely, that his work over the preceding ten years comprises "replies to criticisms raised by communitarians and others" (1996, xix; cf. Sandel 1994, 1767–68 n. 12). But, whether in response to the communitarian critique or not, Rawls has abandoned the position that a fully just liberalism depends on what Sandel calls the deontological doctrine of the self, human nature, freedom, and morality. According to the introduction to *Political Liberalism*, *A Theory of Justice* faced the "serious problem" of being "inconsistent with realizing its own principles under the best of foreseeable conditions" (xviii, xix). For Rawls had contended that "an essential feature of a well-ordered society associated with justice as fairness is that all its citizens endorse this conception on the basis of what I now call a comprehensive philosophical doctrine" (xviii; Cohen 1993, 270). Rawls had neglected the fact that society, especially modern democratic society, is characterized by a variety of conflicting "comprehensive doctrines," some of them religious rather than philosophical. He was forced to accept the fact that it is unreasonable to "expect that in the foreseeable future one of them, or some other reasonable doctrine, will ever be affirmed by all, or nearly all, citizens" (xviii).

This is the apparent starting point for Rawls's revised project of "political liberalism," which seeks to do justice to these prior commitments or to the fact of these prior commitments. Political liberalism will accept, and even affirm as good, the pluralism of modern democratic society (at least for "the foreseeable future"). It will limit its purview to the "political" and avoid any attempt to lay out or evaluate any "comprehensive doctrine." This means that political liberalism attempts to avoid being based in any particular conception of the self or soul, of freedom, morality (as distinguished from justice), nature, the divine, and so forth. It is as neutral with respect to these matters as the liberalism of *A Theory of Justice* is to the question of the good life. Rawls can see the doctrine of *Political Liberalism* as a continuation of the doctrine of *A Theory of Justice,* since political liberalism extends *Theory's* neutrality beyond the good to matters of comprehensive doctrine, and does so on the basis of its neutrality to the good.

### Rorty's Appropriation of Rawls

It is not hard to see how Rorty might claim an alliance with Rawls's new project. We have already discussed Rorty's account of that alliance. Here we will concentrate on how Rorty takes Rawls further than Rawls wishes to go. As we saw in the previous chapter, Rorty struggles with the question of liberalism's neutrality. He wishes for liberalism to be "metaphysically" neutral, but he has drunk too deeply at the antifoundationalist well not to confess that liberalism is ethnocentric and hence nonneutral. Specifically, Rorty understands liberalism to be essentially secular and nontheistic, if not metaphysically atheistic. To Rorty's mind, liberalism is inherently suspicious of religion and tolerates it as a "compromise." Rawls, on the other hand, is determined that liberalism not be a compromise with religion (1996, 171; cf. 163). He does not understand "political liberalism" to be essentially opposed to religion. He is more intent than Rorty on giving an account of liberalism that permits believers to embrace liberalism on their own terms, i.e., on religious terms.

Rorty wishes to promote a "postmetaphysical culture," by which he means a culture that is indifferent to the truth of what Rawls calls comprehensive doctrines, as well as to whether or not liberalism is well grounded. Rawls seeks a nonmetaphysical doctrine of liberalism but not a "postmetaphysical culture." Rawls's doctrine of liberalism is to be nonmetaphysical in that it does not ground itself in any (single) comprehensive doctrine. But this does not mean that Rawls, like Rorty, is unconcerned whether or not citizens believe that liberalism is well grounded. Rawls leaves it to the citizenry privately to do the grounding, which he assumes they will do in various, albeit "conflicting and incommensurable" (1996, 135), ways. He assumes that his liberal theory of justice will be the product of an "overlapping consensus," overlapping from and remaining firmly rooted for the various citizens in any of a variety of comprehensive doctrines about what Rorty calls "matters of ultimate importance."

Rawls does not wish to promote skepticism or indifference regarding matters of ultimate importance. His desire to avoid skepticism and indifference stems, in the first place, from a desire to describe a political doctrine that is as open and tolerant as possible. It also stems, however, from the recognition that skepticism and indifference are swampy earth on which to build a stable politics. He states that an overlapping consensus of views holding to firm religious, philosophical, and moral doctrines "appears far more stable than one founded on views that express skepticism and indifference to religious, philosophical, and moral values" (1985, 250).

Rorty disagrees, at least so far as the political value of indifference is concerned. Liberalism's political indifference to theology has bred a widespread indifference to theology among liberal citizens and a "decline of religious faith" (1989, 85). Some, such as Tocqueville, had thought religious faith necessary for the health of liberal society. This view, according to Rorty, has become manifestly false. Liberal society has in fact been strengthened by the decline of religious faith. By "analogy," liberal society will be strengthened by the decline of faith in the grounding of liberal society itself. This loss of faith is not characterized by angst or some other romantic longing. It is characterized, rather, by indifference.[4]

From Rawls's point of view, such a liberalism has demanded too much, so to speak, and therefore excluded too many. To put it in un-Rawlsian terms, Rawls sees that indifference to foundations is not truly antifoundational. Despite Rorty's intentions, a liberalism of indifference makes too strong a *foundationalist* claim. Rawls states: "It would be fatal to the idea of a political conception [of justice] to see it as skeptical about, or indifferent to, truth. . . . Such skepticism or indifference would put political philosophy [and the liberalism it represents for Rawls] in opposition to numerous comprehensive doctrines, and thus defeat from the outset its aim of achieving an overlapping consensus" (1996, 150). If liberalism is to be open to a genuinely profound plurality of comprehensive doctrines, if liberalism is to be truly liberal, it must not promote, or acknowledge its own, indifference to the truth of comprehensive doctrines, let alone to the truth of liberalism itself.[5]

Rorty is correct to this extent: Rawls has of late offered what might be called an antifoundationalist theory of liberalism. Fish defines foundationalism as "any attempt to ground inquiry and communication in something more firm and stable than mere belief or unexamined practice" (1989, 343). Antifoundationalism, in contrast, "teaches that questions of fact, truth, correctness, validity and clarity . . . are intelligible and debatable only within the precincts of the contexts or situations or paradigms or communities that give them their local and changeable shape" (344). Fish cites Robert Scholes's statement that foundationalism "is lying in ruins around us." Fish himself hesitates to go this far, but he does agree that the argument supporting antifoundationalism "is the *going* argument" today (345). It is understandable why Rawls might not wish to watch liberalism go down with what appears to many a sinking ship. Thus Rawls, in sharp contrast to the foundationalist liberal philosophers of the Enlightenment, disavows "philosophical claims . . . to universal truth" (1985, 223). Rawls states: "We start by looking at the public culture itself as the shared fund of implicitly recognized basic ideas and principles" (1996, 8). Rawls bases his political "philosophy" on (or subordinates it to), as Rorty puts it, "the way we live now" (1991a, 265), rather than on permanent and universally valid principles. Thus "justice as fairness is a political conception in part because it starts from within a certain political tradition" (Rawls 1985, 225). Tradition, as opposed to what is clear and evident to human beings as such, seems to be the source of Rawlsian liberalism. This means that "political liberalism is not a form of Enlightenment liberalism" (Rawls 1996, xl). By acknowledging its source in tradition, political liberalism breaks with the liberal tradition.[6]

Rawls, then, would appear to have capitulated to some fundamental theoretical demands of Rorty, Fish, and their fellow antifoundationalists. He does not attempt to ground liberalism in anything more firm and stable than mere belief or unexamined practice. Rawls seems content to present liberalism as the antifoundationalists insist it must be: as arising out of a local historical context. If Rawls does not profess, as Fish seems to do, that antifoundationalism is the "correct picture of the human situation" (Fish 1989, 346) or even speak of antifoundationalism, it is perhaps because he does not wish even to broach such a fundamental question. Fish says that "the quarrel between rhetorical [antifoundational] and foundational thought is itself foundational; its content is a disagreement about the basic constituents of human activity and about the nature of human nature itself" (1989, 482). Perhaps in this respect, Rawls is the purer antifoundationalist, for refusing even to broach the topic of foundationalism versus antifoundationalism.

We may say, then, that Rawlsian liberalism, like Rortian liberalism, officially eschews foundational concerns. It does not appeal to Nature or Nature's God or make any pretense to follow the Enlightenment in the attempt to justify liberal politics through a comprehensive doctrine of man and nature. Political liberalism denies the exclusive claim of any comprehensive doctrine. Its antifoundationalism is seen in Rawls's description of his political conceptions as "freestanding" — freestanding of its own foundations or justification. This does not mean, Rawls would hasten to add, that "political values are separate from, or discontinuous with, other values" (1996, 10), i.e., with comprehensive doctrines of citizens considered individually. It is to be the product of (or help to produce) an "overlapping consensus." But the fact that these comprehensive doctrines as wholes (as *comprehensive*) are "conflicting and incommensurable" (135) means that political liberalism cannot officially be justified by appeal to any of them.

Thus the disavowal of the identification of liberal foundations is not simply, and perhaps not primarily, a capitulation to the intellectual fashion of the day. That disavowal becomes the basis or starting point of Rawls's strategy for presenting a liberalism that is more open than any foundationalist liberalism could be. This strategy is represented by Rawls's notion of "public reason," where foundational concerns remain a strictly private, or at any rate politically irrelevant, matter.

Rawls thus at times allows himself to make distinctly ahistorical claims. Far from being a merely historical phenomenon, as Rorty would insist, public reason with its limited scope "is part of the idea of democracy itself" (Rawls 1997, 765). Precisely because political liberalism takes no official stand respecting its foundations, it may embrace the widest possible variety of comprehensive doctrines. According to Margaret Moore, Rawls's "political not metaphysical" liberalism "reject[s] the derivation of liberal principles from a neutral starting-point" (1993, 4). She means that Rawls no longer intends for his doctrine to be "applicable to all people in all types of societies" (115). Rawlsian liberalism is in this sense not neutral, for it is built upon the needs

and opinions of a particular people in a particular historical setting. Yet precisely in this move away from universalism, Rawls has attempted a still more
radical neutrality. Rawls promotes a notion of liberal "public reason" that
would be perfectly neutral with respect to the truth of all comprehensive doctrines, while avoiding indifference or skepticism. Rawls admits that liberalism
is not neutral in its effects: not all comprehensive views will find liberal society fertile soil (1996, 195–200). But the resistance of political liberalism to
these views is simply a matter of practical incompatibility. It is not premised
on their being false. When "public reason" functions as it should, "political
liberalism avoids reliance" on "questions of truth" (395). With respect to religion, "public reason" will accomplish this feat by "tak[ing] the truth of religion off the political agenda" (151). Yet this is surely an odd way for liberalism to demonstrate the lack of indifference to truth that Rawls insists upon.
This is only one indication of the inevitable failure of Rawlsian neutrality. As
we will see below, in fact, Rawls's partial capitulation to antifoundationalism
(which, I have argued, entails his attempted neutrality) only leaves him more
vulnerable to Fish's critique, to which we will turn in the next chapter. Yet
from Rawls's point of view, this neutrality is the only way, apart from a revolutionary fanaticism that is obviously illiberal, to avoid compromise — by
transcending the contentious level on which compromise becomes politically
necessary. A fully principled solution (a fully just solution) is possible only if
the question of truth can be set aside. A compromise cannot be fully just.

### Religion and the Restrictions of "Public Reason"

Let us then take up Rawls's doctrine of "public reason," which is to provide
the solution to the political problem of the incompatibility of comprehensive
doctrines. When citizens of a liberal democracy deliberate in accordance with
public reason about fundamental political questions, they are to make the
case for whatever position they happen to hold in terms that their fellow
citizens who hold conflicting comprehensive doctrines might accept. What
this means for Rawls is that they are not to make their case in terms which
would require their fellow citizens to abandon or fundamentally revise their
comprehensive doctrines. They are to accept "the fact of reasonable pluralism." They are, it seems, not to attempt to convert their fellow citizens to
their comprehensive view (not in a political context, at least) or argue so that
agreement would depend on conversion. Thus those arguing in terms of public reason must not appeal to controversial aspects of their own comprehen-

sive views, since they can know beforehand that such an appeal will not provide the basis of a consensus. The same restriction applies to rationalist or secular comprehensive views and to religious views alike. Thus Rawls can claim that public reason, despite the fact that it allows no distinctly religious forms of justification, is not secular.[7] Rawls presents a stark alternative: either liberalism proceeds on the basis of public reason aiming at consensus and whatever that might entail, or the resulting legal institutions will be the product of an illegitimate imposition.

Rawls borrows the term "public reason" from Kant. According to Kant in "What is Enlightenment?" "the public use of man's reason must be free" while "the private use of reason may quite often be very narrowly restricted" ([1784] 1970, 55). Rawls admits that his distinction between public and private reason differs from Kant's. In fact, he turns Kant's doctrine on its head. For Rawls, it is private reason that is free to lead where it may, while public reason is always restricted, and may be narrowly restricted. Kant justified the freedom of public reason on the grounds that "it alone can bring out enlightenment among men." By enlightenment, Kant meant "the use of [one's] own understanding," "without the guidance of another" (54). This applies above all, he states, "in religious matters," which are "the focal point of enlightenment" (59).[8]

Enlightenment is not the goal of Rawlsian public reason; and, far from being the focal point, religious matters are removed from consideration by public reason altogether. According to the restriction laid down by, or defining, Rawlsian public reason, liberalism does not "question the possible truth of affirmations of faith" (1996, 63). The truth or falsehood of comprehensive doctrines is simply not at issue. As Joseph Raz puts it, "The beliefs, attitudes, and institutions which constitute public culture may well have a sound foundation in some comprehensive, possibly universal, moral theory. Alternatively, they may lack sound foundations. Neither matters" (1990, 9). Remarkably, Rawlsian liberalism aspires to be neutral not only with respect to the truth of liberal views but with respect to illiberal views as well. In fact, Rawls sets as one of the primary tasks of the book *Political Liberalism* the full inclusion of "nonliberal and religious views" (1996, xl). Thus: "We try, so far as we can, neither to assert nor to deny *any* particular comprehensive religious, philosophical, or moral view, or its associated theory of truth and the status of values" (1996, 150, my emphasis). "Central to the idea of public reason," Rawls states, "is that it neither criticizes nor attacks any comprehensive doctrine, religious or nonreligious, except insofar as that doctrine is incompatible with the essentials of public reason and a democratic polity" (1997, 766). This exception does not entail challenging the truth of the doctrine in question, but only its "reasonableness"; and, as we will see, it is crucial for Rawls that "truth" and "reasonableness" have no necessary relation.

More than this, Rawlsian liberalism's desire to refrain from touching upon the truth of any comprehensive doctrine whatever entails a silence about its own truth. Rawls assumes that citizens will embrace liberalism as true, but their understanding of its truth is left up to each individually in ways that Rawls assumes will inevitably contradict one another. Political liberalism must officially refrain from speaking to its own truth, since this could not be done without aligning with one of the conflicting doctrines and thus alienating in some way those who embrace liberalism from other causes. Thus liberalism, insofar as it is political and not metaphysical, by Rawls's understanding of those words, must officially bracket the issue of even its own truth.[9]

As we noted above, this does not mean that Rawls wishes citizens to be unconcerned with the truth of the basis of their own ways of life or of liberalism. On the contrary, liberalism would be weakened by skepticism or indifference to the truth. From the point of view of a given citizen, liberalism is the right political order justifiable on the basis of principles believed to be true. For each citizen, the political is part of his or her comprehensive doctrine, as must be the case if that doctrine is to be truly comprehensive. Political liberalism is to be the product of an "overlapping consensus." But since comprehensive doctrines contradict one another, there can be no justification of liberalism that is essential to it. Liberalism is essentially baseless. This means that the justification of liberalism cannot be part of liberalism proper, since no justification is part of the overlapping consensus. Thus, although when understood as an overlapping consensus liberalism may be said to have numerous bases, when understood in terms of that consensus alone liberalism is without a basis, or "freestanding."

This, indeed, must be a crucial point of consensus. Liberalism cannot be seen as simply continuous with the comprehensive doctrines of citizens. Its freestanding character must also be recognized. Indeed, when considered *politically* (i.e., not in the context of one's comprehensive doctrine alone), liberalism must be considered strictly freestanding and not as being justified on the basis of any comprehensive doctrine, including one's own. If citizens consider the question of the truth of liberalism, of its basis and justification, they must agree to consider it as a nonpolitical question.

How are we to arrive at this consensus to disregard politically questions of truth? Why should we agree to the restrictions of public reason? Public reason, according to Rawls, proceeds on the basis of the recognition that the profound incompatibility of comprehensive views is an insuperable feature of liberal democratic society (1997, 765–66).[10] It seems reasonable to assume that this situation first comes to sight as a grave political problem, since "citizens realize that they cannot reach agreement or even approach mutual understanding on the basis of their irreconcilable comprehensive doctrines" (1997, 766). We would naturally wish for a common political life based on the whole truth and dedicated to supporting the right way of life. But reasonable persons recognize the need to live together in as just and equitable a manner as possible, where citizens disagree about the whole truth and the right way of life. And the necessity of living together in these circumstances involves recognizing the "need to consider what kinds of reasons [we] may reasonably give one another when fundamental political questions are at stake" and when the reasons that would otherwise be considered decisive on the basis of our comprehensive views of life are seen as an impossible basis of agreement.

This is indeed a reasonable starting point. But we have not yet arrived at anything distinctive to political liberalism. In the face of intractable disagreement in political life, reasonable people are willing to accept a pragmatic compromise. Reasonable people have always been prepared to do so, even before liberalism was invented. Such compromises entail a certain bracketing of fundamental issues, to be sure, but not the bracketing of public reason. For, as we noted above, Rawls insists that the consensus determined by public reason must not be seen as a compromise. Rawls seeks a consensus, and a compromise is not a true consensus.

A true consensus is of the utmost importance, from Rawls's point of view, because the very legitimacy of the regime and its laws are at stake. Political decisions affect everyone. The political is not just one subcategory of concerns among many. It is uniquely authoritative, a fact that is indicated by its unique claim to the use of coercive force. The political alone is the realm of "coercive norms" (1997, 767):

Political power is always coercive power backed by the government's use of sanctions, for the government alone has the authority to use force in upholding its laws. . . . This power is regularly imposed on citizens as individuals and as members of associations, some of whom may not accept the reasons widely said to justify the general structure of political authority — the constitution — or when they do accept that structure, they may not regard as justified many of the statutes enacted by the legislature to which they are subject. This raises the question of legitimacy of the general structure of authority with which the idea of public reason is intimately connected. (1996, 136)

If the law is not to be an imposition on those who reject its legitimacy, and if consent is the sole basis for legitimacy, then the need for some sort of "public reason" to legitimate the law, and indeed the basic structure of liberal democratic society, becomes apparent.

We are forced, then, to correct our earlier presentation. It is not the case that Rawls has altogether banished justification from the political realm, on the grounds that our justifications contradict one another. He has banished only a certain sort of justification, viz. justification rooted in a contentious comprehensive view, on the grounds that all such justifications are politically illegitimate. A law is legitimate, Rawls implies, only if all those who are subject to that law's coercion recognize its legitimacy. In any case, public reason seeks the universal justification on other grounds that are not available on the basis of any comprehensive doctrine: "on matters of constitutional essentials and basic justice, the basic structure and its public policies are to be justifiable *to all citizens*, as the principle of legitimacy requires" (1996, 224, my emphasis).

Appeal to one's own contentious comprehensive view is illegitimate. But for Rawls this is not simply a matter of avoiding non-self-evident assertions, of providing reasoned arguments. Such a requirement, it could be pointed out, is part of reason per se. Reason as such is in this sense essentially "public." But as Stephen Macedo points out, some arguments are too sophisticated, complex, or subtle to be understood by the general public. Public reason "moderat[es] the aims of philosophy so as to insure the wide accessibility of the relevant forms of reasoning and evidence"; it should not be "excessively subtle and complex" or "too difficult" (Macedo 1990, 48–49).[11] According to Aristotle, this disproportion between fully rational argumentation and what is "accessible" to the public indicates the need for rhetoric. Rhetoric, while often used to manipulate audiences for some unjust purpose, is nevertheless a necessary art for just human beings as well. Aristotle states that, "with some, even if we should have the most exact knowledge, it is not easy to persuade speaking from that [knowledge]. For speech in accordance with knowledge belongs to education, and this is impossible; yet it is necessary that persuasions *[pisteis]* and arguments *[logous]* arising from commonplaces be made, as we said in the *Topics* about addressing the many. . . . The work of rhetoric . . . is among the sort of hearers who are not capable of seeing many things together or reasoning for long" (*Rhetoric*, 1355a24–29, 1357a1–4, my translation). "Public reason" differs from rhetoric because it must be transparent and avoid dissembling or irony. Public reason differs from reason proper in its end. Both seek to avoid dogmatic assertions. Reason proper does so because it aims at the truth. It would rather be right than in agreement. Public reason seeks to avoid dogmatic assertions, or appeals to controversial doctrine, because it aims above all at consensus.[12]

The overriding goal of public reason is consensus. What it seeks consensus about is "the good of the public and matters of fundamental justice" (1996, 213). But if these were the overriding goal, we would have no cause to hope that reason would lead to the consensus that legitimacy requires and not to the same variety of conflicting conclusions to which it leads in other important areas of human life. What is special about public reason is less its subject matter than the "accessibility" of its arguments, although the requirement of accessibility is absolute only where the subject matter is the political order. No attachment to the public good or justice can supersede the higher goal of consensus.

The priority of consensus confronts us again with the difficulty of Rawls's task. Rawls's task is to convince his audience that their participation in a constitutional democracy morally obligates them not to endorse political positions that depend on their comprehensive view of life and the common good where that view is in fundamental conflict with the comprehensive views of their fellow citizens. And because of the (permanent) fact of pluralism in liberal society, this means that in political considerations one ought never to consider what is best in light of the whole truth. Rawls states that "those who believe that fundamental political questions should be decided by what they regard as the best reasons according to their idea of the whole truth . . . will of course reject the idea of public reason" (1997, 771). Rawls seems to realize that it is a lot to ask of those who are devoted to doing what is best for their political community not to act according to what they consider the best reasons. After all, is that not a most reasonable, indeed obvious, thing for a good citizen to do? Is Rawls asking us to act for (what seem to us) inferior reasons? Does justice not demand that we seek the best outcome possible? Does Rawls's scheme, by seeking to subordinate the good of society in light of the whole truth, not seek to *weaken* the hold of justice on us? How can we reformulate or "construct" a notion of basic justice that demotes considerations of what is best? Could a truly just order be something other (i.e., worse) than the best order, the best in light of the whole truth? Rawls shows that he is not oblivious of the power of such concerns: "How can it be either reasonable or rational, when basic matters are at stake, for citizens to appeal only to a public conception of justice and not to the whole truth as they see it? Surely, the most fundamental questions should be settled by appealing to the most important truths, yet these may far transcend public reason!" (1996, 216).

How can Rawls persuade us to formulate basic principles of justice that accord with the more narrow, and perhaps lower, horizon of public reason? Rawls states that he will try "to dissolve this paradox and invoke a principle of liberal legitimacy" — the notion of legitimacy mentioned above. He appeals, in other words, to a basic principle of justice. As it turns out, Rawls's notion of liberal legitimacy justifies public reason alone. Public reason will "appeal only to presently accepted general beliefs and forms of reasoning found in common sense, and the methods and conclusions of science when these are not controversial" (1996, 224). This obviously begs the question of whether there are any universally accepted general beliefs and forms of reasoning of the sort capable of serving as the basis of fundamental political agreement.[13] Is not the absence of precisely this sort of belief the problem public reason is intended to solve? It seems instead that certain opinions about what justice is — reciprocity, equal respect, fairness — lead to the principles governing public reason. Public reason, in other words, already seems to be the product of a consensus on matters of "basic justice" — precisely the matter on which it is the work of public reason to seek a consensus. If so, the capacity of people to come to an agreement despite their supposedly profound differences is not so amazing, since Rawls has from the outset included as parties to the discussion only those liberals who do not differ on the crucial political question at issue.

The consensus that is the goal of public reason depends upon a *prior* consensus regarding the overriding political value of consensus as such. It depends on a pre-existing agreement regarding the priority of consensus to the good or, to be more precise, consensus as the good. Rawls's "overlapping consensus" presupposes itself. Perhaps this is the ultimate rationale for Rawls's uneasy historicism: if we limit our scope to modern Western democratic societies, we can begin by presupposing a massive agreement about the value of liberalism. To be fair to Rawls, however, we should remind ourselves that the express task of "political liberalism" is to embrace "nonliberal and religious" comprehensive doctrines (1996, xl). Yet even there we find that "[political liberalism] takes for granted the fact of reasonable pluralism of comprehensive doctrines." *Reasonable* pluralism is not the same as "pluralism as such" (24). Does "reasonable" mean anything for Rawls other than liberal? Has Rawls not taken for granted the exclusion of those comprehensive doctrines that are not already liberal? But if that is the case, what sense can we make of Rawls's aim of including "nonliberal and religious" comprehensive doctrines? In order to see how Rawls addresses this difficulty, it is necessary to look briefly at his understanding of the "reasonable."

### On Rawls's "Reasonableness"

Rawls is, of course, aware that political liberalism will not satisfy all parties. There will remain those whose beliefs about the basic organization of political life will not overlap with others' in a liberal consensus. There are those who would, if only they could, establish laws that contradict basic liberal principles. If "political liberalism" does not wish to speak to the truth or untruth of the beliefs of these foes of liberalism, how, as Rawls poses the question, is political or freestanding liberalism possible? Is it not inevitable that liberalism be forced to speak to the truth of such nonliberal beliefs? Must not liberalism either make the case for its own superior rationality or be forced, as Rorty says, to assert itself, i.e., be dogmatic at the risk of being illiberal?

Rawls's alternative to arguing for, or even affirming, liberalism's own truth and the untruth of nonliberal beliefs that will not go along is to declare those nonliberal beliefs "unreasonable." "Reasonableness" becomes a massive concept for Rawls, and one cannot proceed very far in *Political Liberalism* without clarity about what it means, for Rawls, to be reasonable. Here we will limit ourselves to pointing out that reasonableness for Rawls does not primarily have to do with the good use of one's reason. One is reasonable not for having reasoned well: one can, according to Rawls, be "perfectly rational" while also being "highly unreasonable" (1996, 48). Instead, one is reasonable for having "the desire to engage in fair cooperation as such" (51). Being reasonable is a moral matter and cannot be arrived at rationally (53–54). Rawls's opinion of the matter is perhaps clearest when he states that "reasonable persons . . . are not moved by the general good as such but desire for its own sake a social world in which they, as free and equal, can cooperate with others on terms all can accept" (50). Reasonable persons are not moved by the general good as such: they are willing, it seems, to subordinate the good of the community to their sense of fair cooperation with others. Does this then mean that they may consciously act in a way contrary to the general good, in a way that is not only bad for themselves but bad for all involved? According to Rawls, concern for the good — not simply one's own private good, but also the good of the whole — is characteristic of the rational rather than the reasonable (50–51).[14] Yet can an action taken in knowledge that it is bad for all concerned possibly be reasonable? We are led to conclude that a belief may, for Rawls, be false (bad for society) but reasonable. More remarkably, it seems that a belief may be true (good for society) but unreasonable.

It is true that a key ingredient of the reasonable, according to Rawls, is the "willingness to recognize the burdens of judgment" and their consequences for politics; and the burdens of judgment could easily be interpreted as meaning to encourage a certain skepticism regarding the truth. But Rawls hopes that the implications of the burdens of judgment can be drawn up short of such skepticism. The burdens of judgment are meant to explain why there is radical disagreement with respect to comprehensive doctrine. There are various possible explanations for the disagreement, including that "people hold views that advance their own more narrow interests," or alternatively that "people are often irrational and not very bright" (1996, 55). "Such explanations," Rawls admits, "explain much," but "they are too easy and not the kind of explanation we want" (55). We want an explanation that is "compatible with everyone's being fully reasonable," though this requires that we "work at first within ideal theory" (58, 55). Thus the burdens of judgment are meant to address the question of why there is radical disagreement with respect to comprehensive doctrine, despite the fact that everyone shares a "common human reason" and "similar powers of thought and judgment" (55). There are various suitable explanations, such as the difficulty of assessing the often conflicting and complicated evidence on which one can judge comprehensive views, and the fact that different life experiences shape our views to a degree that is impossible to know (56–57). These "burdens of judgment" weigh on all of us equally: no one must be supposed to have pursued or to be capable of pursuing these matters more deeply than any of the rest. One might suppose that Rawls is enlisting a certain skepticism about, not only the capacity to know, but even to progress in one's understanding.[15] Rawls denies, however, that the burdens of judgment indicate any manner of epistemological skepticism. The burdens of judgment are meant to indicate only the impossibility of reaching a political consensus on matters of comprehensive doctrine, while continuing to allow for the possibility of equal respect. They do not suggest "that we should be uncertain, much less skeptical, about our own beliefs" (63).[16] The burdens of judgment provide the kind of explanation we want because they help us to allow that, although our fellow citizens are, from our point of view, profoundly wrong about many fundamental matters, our disagreement cannot be traced to any moral or intellectual deficiency on their (or our) part.

To return to the question of nonliberal religious citizens, their views are excluded by Rawls, not for being false, but for being unreasonable. More precisely, Rawls implies that comprehensive doctrines themselves can be neither reasonable nor unreasonable. Only people, through the manner in which they hold or act upon their comprehensive doctrines politically, can be reasonable or unreasonable. This enables Rawls to claim that, in order to be welcomed within the liberal fold, one need not abandon one's core beliefs. Rawls "does not argue that we should be hesitant and uncertain, much less skeptical, about our own beliefs" (1996, 63). Rather, we need only be reasonable in how we *act* upon our beliefs, or in how we interpret their political ramifications or lack thereof. Rawls's goal appears to be that every human worldview could incorporate political liberalism while remaining essentially intact. No one is excluded a priori: "Since we assume each citizen to affirm some [comprehensive doctrine], we hope to make it possible for all to accept the political conception as true or reasonable from the standpoint of their own comprehensive view, *whatever it may be*" (1996, 150, my emphasis).

Macedo, in a defense of the Rawlsian posture to nonliberal religion, states that "the political liberal offers a bargain to moderates in all comprehensive camps, whether fundamentalist Protestant or autonomy-pursuing liberal" (1995, 482). Even fundamentalists, then, are not necessarily beyond the Rawlsian pale — with one proviso: liberals "should insist on political respect for fundamentalists who acknowledge the political authority of liberal public principles" (487). As Macedo goes on to observe, this means that "the question of religious truth must be bracketed." Since the question of religious truth is bracketed, if a person rejects liberalism, it is not due to a fundamental conflict with liberal principles. It is due only to a lack of "reasonableness" on the part of the believer.

### The Collapse of Freestanding Liberalism

Fish's objection to such a project, which we will take up in greater detail below, is simple and powerful. The proviso attached to the "political respect" (toleration?) of fundamentalists is tantamount to a demand that they abandon their fundamentalism. Does it not partly define the fundamentalist to believe that God has issued certain moral commandments that are unambiguous and nonnegotiable, or truly fundamental? If so, a fundamentalist who "acknowledges the political authority of liberal public principles" is no longer a fundamentalist. Rawls seems to suppose that a fundamentalist can believe in the unambiguity of God's commandments for human life — believing, as he puts it, without hesitation, uncertainty, or skepticism — while nevertheless putting those commandments aside politically. But the willingness to set God's will for human life aside in the political realm requires not merely a change in attitude toward one's beliefs; it requires a change in one's beliefs concerning God's will. One must come to believe that it is consistent with God's will that it be set aside in politics. Liberalism depends on religion's being substantively transformed, not bracketed. Liberalism cannot simply preserve the private realm intact. Thus Macedo, his defense of Rawls's political liberalism notwithstanding, has emphasized what he calls liberalism's "transformative agenda": "If a constitutional regime is to succeed and thrive, it must constitute the private realm in its image, and it must form citizens willing to observe its limits and able to pursue its aspiration" (1998, 58).[17] Or as Rorty puts it in the same essay in which he defends Rawls, citizens of a liberal democracy "must abandon or modify opinions on matters that have hitherto given sense and point to their lives, if these opinions entail public actions that cannot be justified to most of their fellow citizens" (1991a, 175).

Rorty's statement underscores a further part of Fish's argument. Not only does liberalism seek a change of belief, it seeks that change just where it matters most to the nonliberal believer. Liberalism seeks to bracket what, for the nonliberal believer, are the least "bracketable" beliefs: "The boutique multi-culturalist [such as Rawls] will withhold approval of a particular culture's practices at the point at which they matter most to its strongly committed members: a deeply religious person is precisely that, *deeply* religious, and the survival and propagation of his faith is not for him an incidental (and bracket-able) matter, but an essential matter, essential too in his view for those who have fallen under the sway of false faiths" (Fish 1999a, 58). Fish's last phrase stresses that the beliefs in question are not understood by the believer to be a merely personal matter. The liberal who, to borrow Jefferson's famous expression, is concerned only that his neighbor who believes in no god or twenty gods not pick his pocket or break his leg (Jefferson [1787] 1954, 159), also has little concern that his neighbor has strayed from the right way, has a distorted and harmful soul, or is damned for his error.[18] Perhaps this lack of concern is possible only if one no longer believes that one's neighbor's error carries any such consequences. But that is precisely the point: a change of *belief* is required. It is not enough to respond that one may still be concerned but limit one's actions to verbal persuasion. For as Rawls states, "a fundamen-tal difficulty is that since under reasonable pluralism the religious good of salvation cannot be the common good of all citizens, the political conception must employ, instead of that good, political conceptions such as liberty and equality together with a guarantee of sufficient all-purpose means" (1996, xli). This is indeed a fundamental difficulty for political liberalism, a difficulty presented only a page after Rawls announced his purpose in the book of embracing "doctrines taken to be nonliberal and religious." What does it mean to say that the religious good of salvation cannot be the common good of all citizens? What would the good of salvation be if not the common good of all citizens? Surely some believers will not find what Rawls calls the "very great virtues . . . of tolerance and being ready to meet others halfway" (157) so great that they outweigh (or rather replace) the moral imperative to do whatever we can to ensure the salvation of our fellow human beings.

This fundamental difficulty proves to be one that Rawls's political theory cannot solve. Recall that Rawls had stated that "we try, *as far as we can*, neither to assert nor deny any particular comprehensive religious, philosophical, or moral view, or its associated theory of truth and the status of values" (1996, 150, my emphasis). It may, he admits reluctantly, become necessary to justify liberalism before nonliberals, which means entering the fray of comprehensive doctrines and addressing those questions of truth and falsehood that he had hoped to bracket:

> In affirming a political conception of justice we may eventually have *to assert* at least certain aspects of *our own* comprehensive religious or philosophical doctrine (by no means necessarily fully comprehensive). This will happen whenever someone insists, for example, that certain questions are so fundamental that to insure their being rightly settled justifies civil strife. The religious salvation of those holding a particular religion, or indeed the salvation of a whole people, may be said to depend on it. At this point we may have no alternative but to deny this, or to imply its denial and hence to maintain the kind of thing we had hoped to avoid. (152, my emphasis)

In what follows the admission that the appeal to comprehensive doctrine may be unavoidable, Rawls tries again to avoid having to pronounce on (let alone investigate) the truth or falsehood of the condemned religious belief/practice. But this avoidance proves to be merely a holding of the tongue, not to say a dissembling: "Of course, we do not believe the doctrine believers here assert, and this is shown in what we do" (153). This final admission is explosive. For since the liberal state must act, and since it cannot take any religious prescription as authoritative for its actions, the liberal state *in principle* denies that there are any true, politically relevant religious prescriptions. Liberalism rests on a theological premise.

At this point, Fish can declare the brand of liberalism represented by Rawls's political liberalism theoretically defeated, undermined by its own premises. For the pretense of neutrality is over, if only for an instant. Liberalism cannot avoid the need to justify itself, thereby transgressing the boundaries of "public reason." Liberals are forced to delve into their "comprehensive doctrines," which contradict one another and which are not themselves amenable to "public reason." They must be, as Rawls says, asserted. They can only be asserted, where political philosophy has abandoned the goal of inquiring into the truth. We inevitably end up outside the land of "overlapping consensus," without recourse to a reasoned solution. Rawls began with the premise that an official dependence on any comprehensive doctrine makes political liberalism impossible, since it would "defeat at the outset [political liberalism's] aim of achieving an overlapping consensus" (1996,

150). But liberalism must enter the fray of conflicting views, precisely because the conflict of views is deep and permanent — precisely because of one of Rawls's basic premises.

But the difficulty is not simply that other sub- or suprapolitical considerations are relevant to politics and cannot be ignored. The difficulty is not that political liberalism is forced to go outside the confines of the political in order to defend a liberalism that is otherwise justifiable on strictly political terms. The more immediate and more important difficulty is that liberalism is challenged by those who dispute its understanding of the political itself. Rawls states that political liberalism's public reason "concerns how the political relation is to be understood" (1997, 766). Yet immediately following this claim he states that those who disagree with political liberalism on the answer to the question of the political relation will be ignored. There are those for whom "the political relation may be that of friend or foe, to those of a particular religious or secular community or those who are not; or it may be a relentless struggle to win the world for the whole truth. Political liberalism does not engage those who think this way" (1997, 766–67). For the sake of what does the political order exist? This is a *political* question, not to say *the* political question. But it is a question on which so-called political liberalism refuses to engage other views, on the remarkable grounds that to do so would carry it beyond the political. "Political liberalism," by avoiding *the* political question, reveals itself to be essentially antipolitical.[19]

Political liberals will, one assumes, defend liberalism with arms; but they will not do so with words. To engage others with words, Rawls fears, would be to engage others on the ground of bare assertion and not with reasoned argument. Liberalism would be forced to appear, or rather to be, dogmatic. Does this reveal Rawls's suspicion that liberalism can only be defended with dogmatic assertion? However that may be, "public reason" cannot itself be justified or even argued for with public reasons. It can only be asserted. If liberalism did engage others, it would not be demonstrating its own grounds, since it would not then be on its own ground — the ground of reasonable democratic consensus — but rather on the ground of dogmatic assertion. So political liberalism ignores its foes. It ignores them since it is not characteristic of political liberalism to conceive of the political relation as consisting of friend and foe. Liberalism does not even recognize its opponents as foes. Liberalism's opponents may vary tremendously in their reasonableness, and some may indeed be the most dangerous kinds of fanatics. But they at least are willing to say *something* in their own defense. By covering its eyes, ears, and mouth, does not political liberalism exhibit a most naked sort of dogmatism?

### The Comprehensive Claim of the Political

In narrowing the scope of the political as part of a project of broad inclusion, Rawls is forced to present the political realm in two ways that fit uneasily together. In order to make political liberalism acceptable to one who takes his or her comprehensive view seriously, as Rawls allows and even encourages, he must present the political as a small, unthreatening, even superficial aspect of one's comprehensive view: "It is only by affirming a constructivist conception — one which is political and not metaphysical — that citizens generally can expect to find principles that all can accept. This they can do without denying the *deeper* aspects of their reasonable comprehensive doctrines" (1996, 97–98, my emphasis). The political, it seems, does not go very deep. Some superficial aspects (the political aspects) might have to give way to liberal political principles; but the deeper aspects — the sub- or suprapolitical aspects — can remain intact and strong. Thus reasonable pluralism is not distinguished from pluralism as such by the relative superficiality of the disagreement. Reasonable liberals too are "profoundly divided" (1996, xx).

And yet, as we have already seen, this cannot quite be the case. The *political* of political liberalism is of far greater scope than it initially claims to be. It is my contention that Rawls does not adequately recognize the *comprehensive* nature of the political. The political comprehends the individuals and associations within it in a uniquely authoritative way.[20] A sign of this is the fact that, as Rawls observes, "the government alone has the authority to use force in upholding its laws" (1996, 136). The political represents "coercive norms" (1997, 767). This is a matter not just of force but more importantly of right — at least of claimed right. That right is the most sovereign in the land, and the character of the political order that claims it cannot help but shape the character of those associations and individuals who live under it. It does not matter whether the vehicle for enlisting that support is the "state." For the political order, as liberalism perhaps uniquely demonstrates, exercises its moral influence willy-nilly. Thus, Macedo owns, "it is in this sense that liberalism may be said to 'silence' the 'religious voice': not through direct censorship and the heavy hand of state oppression, but rather through a wide array of sometimes subtle expectations about appropriate forms of speech and reasoning which amount to a system of unequal psychological taxation sufficient to drive out certain patterns of deeply held belief and practice, not all at once but over the course of generations" (1998, 72; cf. Tocqueville [1835] 1945, 1:269ff., 2:13).

Without recognizing the comprehensive aspect of the political order, Rawls's project seems implausible to say the least. For he expects that a citizen may believe in a "religious and nonliberal" comprehensive doctrine without being "hesitant and uncertain, much less skeptical" (63), and at the same time deny that "the most fundamental questions should be settled by appealing to the most important truths," truths that "may far transcend public reason" (216). Either Rawls is in for a rude awakening when nonliberal believers, and others besides, actually seek to determine the most fundamental questions in light of what they hold to be the most important truths, or else he has greatly underestimated the extent to which liberal principles transform comprehensive doctrines so as to establish *themselves* as the most important truth. Locke, who is far more aware of the transformation of religion that liberalism requires, begins his *Letter Concerning Toleration* by asserting that toleration is "the principal criterion of the true church" (1963, 6). This is not to say that various sects under a liberal regime may not have various doctrines. But they agree that those matters are secondary to the most important thing: toleration.[21] The most important thing ipso facto trumps, and therefore determines what is seen as the right way of life. The right way of life is the tolerant way of life. Political liberalism's priority of the right to the good constitutes a singular view of the good, even as its self-understanding obscures the fact. No doctrine is so important as to override the principle of toleration. Toleration displaces all other doctrines as the core of the true religion. Put otherwise, doctrine, or the question of the *true* doctrine, becomes far less important under a liberal order. Thus what we find in liberal society is not, as Rawls presents it, a limited political consensus that leaves the deep pluralism of comprehensive views essentially intact. We find instead that the liberal political consensus has radically transformed those comprehensive views. As Macedo puts it, "liberal politics is pervasive because public reasons, liberal norms of respect for the rights of others, override competing commitments and claim authority in every sphere of our lives" (1990, 264). Liberalism, by the fact that it is a political doctrine, is a comprehensive doctrine. Reasonable pluralism is a superficial pluralism.[22]

Once we take Rawls's claims regarding the depth of reasonable pluralism with the appropriate grain of salt, the degree to which he seeks something like the uniformity we have been speaking of emerges more and more clearly. Indeed, even though at first glance, as we noted at the outset of the chapter, Rawls appears to step back from pursuing the sort of comprehensive consensus that Enlightenment liberalism allegedly sought, it becomes evident as his project unfolds that Rawls seeks a *deeper* uniformity than Enlightenment liberals sought or even thought feasible or compatible with liberal principles. To begin to see this, it is helpful to contrast Rawls's approach to the political problem posed by pluralism with Madison's approach in Federalist 10.

To begin, Madison speaks of faction rather than pluralism. He contends that, while "the latent causes of faction are . . . sown in the nature of man," factions thrive in a free political society: "Liberty is to faction what air is to fire, an aliment without which it instantly expires" (Hamilton, Madison, and Jay 1961, 58). Here Madison's teaching resembles Rawls's. Madison, however, considers the "propensity" of "popular government" to break into factions as "a dangerous vice" (56). Rawls, in contrast, insists that "the fact of reasonable pluralism" — the focus of his concern — "is not an unfortunate condition of human life," or of life in a free society (1996, 37). It is not unfortunate because reasonable pluralism is "the inevitable outcome of free human reason" and the outcome of free human reason, it seems, cannot be unfortunate (37; cf. xxvi–vii; Cohen 1993). Reasonable pluralism is "not simply the upshot of self- and class interests, or of peoples' understandable tendency to view the political world from a limited standpoint" (37). Reasonable pluralism represents not the clash of petty and narrow interests but rather the high level incompatibility of comprehensive views of the whole of life — respectable, reasonable, public-spirited views. Madison, on the other hand, hardly seems to suppose that such pluralism exists. At any rate, the problem of faction as he understands it is precisely one of narrow interests.

According to Madison, man's reason is never divorced from his narrow interests. Self-interest distorts reason and leads men's reasoning in contradictory directions: "As long as the reason of man continues fallible, and he is at liberty to exercise it, different opinions will be formed. As long as the connection subsists between his reason and his self-love, his opinions and his other passions will have a reciprocal influence on each other; and the former will be objects to which the latter will attach themselves" (58). And the problem is only made worse by the "diversity in the faculties of men, from which the rights of property originate." "The protection of these faculties," these unequal faculties, "is the first object of government." The material inequality thus secured influences "the sentiment and views of the respective proprietors," producing "a division of society into different interests and classes." Here, "sown in the nature of man," are the "latent causes of faction," including the "zeal for different opinions concerning religion, concerning government, and many other points, as well of speculation as of practice." The higher sort of disagreement that is Rawls's concern is, Madison suggests, traceable to these baser causes. Religious and moral disagreement, however intractable it may be, is not "deep." At any rate, neither morality nor religion can reasonably be expected to moderate the effects of base self-interest: "If the impulse and the opportunity be suffered to coincide, we well know that neither moral nor religious motives can be relied on as an adequate control" (61). Accordingly, Madison's famous solution asks nothing, so to speak, of the various partisans:

> Extend the sphere [of society], and you take in a greater variety of parties and interests; you make it less probable that a majority of the whole will have a common motive to invade the rights of other citizens; or if such a common motive exists, it will be more difficult for all who feel it to discover their own strength, and to act in unison with each other. (64)

The Madisonian solution would accept human nature as it is. The Madisonian solution is unconcerned with making citizens more just. It is unconcerned with the virtue, the quality of soul, of the citizens. It implies that a moral solution is utopian or naive.

The Rawlsian solution, in contrast, in emphatically moral. This is because Rawls's understanding of the problem is moral. Madison is indeed vulnerable to the criticism that there are serious moral and religious differences of opinion that cannot plausibly be traced to a mundane clash of material self-interests. One can recognize the enormous political importance of self-interest, while finding that Madison's hard-bitten realism rings artificial. The problem Rawls addresses is not principally one of clashing interests. The problem for Rawls is that moral, decent, public-spirited people disagree about fundamental issues. But precisely because his audience is moral, decent, and public spirited, Rawls can propose a moral, decent, and public-spirited solution.[23] The Rawlsian solution is to stand in contrast to a "modus vivendi" (literally, a measure or manner of living). Rawls borrows the term from international relations studies, where it represents an "equilibrium point," an agreement whose

> terms and conditions . . . are drawn up in such a way that it is public knowledge that it is not advantageous for either state to violate it. . . . But in general both states are ready to pursue their goals at the expense of the other, and should conditions change they may do so. . . . A similar background is present when we think of social consensus founded on self- or group interests, or on the outcome of political bargaining: social unity is only apparent, as its stability is contingent on circumstances remaining such as not to upset the fortunate convergence of interests. (1996, 147)

Rawls is concerned that a modus vivendi is by nature unstable.

But his deeper concern is that, even if a modus vivendi could produce a stable society, "in this case we do not have stability for the right reasons, that is, as secured by a firm allegiance to a democratic society's political (moral) ideals and values" (1997, 781). Rawls is not satisfied if a citizen obeys the laws, respects the rights of others, serves in the military when called, etc. He is not concerned with outward acts only. Rawls is concerned that citizens do what they do "for the right reasons." He is concerned with what is in the citizen's heart. He seeks "*wholehearted* members of democratic society who endorse society's intrinsic political ideals and values and do not simply acquiesce in the balance of political and social forces" (781, my emphasis). We might have been led to believe that what counts as being "for the right reasons" was to be a matter left to the various comprehensive doctrines, beyond the purview of political liberalism. But the "right reasons" turn out to be a chief concern, even the defining concern, of political liberalism.

The liberalism of the Enlightenment, what Rawls considers comprehensive liberalism, feared that such intimate concern for what is in the hearts of citizens ran too great a risk of oppression and intolerance. That was the stuff of theocrats and would-be theocrats, for whom outward conformity to the law was not enough. Hobbes set the tone for the early liberals when he insisted that God alone can know what is in the heart — God, not our fellow citizens, not the priests, not the sovereign. The law, according to Hobbes, does not represent an entire way of life. What the law does not specifically determine is left for each to determine as he wishes; and the law cannot determine the heart. The right of conscience, if not the right of speech or outward expression of the conscience, is by nature absolutely inalienable. All the sovereign can demand, and all that he need demand, is outward compliance. Moreover, the concern for the souls of our fellow citizens, Hobbes teaches, is not natural. Our natural unconcern for our fellows does not much allow for mutual respect, the desire for great social cooperation, or other greater aspects of community; but it is, the early liberals believed, the surest ground of toleration. Political liberalism seems to have attempted to combine an unconcern for our fellow citizens' souls with a revived concern for their souls — that they be suitably tolerant, suitably just.

As we noted at the beginning of the chapter, Rawls's political liberalism presents itself as more open, more inclusive, and therefore more liberal than its "comprehensive" predecessors. Rawls seems to ask very little indeed. No comprehensive doctrines are in themselves out of bounds, and therefore no fundamental change of belief is sought. But Rawls asks more than he knows. Bracketing so very much of one's comprehensive view from consideration in the political realm requires a radical transformation of that comprehensive view. "Bracketing" is not simply bracketing; it is transforming. To use our earlier example, in order to set aside consideration of God's will for human life when deliberating about how we humans should live together in political society, one must believe or come to believe that it is compatible with God's will that it be set aside in this way. This belief, according to Rawls's scheme, is not properly "political." But this belief is necessary to justify or support the bracketing, even as it reveals that there in fact has been no real bracketing. The political molds the subpolitical in a way that cannot be made sense of in the context of the doctrine of "political liberalism."

And yet political liberalism depends on this liberalizing transformation. To be more precise, it depends on the crucial transformation already having taken place. It is only because Rawls takes it so much for granted that he can mistake liberal pluralism for deep pluralism. And bear in mind that reasonable pluralism only includes those who are attached to liberal principles "for the right reasons." It is even narrower than the pluralism actually found in liberal society, to say nothing of "pluralism as such." But this does not mean that the scope of political liberalism is identical to that of the liberal moral transformation. The scope of political liberalism is, ironically enough, narrower. For it is not even clear if those whom Rawls describes as comprehensive liberals meet political liberalism's strict moral "standard." Recall that a crucial point of consensus is the freestanding character of liberal principles.

That is, all must agree on the irrelevance for politics, in the strict Rawlsian sense, of contentious elements of their comprehensive views. This applies to those whose comprehensive views are liberal — the Lockean, the Deweyan, the "pre-political" Rawlsian — as well as those holding religious and nonliberal views whom Rawls also seeks to include. Citizens must not see whatever it is that justifies liberalism (for them) as a necessary part of the political conception of justice, i.e., as essential to liberalism. For their fellow liberal citizens disagree profoundly with them on that score. Therefore the "comprehensive liberal" must alter his view of what liberalism is about. A Dewey may still see liberalism as having the same "comprehensive" significance for himself and those like-minded. But liberalism can no longer be what it primarily was for Dewey: a universal political and cultural project of rational liberation and control. What such a revised Deweyan liberalism would look like is a question that lies outside the purview of political liberalism. But it seems that Deweyan liberalism would have to be abandoned. Matters that were once seen to be politically essential, even for liberals, must now be seen to be politically irrelevant or not political at all.[24]

Though this consequence of Rawls's scheme is ironic, given his intentions, political narrowness is not objectionable if there are good reasons for it. But Rawls's reasons are not altogether good ones. Rawls's project is driven by the notion that justice requires equal respect. Few would question the nobility of that goal. But the disagreement on important matters that Rawls identifies with pluralism seems to go naturally with unequal respect. Abstracting from the moral desire for equality, people appear naturally inclined to respect less those whom they believe to be wrong about the most important matters. Rawls uses the moral desire for equality in the attempt to overcome that inclination, which is unreasonable or immoral from the point of view of that desire. Rawls's means of achieving this democratic goal are less than admirable. For the consensus he seeks quickly devolves into consensus for consensus' sake alone. The "virtue" of getting along, of not insisting on anything (too) controversial, is elevated by Rawls to the highest possible plane. Rawls's "reasonable pluralism" flatters us into believing that we remain true to ourselves on a deep level, even while there is nothing we will not concede for the sake of an "overlapping consensus." Rawls's pluralism is a Trojan horse of conformity. Nothing, Rawls tells us, can be so important that it is worth disrupting the peaceful scheme of social cooperation. Nothing is so important that it is worth not getting along, not going along.

*Conclusion*

When confronted with conflicting "comprehensive views," moral views, views of justice, a simple appeal to one's own ways is insufficient. To this extent, Rawls is surely correct. But when this "fact of pluralism" is confronted squarely, justice becomes a question, indeed a problem — which is the right way? This has been *the* question of political philosophy from the time of its inception; and a most reasonable one it is in the face of the problem of justice. The question of justice cannot be abstracted from questions of "comprehensive doctrine," including those religious "doctrines" that make claims on our lives as a whole. Rawls, however, despite his best intentions, wishes to deny that this "pluralism" poses a problem, and he does so in two ways. Rawls denies the problem of justice first insofar as, for him, political philosophy becomes indifferent to which of the conflicting ways is the right way. It tries to get around that problem by bracketing the question — the political question — of which is the right way. So each "way" is left untouched, unevaluated in its goodness and badness. Political liberalism may seem, then, to stand silent on the great political question confronting us as human beings. Yet clearly political liberalism does not stand silent on the question of justice. Thus, Rawls also denies the problem of justice in a way that contradicts the first form of denial: by offering political liberalism itself as the solution, the one right way. He implies that no alternative to liberalism even has a reasonable case to make on its own behalf. Only the liberal, or the "political liberal," way is reasonable. But in claiming to be the one right way, political liberalism becomes another of the claimants to justice. As such, it too would appear to be "incommensurable" with the rest. It cannot encompass them by making itself "merely political," since the meaning of "the political" is the question. Political liberalism therefore is not radically open to religious comprehensive views as it supposes, nor could it be. Rawls seems to suppose that the sort of neutrality to which political liberalism pretends is necessary for genuine toleration, and hence genuine liberalism. Yet precisely the identification of neutrality with toleration and liberalism leaves liberalism vulnerable to the devastating critique of Stanley Fish. Fish shows that liberalism thus understood is most vulnerable in its posture to religion.

# 6

## STANLEY FISH AND
## THE DEMISE OF
## THE SEPARATION OF
## CHURCH AND STATE

Rawls's case for the substantive neutrality of liberalism seems to depend on the contention that substantive disagreement — disagreement on life's ultimate questions — is deep and intractable. Precisely insofar as we come to accept this obvious fact, we can begin to see the need for a way of getting on politically that has as little as possible to do with such massive questions. We see the need, in other words, for a politics that is neutral with respect to life's ultimate questions. And this neutrality means, of course, a politics of toleration. The liberal state, as a matter of principle, takes no stand on distinctly religious questions. The Supreme Court, for example, has nothing to say whatever about the way to salvation of the soul.

But neutrality, in liberal thought, often carries a moral significance beyond that arising from the practical need of getting along politically. What may seem to be at stake in the question of liberal neutrality is the political or moral virtue of toleration itself. Toleration of some sort is, of course, possible without any pretense of neutrality. A country with an officially established religion may allow the free exercise of other religions. Free exercise does not depend on separation. But a political regime with an established religion may seem to some to be, on a deeper level, intolerant of other religions, or tolerant only in the sense of forbearing — what is sometimes called "mere toleration." Believers in other faiths may be viewed, by themselves and others, as somehow less than full citizens. Forbearance is indeed the most basic meaning of toleration, but it is not the lofty and overriding moral virtue that liberals may wish toleration to be. For that reason we may become suspect of anything that threatens the noble virtue of toleration in our own hearts, including taking a stand ourselves on the ultimate questions — our own private "establishment." We thus return to the notion that liberalism requires a full-fledged neutrality — a neutrality that tolerates without provisos that would curb, look down upon, or otherwise reduce those differences that a liberal state would tolerate. There is a moral ideal driving the case for liberal neutrality.

But when the ideal of a toleration that transcends mere forbearance is expressed in terms of neutrality, it becomes immediately problematic. As ideal, as a lofty moral principle, toleration is no longer neutral with respect to life's ultimate questions but offers itself as an important part of the answer to those questions. Precisely the moral impulse that gives rise to the goal of pure neutrality in the first place reveals that neutrality to be false. Toleration is not neutral. The paradoxical question then arises: Is toleration tolerant? Must not toleration continually push aside and suppress other competing principles, which are recognized as intolerant? Is toleration as a moral virtue possible, or even coherent?

No one in recent years has pursued this critique of liberal toleration more forcefully than Stanley Fish, who concludes from it that "liberalism doesn't exist" (1994, 138). For, as he puts it, "liberalism's attempt to come to terms with illiberal energies — especially, but not exclusively, religious ones — will always fail because it cannot succeed without enacting the illiberalism it opposes" (1999b, 242). According to Fish, intolerance — drawing a line between you and your opponents, between right and wrong, and seeking to exclude and defeat the wrong — is an inescapable part of human life, or, at least, necessary for any genuinely moral life. Liberals also exclude those who are not like-minded. They too are illiberal. But, Fish contends, they are either dishonest about it or do not know themselves.

Fish's critique of liberalism evolved from his work in legal theory, above all from his critical work on the First Amendment (see especially Fish 1994). There he agues that the principles of the First Amendment are impossible to achieve or even coherently articulate and that frequently they are obstacles to genuinely moral and principled outcomes. Because the First Amendment embodies core principles of our liberal constitutional form of government, Fish has turned his attention to liberal political theory, exposing its failure to explain how liberalism can bracket off our profoundest moral and religious disagreements from the political realm. According to Fish, the failure of such attempts is indicative of, if not identical to, the failure of liberal rationalism as such. Liberalism and rationalism together form the object of his critique. And, as the passage quoted in the previous paragraph shows, Fish understands liberalism's chief task in establishing itself to be the suppression and exclusion of religion. The separation of church and state is not, in Fish's account, principally a means of protecting religion; it is a means of keeping religion out of power, where it counts. Liberalism does not stand apart from matters of faith. Liberalism is itself a competing faith, albeit a furtive one. And the ground of competition is above all the hearts and minds of believers themselves, who, according to Fish, time and again fail to recognize how liberalism entices them into betraying their moral and religious convictions in the name of ostensibly neutral principles. While Fish denies that his antifoundational critique recommends any course of action or political institutions, his argument leads him to the conclusion that liberal doctrines on religion, as they present themselves, are incoherent. The ramifications of his critique are therefore radical: Nothing, so to speak, can be ruled out — not religious orthodoxy or even theocracy.

I mean to offer a limited defense of liberalism against Fish's critique. Fish represents, not the nonliberal, but the antiliberal — that is, the simple negation of liberalism — and the simple negation of liberalism does not signal a genuine transcendence of liberalism. He has underestimated the conceptual and moral power of liberalism. This underestimation is largely the result of mistakenly identifying neutrality as the essence of liberalism. Liberalism does not rest on a neutral basis. Fish's critique of liberal neutrality, while effective in the case of some liberal theory, such as Rawls's "political liberalism," cannot be fatal to liberalism as such.

### Fish's Critique of Liberalism

According to Fish's presentation, liberalism begins by accepting the fact that human beings are in perpetual disagreement about the most important things, in particular those things around which human social or political life should be organized. Liberalism accepts the fact that the sort of disagreement that ordinarily leads to civil strife cannot be resolved. It then attempts to bracket off all those things about which people are inclined to fight — "the truly meaningful things" — and to design a politics limited to the lowest common denominators, "the set of truly nonmeaningful things" (1999b, 270). It is precisely the truly meaningful things, above all religious imperatives, that do not admit of compromise. If, therefore, politics could concern the truly unmeaningful matters only — those matters Locke refers to as theologically "indifferent" — people would be much more likely to negotiate peacefully and compromise. We can have our high-order disagreements but live in peace.

In order to persuade all parties to sign on, liberalism cannot present itself as partisan. Indeed, "liberalism . . . defines itself by . . . its not being the program of any particular group or party" (1994, 138). Liberalism promotes peaceful adjudication concerning the truly unmeaningful things and toleration concerning the truly meaningful things. But liberal adjudication inevitably involves drawing a line between the meaningful and unmeaningful things, and that line is among those things hotly contested. What is truly unmeaningful to some is truly meaningful to others. For example, to a Hindu cows are sacred, whereas to a Christian they are a matter of theological indifference. Therefore, liberalism cannot leave behind the sorts of disputes it intends to bracket. And it cannot leave them behind for precisely the reason it itself has identified: "the inescapable reality of contending agendas or points of view" (1994, 296).

Moreover, in order to make its case for the bracketing of beliefs of utmost importance, liberalism must promote the belief that this bracketing itself is of the utmost importance. Everyone is required to keep in check his own convictions — thinking of his religion, e.g., as, in Jefferson's words, "a matter that lies solely between man and his God" (Jefferson 1943, 518) — and to do so out of deference to the rights of others. Liberalism fosters a view of convictions as relevant only for oneself (a merely personal viewpoint), which is to denigrate them. Put otherwise, liberalism demands that we recognize rights for what (we believe) is wrong. This is not a mere bracketing of conviction, while neutrally keeping intact the substance of conviction. It signals instead a radical change in the very meaning and therefore the substance of conviction, a radical change that liberalism can never openly acknowledge.

According to "Fish's first law of tolerance-dynamics, . . . toleration is exercised in an inverse proportion to there being anything at stake" (1994, 217). Thus liberalism sets itself the task of turning the natural order of politics on its head. It must turn truly meaningful things, if they are to be tolerated, into things where nothing is at stake, into unmeaningful things. To accomplish this feat, liberalism, by a sleight of hand, displaces all competitors for the organizing principles of public life with its own "neutral" principles: "autonomy, individual freedom, rational deliberation, civility" (1999b, 272). Far from being neutral, however, liberalism has "managed, by the very partisan means it claims to transcend, to grab the moral high ground, and to grab it from a discourse — the discourse of religion — that had held it for centuries" (1994, 138). This moral high ground is a sign that liberalism in fact promotes its own notion of what is truly meaningful, of that around which public life should be organized. In the guise of neutrality, liberalism has managed to replace all other partisan agendas with its own partisan agenda. Liberalism claims to stand above the partisan struggle but necessarily takes part in it. Therefore, according to its own self-understanding, "liberalism doesn't exist."

Although I wish to take issue with what Fish calls liberalism's self-understanding, the position he has identified as liberalism's is no mere straw man. Fish has exposed a prevalent difficulty, which, as he points out, is not merely an abstract or theoretical one. Consider the case, *Mozert v Hawkins County Board of Education*,[1] which, as Fish explains, "pitted Vicki Frost, a fundamentalist Christian and the mother of a gradeschool daughter, against an educational establishment that would require her child to participate in a program of 'critical reading' designed to cultivate the capacity for considering every side of a question, the capacity, in short, of openness of mind" (1997b, 2288). A number of fundamentalist parents objected to the reading program and sought to have their children exempted. The school board voted unanimously to require participation. Frost and other parents brought a suit against the school board, which the parents eventually lost in the 6th Circuit Court of Appeals in 1988.

The parents' suit charged the school board with violating their right of free exercise of religion. The reading series, they said, hindered their ability, their religious duty, to raise their children in the faith. The school board defended itself by claiming that they were not inhibiting the parents' free exercise, since they were not promoting any of the various points of view presented in the readers. They were merely exposing the children to various points of view — mere exposure, neutral exposure. But this response of the school board did not meet the plaintiff's most challenging argument. For the plaintiffs did not base their case on objections to this or that teaching found in the readings. It was not the fact that the reading introduced children to Darwinism or witchcraft, for example, which the parents surely would find objectionable in themselves. They objected rather to the fact of the exposure to a variety of points of view, to the fact of exposure itself. They tacitly conceded, in other words, that the exposure did not attempt to promote any one of the points of view presented. But they denied that such exposure is in truth neutral with respect to points of view. For the notion that children should learn by being exposed to a variety of points of view is itself a distinct point of view, even if it is not identical to any of the ones presented. The courts were persuaded by the argument of the Hawkins County school district superintendent, who claimed that the "plaintiffs misunderst[ood] the fact that exposure to something does not constitute teaching, indoctrination . . . or promotion of the thing exposed."[2] The last official word was "that, by definition, 'mere exposure' to ideas could not violate the right to the free exercise of religion" (Stolzenberg 1993, 598). The courts never responded directly to the plaintiffs' claim that there is no such thing as "mere exposure." According to Fish, "what the children are being indoctrinated in is distrust of any belief that has not been arrived at by the exercise of their unaided reason as it surveys all the alternatives before choosing one freely with no guidance from any external authority. But unaided reason — reason freed from the tethering constraints of biblical commands or parental precepts — is what the parents in the Mozert case distrust." A substantive end reveals itself — the end, it appears, of rational enlightenment.

According to the plaintiffs, by encouraging students to evaluate a wide variety of beliefs critically, tolerantly, and evenhandedly, the schools were effectively serving to undermine the parents' ability to fulfill their religious obligation to raise their children to obey the will of God — obey, not critically evaluate and freely choose. Fish's claim is that the liberal state is incapable of neutrally and tolerantly encompassing beliefs like those of the plaintiffs in *Mozert,* because the very ideal of neutrality and tolerance is partisan and exclusionary and therefore not truly neutral or tolerant: "Openness is an ideology, in that, like any other ideology, it is slanted in some directions and blind (if not downright hostile) to others" (1999b, 156).

Fish takes no exception to liberal thought's starting point, as he understands it: "Liberal thought begins in the acknowledgment that faction, difference, and point of view are irreducible," and with "a strong acknowledgment of the unavailability of a transcendent perspective of the kind provided by traditional Christianity (against whose dogmas liberalism defines itself)" (1994, 16). That is, not only are different worldviews irreducible (there is, after all, an irreducible difference between right and wrong, wisdom and folly), but no human being is authorized or able to judge among them. The trouble with liberalism is that it attempts to put this genuine insight to work in solving or managing the very situation it acknowledges to be permanent. Liberalism is not simply an articulation of the human situation; it is a program for managing, even transcending, the human situation.

Liberalism thus falls back on foundationalism, by which Fish means the "attempt to ground inquiry and communication in something more firm and stable than mere belief and unexamined practice" (1989, 342). Of course, liberalism's foundationalism is no secret: liberalism is the product of the Enlightenment, the Age of Reason. The Enlightenment, indeed, represents the most extreme foundationalism, in its doctrine that the human race can transcend the accidents of nationality, sex, religion, and whatever else divides it through unaided reason or science. However, as soon as reason is seen to be questionable, nay, as soon as reason is seen to rest on faith, we are led with greater clarity than before to liberalism's first premises. Those premises can now be seen to culminate in antifoundationalism, in "the inescapable reality of," the impossibility of transcending or managing, "contending agendas or of points of view or, as we would now say in a shorthand way, of 'difference'" (1994, 296). As Fish presents it, antifoundationalism, which sets itself in opposition to the Enlightenment, is nothing other than a strong affirmation of the premise that liberalism has affirmed weakly from its start in the Enlightenment. We may say that Fish holds to liberalism's beginning premise more consistently than does liberalism itself.

Although foundationalism did not, of course, begin with liberalism, and although liberalism laid the groundwork for antifoundationalism, what is afoot in foundationalism as such nevertheless becomes most evident in liberalism. For the project of transcending the partiality of one's impassioned and merely human beliefs — the movement from opinion to knowledge — requires the attempt to step away from one's beliefs, to examine them impartially and dispassionately, i.e. rationally. True impartiality cannot mean merely adopting some other partial viewpoint. Rather, one must transcend all partial viewpoints to occupy a universal perspective, which is somehow at once the perspective of everyone and no one in particular.[3] Foundationalism culminates in rationalism, which culminates in liberal neutrality among viewpoints. "The principle of rationality that is above the partisan fray . . . is not incidental to liberal thought; it *is* liberal thought" (1994, 137). Liberalism is ever in search of universal, or neutral principles, principles "you would be willing to apply no matter what the circumstances or interests involved"

(1997a, 394n). Fish gives the examples of equality and racial colorblindness. His critique of liberalism is "an attack on principle, or, more precisely, 'neutral principle.'"

Instead of formal universal principles, Fish would have us take our bearings by "the norms, histories, and practices of different groups," i.e., of our own group. Fish therefore could with good reason be thought a relativist.[4] After all, the norms and practices, indeed every thought, of every human being, Fish teaches, is the "function" of, or relative to, his "institutional history, personal education, political and religious affiliations" (1994, 18). According to Fish, however, "there is no slide to nihilism or relativism here." On the contrary, "for me it is relativism when you slide away from the norms, histories, and practices of different cultures and groups and emphasize instead formal universal principles like equality and colorblindness" (1999b, 24).[5]

Fish illustrates what he means with Justice Powell's extreme, but for that reason revealing, statement in *Gertz v Robert Welch, Inc.* (1974): "Under the First Amendment there is no such thing as a false idea" (quoted at Fish 1999b, 24). The First Amendment, according to Powell, does not set out to distinguish true beliefs from false. Rather, it transcends the level of that partisan dispute, adjudicating in matters of speech, religion, and so forth in a manner that is neutral toward all points of view. Powell's statement, Fish claims, is a clear example of a neutral universal principle at work, "for it refuses to put the power of the state behind this or that point of view and insists that government maintain a strict neutrality between the various combatants in the wars of . . . truth" (25). He continues: "The logic is clear and apparently compelling until you realize that it is the logic of relativism and that it undermines the possibility of saying that some things are true and others false" (25). According to Fish, it is only from the partial perspective of commitment that we can pronounce true and false, right and wrong. It is impartial universalism which, precisely because it is impartial and universal, leads us to stifle or obscure or deny our beliefs, by granting all beliefs equal status, a move that culminates in relativism or nihilism. Furthermore, "an argument from principle easily becomes a recipe for inaction, for not doing anything in the face of an apparent urgency" (25), at "the cost of nothing less than the *moral* — not neutral — principles that lead us to judge one course of action better than another" (26). "The alternative to the neutral principle is a real [i.e., moral] principle" (1997a, 394n). In one sense, neutral universal principles are like any other morality — being equally rooted in partial faith, equally functions of historical contingencies, equally exclusionary. Yet they are not *real* principles. They can never fully displace real moral principles, since we cannot escape the need to judge what is the best course of action. They can, however, obscure the fact that we are so judging and thereby cripple our capacity to judge well, or at any rate to judge in clear view of our own moral commitments. These are the consequences that make up "the trouble with principle."[6]

We may become aware of our moral commitments, but we can neither evaluate nor freely choose them. We cannot step back, as the foundationalist would do, from our own most fundamental beliefs, our "first principles," or "basic conception of what the world is like (it is the creation of God; it is a collection of atoms)" (1994, 136, 137). We cannot reason about them, because they are the basis of any reasoning we can do:

> If you propose to examine and assess assumptions, what will you examine and assess them *with*? And the answer is that you will examine and assess them with forms of thought that themselves rest on underlying assumptions. At any level, the tools of rational analysis will be vulnerable to the very deconstruction they claim to perform. You can never go deep enough, for no matter how deep you go, you will find reasons whose perspicuity is a function of just those factors — institutional history, personal education, political and religious affiliations — from which Reason supposedly stands apart. (18)

Thus the question of our responsibility to assess the soundness of our assumptions need never arise. Reason follows from "first principles," or at any rate from what we believe to be first principles. Thus reason cannot determine first principles.[7] A choice between alternatives that did not assume some standard on which to base the choice would be not free but purely arbitrary. To repeat, according to Fish it is rationalism, not antifoundationalism, that culminates in nihilism. Yet all human thought depends upon some "first principles," the adequacy of which are not rationally assessable. This is as true of the fundamentalist Protestant as it is of the modern natural scientist. They are separated by a fundamental conflict of faiths. Empirical verification is no more subject to rational justification than biblical inerrancy (136; cf. 1999b, 244). In the end, we have recourse to nothing "more firm and stable than mere belief or unexamined practice" (1989, 342). But, Fish insists, it is precisely because deliberation about our most basic assumptions is impossible that we are *never* deprived of some basis for judgment. That basis, however sound or unsound it may be, is not subject to our choosing or evaluation. Rather it seizes us, and it does so whether or not we are fully aware of it.[8]

## Rorty and the Antifoundationalist Projects

Fish, of course, is not alone in thus criticizing liberal rationalism. Rorty, for example, would likely endorse Fish's critique as I have presented it so far, although with a few significant qualifications. Fish understands the critique of liberal rationalism to signal the demise of liberalism as such. If rational (neutral) adjudication among beliefs is impossible (as both Rorty and Fish agree that it is), then, according to Fish, liberalism is impossible. As we have already seen, however, Rorty believes that if we (liberals) drop all pretensions of rationality (neutrality), we can simply embrace liberalism as our own, as what we like or are committed to. After all, if we all are necessarily committed to *something,* must not we late-twentieth-century Westerners own to our commitment to liberalism? Is that not where our hearts lie?

But, as we saw in chapter 4, Rorty goes well beyond this in tracing the significance of the critique of rationalism for liberalism. Rorty does not leave it at "It's got to be some commitment; why not liberalism?" For Rorty, the critique of rationalism, which is part of the broader critique of foundationalism, can strengthen liberalism in much the same way that the Enlightenment's attack on theology did. Thus antifoundationalism becomes part of a positive liberal project.

Fish, however, objects to any attempt to turn antifoundationalism into a practical project. Fish contends that "if you take the antifoundationalism of pragmatism seriously . . . you will see that there is absolutely nothing you can do with it" (1994, 215).[9] Rorty hopes that if we recognize the "radical contingency of all values," we will become less dogmatic about our own beliefs and more tolerant of the beliefs of others. "[Rorty's] idea," Fish explains, "is that if people would only stop trying to come up with a standard of absolute right which could then be used to denigrate the beliefs and efforts of *other* people, they might spend more time sympathetically engaging with those beliefs and learning to appreciate others" (1994, 216). Antifoundationalism is to make one less serious about one's own beliefs and thereby less serious in one's disapproval of, more tolerant of, and possibly even admiring of, the beliefs and practices of others. Whereas Rorty intends to make us less serious about our beliefs, Fish intends to make us more serious about them.

Yet Fish sees the difference between Rorty and himself as more than one of intentions. Rorty hopes that these "consequences of pragmatism" will follow "naturally" from the "pragmatist insight." Rorty hopes, in other words, that the "consequences of pragmatism" are *not* "radically contingent," but predictable or manageable. Fish objects that to speak of the consequences of pragmatism, as Rorty does, is to contradict the basic premise of pragmatism (understood here as equivalent to antifoundationalism). For Rorty, intrinsic to pragmatism, for the reasons mentioned in chapter 4, is the practice of "redescription" and the "skill at imaginative identification" with others. Pragmatism, Rorty hopes, entails the "ability to envisage, and the desire to prevent, the actual and possible humiliation of others — despite differences of sex, race, tribe, and final vocabulary" (Rorty 1989, 93). What Rorty describes, however, is not so much a skill or ability (a sort of knowledge that can be mastered) as a moral outlook, which Rortian pragmatism teaches is the product of "radical contingency" (which cannot be mastered). According to Fish, if one does come to adopt Rorty's moral agenda, that change will not follow "naturally" from the recognition of the "pragmatist insight." It will, rather, come about through the mysterious dispensation of a "conversion experience." Fish states: "This 'conversion' experience, if it occurs, will not be attributable to a special skill or ability that has been acquired through the regular practice of redescription — through empathy exercises — but rather to the (contingent) fact that for this or that person a particular argument or piece of testimony or preferred analogy or stream of light coming through a window at the right moment just happened to 'take'" (1994, 217). To repeat, we cannot according to Fish freely choose or evaluate our deepest held beliefs. They seize us for reasons beyond our understanding or control.

The clearest sign that Rorty hopes to put antifoundationalism to work in overcoming the very situation asserted by antifoundationalism to be unavoidable is Rorty's description of his project as one of "de-divinization." According to Fish, however, Rorty's secularism rests on faith no less than theism (or theocracy), and being aware that it rests on faith does not make it rest any less on faith. Rorty's disbelief in God and belief in "creative redescription" and "imaginative identification" are no more self-evident or enlightened than any expressly religious faith. Perhaps liberal culture will change as Rorty hopes it will. But whatever changes may come about, "we will not have escaped semantics (merely verbal entities) and metaphysics (faith-based declarations of what is) but merely attached ourselves to new versions of them" (1994, 212).

Rorty, of course, feels the pressure of such an objection, which is why he is at such pains to explain how he is not offering an account of what is. The "atheism" that he avows is not metaphysical (he is not claiming that there is no God) but is rather a creative description of the "world." But can Rorty deny that "creative atheism" presupposes disbelief in God (metaphysical atheism), or at least in a god of a certain kind? That is, someone who believes that God is concerned that we live in a certain manner and that we recognize and honor his true nature would view Rorty's "creative redescriptions" as great folly or sin. In response to a similar charge by Michael Sandel against John Rawls (specifically, that Rawls necessarily makes a metaphysical claim), Rorty responds that the charge is "accurate, but not really to the point" (1991a, 182n.). Speaking for Rawls (as well as Jefferson and presumably himself) Rorty says, "I have no arguments for my dubious theological-metaphysical claim, because I do not know how to discuss such issues, and do not want to" (182). But Rorty's theoretical "don't ask, don't tell" policy serves only to obscure what is nevertheless there: the fact that his project depends upon a "dubious theological-metaphysical claim." Rorty's theological-metaphysical claim and the way of life it is meant to support are left conveniently unexaminable. On this, Rorty and Fish agree. But Fish does not agree that Rorty's liberal culture would or could be "postmetaphysical" in the sense that both Fish and he understand "metaphysics." [10] Fish affirms that human beings necessarily hold opinions about what is.

Rorty, in the manner typical of the liberal neutrality Fish criticizes, seeks to bracket what he calls "matters of ultimate importance" (Rorty 1991a, 175) and establish a political order of "procedural justice" (209). Thus, even while frequently admitting that liberalism is merely one sectarian competitor among many and denying that liberalism could ever rise above the partisan fray, Rorty falls back into a rationalistic neutral proceduralism. Rorty has not left behind the fallacy of liberal rationalism; he has only reproduced it in a more dramatically self-contradictory way. That is, having affirmed in a more radical way than Locke and Jefferson, for instance, ever would have entertained the "irreducible difference" among world views, Rorty proceeds to seek a political (and theoretical) plane that transcends the plane of intractable dispute. To be fair to Rorty, we must say that this is an issue with which he constantly struggles — affirming liberalism's ethnocentrism, while seeking a liberalism that is more open than ever before to what lies outside itself. Nevertheless, ignoring one's basic assumptions about "what is" does not make them or their potential difficulties go away. Rorty's liberalism is thus utopian in a stricter sense than he is willing to admit — not in terms of its perfection but rather in terms of its impossibility.

Fish is a still harsher critic of another group of theorists who want anti-foundationalism to serve a different moral-political project — the proponents of multiculturalism, including "the politics of difference," who object to liberalism's overt or covert assimilationism in the guise of neutrality. Fish identifies milder and stronger versions of multiculturalism. He calls the milder variety of multiculturalism, which admits the need of some degree of political assimilation — the sort of multiculturalism that liberals like Rorty and Rawls might be able to abide — "boutique multiculturalism":

> Boutique multiculturalism is the multiculturalism of ethnic restaurants, weekend festivals, and high profile flirtations with the other in the manner satirized by Tom Wolfe under the rubric of "radical chic." Boutique multi-culturalism is characterized by its superficial or cosmetic relationship to the objects of affection. Boutique multiculturalists admire or appreciate or enjoy or sympathize with or (at the very least) "recognize the legitimacy of" the traditions of cultures other than their own; but . . . the boutique multiculturalist resists the force of [the] culture he appreciates at precisely the point at which it matters most to its strongly committed members. (1999b, 56, 57)

There is a limit to the boutique multiculturalists' tolerance. They will not shy away from affirming the need for some degree of assimilation, at least concerning fundamental moral and political matters.

Fish contrasts the boutique multiculturalists with the "strong multiculturalists," including those associated with the "politics of difference."[11] Strong multiculturalism views assimilation as an evil. It thus prefers the active encouragement of the flourishing of the variety of cultures to "mere toleration" of them, which is indifferent to their flourishing or dying. Fish states: "The politics of difference is the equivalent of an endangered species act for human beings, where the species are not owls and snail darters, but Arabs, Jews, homosexuals, Chicanos, Italian Americans, and on and on and on" (1999b, 60). Fish finds, however, that when faced with such things as Iran's death sentence placed on Salman Rushdie, the strong multiculturalist reveals that he cannot value cultural distinctiveness as such, turning his back on it "usually in the name of some supracultural universal now seen to have been hiding up his sleeve from the beginning" (61). He "thereby reveals himself not to be a strong multiculturalist at all. Indeed it turns out that strong multiculturalism is not a distinct position but a somewhat deeper instance of the shallow category of boutique multiculturalism." Fish points out that the "strong multiculturalist" had no choice but to abandon the unrealizable goal of radical openness. For if, in the attempt to be a really strong multiculturalist, he does not condemn the death sentence on Rushdie, if he defends the Muslims' "right" to maintain their full "cultural identity," if he goes "all the way," he will find himself saying with the Iranian, "Rushdie must die" (62). He would then no longer be a multiculturalist at all, but a committed Muslim. That is what full "appreciation" of Muslim "culture" would require; and that is what only a true Muslim is capable of.[12]

In Fish's presentation, antifoundationalism entails no inherent obstacle to "going all the way." This means that antifoundationalism is in principle compatible with any worldview. According to Fish, whether we accept or reject the call of Muslim commitment has nothing to do with anything we might learn from antifoundationalism. Antifoundationalism is a theoretical account of where beliefs come from. It cannot be of help in deciding which beliefs to accept or reject. Holding a belief and describing where beliefs in general come from are two "logically independent activities" (1989, 248). Holding a belief, according to Fish, belongs to the realm of practice, and (invoking an age-old rationalist distinction) "practice has nothing to do with theory" (355).[13] Moreover, to repeat, we cannot choose what we believe, since our beliefs are the basis of our choosing. Antifoundationalism may, however, help to clarify what it means to believe and what our own beliefs are, thus removing the obstacles erected by rationalism and liberalism. Antifoundationalism "offers you nothing but the assurance that what it is unable to give you — knowledge, goals, purposes, strategies — is what you already have" (355).

### The Separation of Church and State Doesn't Exist?
Fish thus finds nothing amiss in appropriations of antifoundationalism, such as Stephen Carter's in "Evolutionism, Creationism, and Treating Religion as a Hobby" (1987) and *The Culture of Disbelief* (1993), in the cause of broadening religious involvement in the political sphere. But he criticizes Carter too for failing to adhere consistently to the critique of liberal neutrality that Carter himself lays out. In response to Carter's argument in "Evolutionism," Fish states, "My only quarrel is with its conclusion when he urges a

'softened liberal politics'" which would transcend the difficulties he lists. Fish argues that Carter "could never [work out the details of such a politics] for reasons he himself enumerates" (1994, 134). Since liberalism rests on "a faith . . . in reason as something that operates independently of any particular worldview," it "can only 'cherish' religion as something under its protection; to take it seriously would be to regard it as it demands to be regarded, as a claimant to the adjudicative authority already deeded in liberal thought to reason" (134, 135). Carter seeks a more respectful accommodation of religion by liberalism. But Carter does not recognize that, for a liberalism deeply mistrustful of religion, "accommodation is a much better strategy than outright condemnation, for it keeps the enemy in sight while depriving it of the (exclusionary) edge that makes it truly dangerous; and best of all, one who accommodates can perform this literally disarming act while proclaiming the most high-sounding pieties" (1999b, 257).

The same logic that undermines liberalism, however, appears to undermine antifoundationalism as well. Fish, of course, never makes that move, but he makes it inevitable. Fish states that historian George Marsden's claim that after postmodernism "there is no intellectually valid reason to exclude religiously based perspectives" is a self-defeating argument.[14] He argues:

> It is an argument from weakness — yes, religious thought is without objective ground, but so is everything else; we are all in the same untethered boat — and if a religious perspective were to gain admittance on that basis, it would have forfeited its claim to be anything other than a "point of view," a subjective preference, a mere opinion. . . . If a religious perspective is included because there is "no intellectually valid reason" to exclude it, neither will there be any intellectually valid reason to affirm it, except as one perspective among others, rather than as the perspective that is true, and because true, controlling. (1999b, 260–61)

So long, Fish's argument goes, as antifoundationalism sees the competing perspectives in light of their common lack of objective status, it continues the liberal policy of treating all perspectives as equal — equally marginalized. Since reason is incapable of approving any one perspective, none has a right to predominate. Such an antifoundationalism continues to defer to the authority of a now silent reason.[15]

Fish argues that Carter and Marsden in effect do no more than accuse liberalism of not being liberal enough. But to make this case wins nothing but a debating point, where liberalism still controls the terms of the debate. If religious faith took a seat at the liberal table, it would do so as one of countless equal points of view. It would not and could not come as the authoritative guide of human life.[16] Fish makes the following recommendation:

> To put the matter baldly, a person of religious conviction should not want to enter the marketplace of ideas but to shut it down, at least insofar as it presumes to determine matters that he believes have been determined by God and faith. The religious person should not seek an accommodation with liberalism; he should seek to rout it from the field. (1999b, 250)

Liberalism confronts religion as a competing faith. When believers accept the separation of church and state, they bow to the political establishment of an alien faith. Since according to Fish's logic every act of legislation is the establishment of some faith or other, we are compelled to conclude that, in a manner of speaking, there's no such thing as the separation of church and state. There would appear to remain no principled reason for believers not to seek expressly religious establishment, precisely insofar as they hold their beliefs to be true. Fish, in effect, says to the believer: If you really believe your religion to be true, why not theocracy? Isn't the only alternative to establishing the truth, establishing a lie?

Michael McConnell is probably not alone among modern believers in being wary of such an argument. The alternative Fish poses is too stark. The establishment of a lie could mean the silencing (or worse), even on the subpolitical level, of what does not conform to the established doctrine or practice. The "establishment" of the separation of church and state, whatever its shortcomings may be in comparison to the highest truth, does grant to believers a significant degree of freedom to worship and proselytize. Thus, despite objecting to the strictest privatization of religion, McConnell insists that "we cannot have religious freedom without [the public-private distinction]" (1993, 184). Liberalism grants believers certain rights, which are held privately but which are therefore also out of reach of the arm of the state.

According to Fish, however, the acceptance of liberalism's solution as a matter of principle, as the final word, instead of as a temporary and necessary expedient, amounts to a betrayal of one's faith. Fish says that "we see the spectacle of men like McConnell, Carter, and Marsden, who set out to restore the priority of the good over the right but find the protocols of the right —

of liberal proceduralism — written in the fleshly tables of their hearts" (1999b, 262). McConnell frames his case against the strict privatization of religion as "a plea for old-fashioned broadmindedness" (1993, 166). Fish points out that, in so doing, McConnell "does not realize that broadmindedness is the opposite of what religious conviction enacts and requires" (1999b, 252). McConnell thinks that his opponent is a "liberalism gone sour"; whereas in fact it is (or should be) "liberalism, pure and simple" (253). The believer may be free under liberalism to "practice" his religion. "But of course," Fish objects, "the freedom thus gained is the freedom to be ineffectual. . . . What is not allowed religion under the public private distinction is the freedom to *win*, the freedom not to be separate from the state, but to inform and shape its every action" (254). By signing on to the principle of private freedom of religion as such (as opposed to absolute freedom for the *true* religion), McConnell has already "give[n] the game away to his opponents" (252). If religion accepts its place as one among countless equal worldviews, it has already surrendered on the crucial point, viz. its claim to be authoritative. To put the matter harshly, by accepting religious freedom as a matter of principle, McConnell betrays his faith by assigning it the role of permanent loser.[17]

Thus Fish stands in contrast to Frederick Gedicks, who maintains that, while postmodernism is "good news for religion" in "foreshadowing the end of the secular monopoly on public life," it is "bad news" for "conservative religion," which would make a claim to "exclusivity of Truth" (Gedicks 1991, 144).[18] For to deny religion this claim is again to trivialize it. The religious antifoundationalists' hesitation in following their own antifoundationalist premises all the way results in their not being true to their religious beliefs. It results in their acting as if their religious beliefs were not true. The difficulty is apparent in the following comments of Gedicks and Roger Hendrix:

Whether one who claims [to have had a] religious experience has actually received revelation from God is a question whose truth is not subject to authoritative, objective discourse. Having said that, however, it hardly follows that their claims of divine communication are necessarily false. . . . If the United States is to reach beyond the sterile secularism of modern American public life to a postmodern society in which no discourse is privileged, it must begin to admit the possibility that religious experience truly occurs, not as the pathetic hallucinations of the unbalanced or insecure, but as what it claims to be — God talking to humanity. (1991, 112, 130)

But how can one admit of this possibility, or more importantly believe in its reality, and nevertheless insist that no "discourse" be privileged?

Fish appears to suggest that the believer in revelation must take that revelation to be "privileged discourse," or "true, and because true, controlling" — controlling not just for me, but for my community and, indeed, for human life simply. This means, however, that the believer in revelation does not concede the premise common to both liberalism and antifoundationalism: the "strong acknowledgment of the unavailability of a transcendent perspective of the kind provided by traditional Christianity" (or Judaism or Islam) (1994, 16). The question of where a belief comes from is not extrinsic to the substance of that belief as Fish supposes. If antifoundationalism held consistently leads to the affirmation of a belief as true, and therefore based on *more* than social construction or our own interpretation, it would appear to lead beyond itself, to a recovery of foundationalism, albeit of a distinctly nonliberal (preliberal) variety. This conclusion, moreover, does not apply only to believers in revelation. For we are all, Fish claims, believers in something, in some "first principles" or basic conception of what the world is like. We hold our beliefs to be grounded in "what the world is like," or what is — in the eternal. But does this not mean that we are all foundationalists, or that antifoundationalism doesn't exist?

We must go beyond Fish and ask, how is it that we can come to recognize our beliefs as resting on faith, unless we recognize that they are questionable? And how can we recognize that they are questionable unless we can somehow step away from them, however qualifiedly? Does not antifoundationalism presuppose the capacity of stepping outside our beliefs in order to gain the "insight" that they are not well grounded, adopting a vantage point from which it can be seen that no human belief is well grounded, a vantage point beyond all mere belief? But it is precisely such a vantage point that the antifoundationalist denies.

Fish, in fact, does concede that foundationalism, defined as holding some foundational beliefs, is humanly unavoidable. For Fish, however, this means that we are all foundationalists "only in the sense that we all believe what we believe, and that we take what we believe to be true," being "guided by that which, according to our lights, is really true" (1989, 384). He insists that "by the same argument, we are all conventionalists [antifoundationalists]," since for each of us "true" is "what we take to be true." That is, "it is only 'according to our lights' that the category of the 'really true' acquires its members" (384). How can we make sense of this subtle argument? Fish's argument seems to suggest the following. We cannot *know* that our beliefs are truly well founded, no matter how well founded they may appear to us at a given moment; for we must admit that how matters appear to us is only how they appear *to us* ("*only* 'according to *our* lights'"). And yet, Fish insists, this admission does not alter *how* matters appear to us, including how clearly they appear to us (383). Thus, Fish concludes, the antifoundationalist insight is of no consequence for life.

According to Fish, then, we are all foundationalists in the sense that we all have *faith* in some foundations. Foundationalism in the full sense would require "absolute certainty of the kind that can only be provided by revelation (something I do not rule out but have not yet experienced)" (Fish 1994, 113).[19] But if that possibility cannot be ruled out, antifoundationalism may not be the universal human condition, as Fish nearly everywhere suggests. There are, after all, many who have claimed revelation. Have they all possessed "absolute certainty"? How could they have done so given the contradictions between claims of revelation and even, not infrequently, within a single claimed revelation? Are there not false prophets? Do not even true prophets have need of faith? It would appear that Fish has confused certainty (knowledge) with strong conviction. Furthermore, by affirming that all human thought is grounded in *nothing* more solid than local and temporal contingencies, the antifoundationalist demonstrates that he is not agnostic respecting revelation but rather interprets revelation to be of strictly human origin, which is tantamount to a denial of revelation.[20] The antifoundationalist appears to side with the rationalist on the most fundamental question. Yet probity would appear to require an admission like Fish's that knowledge rooted in more than mere social construction — knowledge of the eternal — cannot be ruled out.

More than this, if the truths possessed through revelation could be held with "absolute certainty," i.e. if they are humanly, or rationally, intelligible, the possibility emerges that the highest truths are intelligible to human beings as such, without the benefit of revelation. It seems that Fish has not ruled out even the possibility that unassisted human reason is capable of discovering the highest truths, or that human beings are not in need of revelation. Why, then, does Fish stick so intransigently to what appears a hasty and unwarranted antifoundationalism? Why does he deliver always the same message of the unavailability of certainty, if the possibility of certainty concerning such an important subject cannot be ruled out?

One possible answer lies in Fish's doubt that he would want certainty. There is another reason for Fish's antifoundationalism, a reason that lies in apparent tension with his desire to give us the courage of our convictions. Fish does not, as it sometimes appears, seek to promote unbridled confidence in one's convictions. He does, after all, deny that there are evident moral foundations. His denial of evident moral foundations is intended to promote a degree of humility. He states: "in a world where certain grounds for action are unavailable, one avoids the Scylla of prideful self-assertion and the Charybdis of paralysis by stepping out provisionally, with a sense of limitation" (1994, 272; cf. 293). Liberalism hides our convictions from us, and thus stunts our ability to act morally. Antifoundationalism helps us discover our convictions, but it also shows us that our convictions are not "anchored in a perspicuous and uncontroversial rule, golden or otherwise." Fish does not underscore the point; yet it appears that antifoundationalism, like reason (or rather with the aid of reason), weakens our moral commitments, or at any rate gives us pause. But it does so with a moral intention: it protects us from "prideful self-assertion." (Antifoundationalism *is* of some consequence for life. See Appendix.) More important (and showing Fish's ultimate hostility to reason), moral "uncertainty . . . is not a defect in our situation but the very ground and possibility of meaningful action." For despite this uncertainty, "we must nevertheless respond to [the moral life's] pressures." And "it is only because the moral life rests on a base of *nothing* more than its own interpretations that it can have a content; for were there a clearly marked path that assured the safety of pilgrims and wanderers, we would have no decision to make, nothing to hazard, nothing to wager" (my emphasis).[21] It is our uncertainty that makes morality a matter of commitment — that makes it *morality* — and not simply the following of clearly laid out rules. Our uncertainty, combined with the need to act, lends our lives nobility that is lacking in a life guided by knowledge.

This line of reasoning is remarkable for its similarity to as well as its difference from traditional arguments for free will. Compare, for example, the following speech of Milton's God in *Paradise Lost:*

> Freely they stood who stood, and fell who fell.
> Not free what proof could they have given sincere
> Of true allegiance, constant faith, or love,
> Where only what they needs must do appeared,
> Not what they would? What praise would they receive,
> What pleasure I, from such obedience paid,
> When Will and Reason (Reason also is Choice),
> Useless and vain, of freedom both despoiled,
> Made passive both, had served Necessity,
> Not Me? They, therefore, as to right belonged
> So were created, nor can justly accuse
> Their Maker, or their making, or their fate,
> As if Predestination overruled
> Their will, disposed by absolute decree
> Or high foreknowledge. They themselves decreed
> Their own revolt, not I.
>
> (3.102–17)

Although the possible reasons for disobedience are not made clear here, the nobility of the moral life as described by Milton's God is compatible with, indeed it presupposes, knowledge of right and wrong, or of God's commands. There still may be uncertainty. But it is uncertainty with regard to whether or not to obey, perhaps due to some confusion about what is good for oneself, rather than with regard to what is right and wrong. After all, if we are ignorant of what is right, how can we be under an obligation to do it? [22]

In Fish's interpretation of *Paradise Lost* (Fish 1967), he makes abundantly clear the centrality of knowledge of what is right from the perspective of the moral life. [23] In his recent writings, however, he has stressed the "conflict . . . between . . . normative obligations" (1989, 11), particularly the conflicting normative obligations represented by competing worldviews. This is surely a legitimate and important problem. Yet in Fish's antifoundationalist account of the problem, not doing the right thing comes to mean doing the right thing from another point of view. It appears that we are simply seized mysteriously by one morality or another (immorality is another morality?). [24] The conflict of principles of justice is understood exclusively as a conflict between differ-ent "moralities" (morality as seen from above), where everyone is always be-ing true to his moral commitments. Clearly Fish has abstracted from some-thing crucial. His approach prevents full recognition of any conflict between the demands of morality and other interests, or the conflict internal to the principles of morality. In Fish's account, the possibility of immorality or wickedness, of willfully doing wrong, has been almost entirely eclipsed. For our beliefs and all that flows from them are simply beyond our choosing. They are "matter[s] of (non-culpable) fact" (1999b, 238). Fish states that "it follows . . . that you can't be faulted either for not having chosen them or for having chosen the wrong ones" (1989, 394). Fish comes close here to denying that we bear any moral responsibility whatever for our way of life and deeds (insofar as our deeds are "functions" of beliefs beyond our control). Fish wishes to place us within the perspective of the morally committed, or to awaken us to our moral commitment. Yet this is impossible so long as one begins with antifoundationalism's view of morality — so long as the alter-native to our moral commitment is an alternative "morality," rather than immorality.[25]

But, one could reasonably respond, do we know what morality is? Suppose we were to conclude that antifoundationalism points to the recovery of some "foundationalism." Must we not ask which one? Has Fish not done us a ser-vice by drawing our attention to the questionableness of our unexamined assumptions? To this I would respond that Fish has not shown our ignorance of moral principles to be a virtue. Antifoundationalism would appear to be, at best, preparation for the direct consideration of the components of the moral life. Only if that move were taken could one be able to determine if the conflict of the principles of morality admits of a resolution. From the perspec-tive of the moral life, clarity regarding the content of morality is of the highest importance. Moreover, the need to act, which Fish leads us to see, makes such consideration necessary. The need for such clarity is implied in Fish's claim that our ignorance concerning moral principles involves risk. Does not this risk entail the risk of being wrong and all that goes with it, such as the per-verting of the soul and the deserving of punishment? Ignorance of the content of morality must be a defect. For might not the result of that ignorance be immorality? Does not an action taken in faith always risk immorality? The morally serious human being cannot rest satisfied with antifoundationalism.

FISH, LOCKE,

AND RELIGIOUS

NEUTRALITY

By Fish's own admission, antifoundationalism offers no guidance or insight regarding the content of moral or religious belief. Fish makes the point repeatedly that nothing follows — no course of action or moral (or immoral) outlook — from the antifoundationalist "insight." Fish's antifoundationalism assumes a posture of perfect neutrality with respect to the variety of beliefs. In this respect it mirrors the liberalism it criticizes. This should not be surprising once we recall that antifoundationalism's insight is, according to Fish, really liberalism's insight. Fish criticizes liberalism for claiming to occupy a position that is neutral with respect to the truth of competing comprehensive views, a position which no human being can hold. Yet Fish's critique of liberalism is equally neutral with respect to the truth of the competing views. It says neither yea nor nay. It is silent about whether some views are not more adequate than others.

We may say, then, that Fish's antiliberalism is just as tolerant as liberalism. Indeed, in a sense Fish is more tolerant, for he is "open" to Christian and Muslim fundamentalists, to say nothing of other illiberals, in a way no liberal could be. His call to arms, as it were, is not issued only to those who share his beliefs. Consider his exhortation, quoted above, to the "person of religious conviction" to "rout liberalism from the field" where the truth as the believer understands it has been determined by his religion. Fish speaks abstractly, neutrally. Is it not of the utmost importance to ask, before issuing such a blanket exhortation, which religion? [1] Fish does not say, for it does not appear to matter to him which religion opposes liberalism, if indeed it is a religion at all. It thus becomes impossible to determine from his critique of liberalism what Fish is for, or what the true basis of his critique is. We can say for sure only that he is against liberalism. In other words, we can say of Fish's critique of liberalism what Leo Strauss said of Carl Schmitt's, that it is "liberalism preceded by a minus-sign" (Strauss 1965, 350). From the point of view of antifoundationalism all beliefs have equal status — they are equally remote from the objective truth. More precisely, their truth is beside the point. Fish, like his apparent antagonist John Rawls, would not deny that one of the competing views might be true (see Rawls 1996, 128–29). But Fish's antifoundationalism, like Rawls's political liberalism, is interested in the competing views only as generic beliefs, not as candidates for truth.

Whenever we do catch a glimpse of Fish's beliefs, they seem to be in general accord with other left-liberal professors.[2] It is possible that this is no accident. Liberalism may have a greater hold on Fish than he recognizes. If so, this would help to explain why Fish fails to do justice to liberalism's *moral power*.[3] For by identifying liberalism with moral neutrality and proceduralism only, he does not see liberal morality for what it is. He too often loses sight of liberalism's emphatically moral claims in the hunt for its dubious claims to neutrality. Yet liberalism does not disguise the fact that it rests on a doctrine of right, i.e. on a moral doctrine. It is in fact liberalism's most massive feature. However sound Fish's critique of liberal neutrality is, it does not go to the heart of the matter.

Too often Fish gives the impression that liberal neutrality defines liberalism. He thus frequently seems to suppose that when liberalism's nonneutrality to high-order disagreements is exposed, liberalism is defeated. Yet as he himself has indicated, such neutrality does not form the foundation of liberalism.[4] Insofar as Fish's critique moves still within a liberal horizon, it is not yet a radical critique of liberalism. That would require the recovery of the preliberal horizon within which the foundations of liberalism were laid and from the perspective of which alone they can be adequately assessed. The neutrality that Fish criticizes and in which he remains entangled is characteristic of the worldview that was constructed upon liberalism's foundations but that also therefore obscures those foundations. The founders of liberal thought certainly were not neutral with respect to the highest truths. Hobbes was not neutral to the metaphysical disputes of the schoolmen. Spinoza was not neutral to teleology. Locke was not neutral concerning the natural purpose and basis of political society. And none were neutral to notions of right. High-order questions could come to be ignored politically only because they had been addressed in a painstaking fashion theoretically. The fundamental question they could not ignore is now ignored in no small measure as the result of the political success of their project, with the effect of distorting our view of liberalism's true basis.

This difficulty is most evident in Fish's account of Hobbes's teaching concerning the basis of the war of all against all in man's natural state. According to Fish, "Hobbes begins, as all liberals do, with the insight that values and desires are plural and therefore a source of conflict," since "no one is authorized by nature to judge his fellows" (1999b, 178). This is possibly a tolerably accurate description, if Fish were giving a material or even economic sense to the word "values." But in our day, when commercial language pervades every aspect of life, "values" suggests "moral values." Fish indicates that he does indeed have in mind a moral meaning when he describes human beings in Hobbes's state of nature as being "committed" to "their visions of the good" (179). Fish thereby reveals that he has gotten Hobbes wrong. According to Fish, the conflict that characterizes man's natural state includes, above all, conflict over the highest things.

Hobbes, however, could hardly be more plain that human beings in the state of nature are at war over the scarce objects of base appetites and vainglory. According to Hobbes, the "high" things are the products of confused and unscientific strategies for securing the objects of base appetites, e.g. through the superstitious appeasement of "invisible powers." Hobbes declares: "from the innumerable variety of fancy, men have created in the world innumerable sorts of gods. And this fear of things invisible is the natural seed of that which everyone in himself calleth religion, and in them that worship or fear the power otherwise than they do, superstition. . . . There is no cause to doubt but that the seed of religion is . . . in man."[5] Hobbes was not neutral to the truth of high-order conflicts, but reduced, or "deconstructed," them, asserting their true basis in base self-interest.

In Fish's presentation, Hobbes leaves high-order disputes intact. His postmodernized Hobbes does not reduce human "values" to selfish interests but leaves "difference" irreducible. As Fish correctly points out, however, Hobbes finds the "independent value" on which political society can be unified in the desire for peace (1999b, 179). Yet this solution makes no sense if high-order conflict cannot be reduced to the conflict of base self-interest. For it is precisely high-order "values" that lead human beings to sacrifice their self-interest and peace, as Hobbes, being an Englishman of the seventeenth century, knew too well. Hobbes's project thus depends upon enlightening the many about their true interests and thereby about their natural rights.[6] A liberalism of *natural right* clearly does not begin from the sort of universal moral parity that Fish would attribute to Hobbes and to liberalism more generally. The true moral principles of natural right were a discovery of the new political science. As Locke makes clear, natural right is not evident to all human beings (awareness of it is not "innate") but has to be discovered: "moral principles require reasoning and discourse, and some exercise of the mind, to discover the certainty of their truth."[7] The fact that there is even greater disagreement about moral principles than about "speculative maxims" does not, Locke assures us, "bring their truth at all in question." This means that Locke, unlike Fish, does not find the simple fact that a view may be contested by someone at some time proof that that view is not rationally evident.[8] (Just as Fish allows no place for immorality, so he allows no place for irrationality.)

Fish is nevertheless intent on presenting a Locke too who teaches "irreducible difference." In the case of Locke such a presentation is rendered somewhat more plausible by Locke's polemics on behalf of toleration, of the sort that Hobbes never felt compelled to employ. The phrase of Locke's that Fish seizes upon is from the *Letter Concerning Toleration:* "Every church is orthodox to itself, to others, erroneous or heretical" (1963, 34).[9] Locke continues:

> . . . if in fact what it believes, it believes to be true, what deviates it condemns *[damnat]* as in error. And so of the truth of doctrine, of the rectitude of worship, the dispute between them is on both sides equal; there is no judge (none who is in Constantinople or on earth) by whose sentence it will be settled. The decision of the question belongs only to the supreme judge of all men, to whom alone also belongs the correction *[castigatio]* of the erring. (34, my translation)

Fish contends that "discussion of this vexed issue has not advanced one millimeter beyond the terms established by Locke in his *A Letter Concerning Toleration*" (1999b, 163). But Fish argues that Locke, in typical liberal fashion, fails to do justice to the insight revealed in the phrase "every church is orthodox to itself," which in Fish's hands equals the antifoundationalist doctrine of "irreducible difference."

How does Fish arrive at this puzzling equation? Fish advances an admittedly plausible interpretation of the passage from Locke's *Letter* quoted above:

Persons grasped by opposing beliefs will be equally equipped ("on both sides equal") with what are for them knock-down arguments, unimpeachable authorities, primary, even sacred, texts, and conclusive bodies of evidence. And since anyone who would presume to arbitrate disputes between believers will himself be a believer for whom some arguments, authorities, and bodies of evidence will seem "naturally" weighty, no one's judgment will display the breadth and impartiality that would recommend it to all parties. . . . It follows then, that the only sensible course of action, if we wish to avoid "all the bustles and wars that have been . . . upon account of religion" [Locke 1963, 105],[10] is to remove religious issues from the table of public discussion, leaving their ultimate resolution to the "Supreme Judge" (or, as we would say today, to the marketplace of ideas) and adopting an official policy of toleration toward all professions of belief. (1999b, 163–64)

Locke accepts the fact that no universal agreement is forthcoming on the question of highest importance for human beings — the question of the way to salvation of the soul. Beginning from this fact, he proposes an organization of political life such that intractable religious disputes are bracketed off from politics, establishing a regime of religious toleration. The liberal state will be neutral to the highest religious truths, neither privileging nor hindering any religious belief.

Fish asks: but is blanket toleration not the same as anarchy? That is, how does Locke avoid leaving us with a "civil authority prevented from dealing with behavior it thinks wrong if those who engage in it say they are moved to it by faith" (1999b, 166)? Locke must admit a limit on toleration. Yet once the liberal admits the need for some regulatory power by the state, the following problem emerges: "how to justify the stigmatization of those doctrines and actions that violate the limits as drawn [by the liberal state]" (167)? Fish states: "It is my thesis that there can be no justification (apart from the power performed by those who determine the boundaries) and that therefore any regime of tolerance will be founded by an intolerant gesture of exclusion" (167). Fish does not mean that the liberal state would have nothing to say in justification of the limits set on toleration. He means rather that the liberal justification would be perceived as no justification at all by those orthodoxies that were not already predisposed to accept the limitations the liberal state requires.[11] Liberalism thus comes to light as merely one more "orthodoxy" — "orthodox," that is, to itself alone; to others, erroneous or heretical.

Fish sets out to demonstrate his thesis by examining Locke's turn to the "particulars" of the limitations of liberal tolerance. Locke states:

> I say first: No doctrines opposed or contrary to human society or to the good mores *[bonis moribus]* necessary for preserving civil society, are to be tolerated by the magistrate. But of these examples in any church are rare: for no sect is wont to progress to such insanity that it would teach doctrines for religion, which manifestly undermine the foundations of society, and are indeed condemned by the judgment of all mankind . . . (1963, 84)

Locke makes clear that civil and temporal authority trumps religious and spiritual authority, whether rooted in the church or the conscience. Conservation of the political order, whose end is the conservation of worldly goods — "external things, such as land, money, furniture, etc." (14) — determines the limit of toleration, and, as we shall see, reveals its ultimate justification as well.

What Fish focuses on is Locke's rhetorical sleight of hand. According to Fish, Locke here makes the quintessential liberal maneuver, to be repeated by nearly every liberal after him. Without drawing attention to the fact, Locke identifies his own judgment regarding the limitations on toleration with the "judgment of all mankind" — the voice of right reason. Fish raises a reasonable objection: "How can you get to the judgment of all mankind, to what we now call 'common ground,' if you begin by declaring that differences are intractable because every church is orthodox to itself" (1999b, 167)? That is, has Locke not already discounted the possibility of a judgment common to all mankind, reserving the authoritative judgment to the "supreme judge"? If so, what else could Locke be doing but attempting to disguise his own personal judgment as the universal and uncontroversial judgment of all mankind?

Fish declares that the problem of finding or making common ground in the face of "irreducible difference" is insoluble. He identifies the four most common attempts by liberal theorists to get around the problem: (1) The common ground is found in vague generalities — such as "be good" — that are so abstract as to be of little or no use in a difficult concrete situation. (2) The common ground is found in contrast to some allegedly universally despised view. (3) The common ground is found in pure proceduralism. And (4) "the common ground is identified with whatever distribution of goods and powers a majority has ratified (or at least not rebelled against)" (1999b, 168). Fish does not make clear which of these he attributes to Locke's teaching concerning toleration. In any case, he omits Locke's answer to the source of political "common ground" as Locke himself presents it, viz. the distinction between the goods of this world and those of the next, or the separation of church and state.

According to Locke, the goods, or good, of the next world is eternal life, or the salvation of the soul. The salvation of souls is, in fact, the sole business of the church (Locke 1963, 56). The security of earthly goods — above all, life and property — is the sole business of the state (14). Church and state are separate because heaven and earth are separate. As Locke initially presents his argument, it is the failure to recognize what we may call the irreducible difference of these two realms, and of their corresponding goods, that leads to volatile religious conflicts here on earth.

But how does the distinction between heavenly and earthly goods lead us to distinguish between church and state? After all, insofar as securing property and eternal life for the soul are both the work of this life, why should the earthly powers of the state not be employed to secure both in this life? Moreover, since "there is nothing in this world that is of any comparison with eternity" (Locke 1963, 80), should not the salvation of souls take absolute priority? Indeed, church and state are not so different in Locke's presentation as they may at first appear. Both are "free societ[ies] of men, joining themselves together voluntarily" (22). And human beings enter both with a view to the preservation of their "propriety" (and what could be more one's own than one's soul?). Both societies operate according to some sets of laws, only through the enforcement of which with penalties can they subsist (20, 24). Why should one's soul not be listed with the rest of one's "propriety" the preservation of which is civil society's raison d'être? Why should there not be one society whose purpose it is to preserve its members' (eternal) lives?

Part of the difference, however, between heavenly goods and earthly goods is the difference in our knowledge of how to secure them. In responding to the "zealots" who claim that there is only one true way to eternal life, Locke asserts that, even if this were conceded, "it is uncertain which is the right one." "In this incertitude of things," why should one trust one's soul to whatever chance magistrate is in power, "who can be as ignorant of the way [as myself], and must certainly be less solicitous about my salvation than I myself" (1963, 48). In short, "is it fit for the magistrate to prescribe a remedy, because there is but one, and it, amidst such a variety, *is unknown?*" (46–48, my emphasis).

Thus Locke does concede, in a manner, that there is no end to theological disputes — disputes about how to secure heavenly goods — owing to the natural limits of human understanding. But the situation is different when it comes to securing earthly goods:

> Since men coming together in a commonwealth, through mutual pacts of assistance for the defense of the things of this life, might nevertheless be deprived of their things, either by the rapine and fraud of their fellow citizens; or by the hostile attack of foreigners; of the latter evil, arms, riches, and a multitude of citizens are the remedy; of the former [the remedy] is a question of laws; the care of and power over all these things is handed over by society to the magistrates. The legislative (which is the supreme) power in any commonwealth had this origin, is established for this use, and circumscribes this limit. (1963, 82)

The remedy for the loss of the soul is unknown. The remedy for the loss of "the things of this life" is known. And the distinction between eternal and temporal goods is known.[12]

A Fishian objection immediately comes to mind: these things are "known" and "unknown" to Locke, no doubt; but the "zealots" (already a term of dismissal) just as surely lay claim to their own "knowledge." They are certainly not zealots because they doubt, as Locke does, the one true way to salvation. Has Locke really done anything more than gainsay his opponents? What else could he do with them, or they with him? Has Locke not simply presented us with yet another "orthodoxy"? Are we not just as far from the "judgment of all mankind" as we ever were?

This objection cannot be shrugged off. Indeed, such an objection must move a rationalist, such as Locke, above all. But Locke cannot be dispatched simply by raising it. For one thing, as we noted earlier, Locke denies that something need be judged true by all human beings in order to be truly known. Permanent and widespread disagreement says nothing whatever about the possibility of true rational knowledge. The fact that there are irrational human beings does not show that there are no rational ones. The fact that there are fools does not show that no one is wise.

True as this is, to what extent does it help Locke's case in the present instance? After all, if Locke and a few of his friends were the only ones capable of knowing the distinction between church and state, or natural right, liberal civil society could never be more than a "city in speech" like Plato's Republic and More's Utopia. According to Locke's presentation of the matter, however, citizens need not master the *Essay Concerning Human Understanding* in order to respect the separation of church and state. All they need is a healthy sense of their own interests — interests that by nature are the most powerful spring of their actions. One need not be an epistemologist in order to know that oneself and one's property are safer in times of peace than in times of war; safer in times of war, when the regime has money and soldiers; and safer in times of peace, when the laws are enforced.

But is the problem Locke faces not the fact that many citizens — in particular those he labels "zealots" — do not understand peace and security to be the highest political ends, combined with the fact that the "zealots" disagree amongst themselves regarding what is the highest political end or the means to it? Is Locke not faced again with what Fish calls "irreducible difference"? Locke's response becomes evident toward the end of the *Letter,* where he answers the objections, not of believers who seek religious establishment, but of those who fear that tolerating religious sects runs the risk that they will flourish and wreak political havoc. According to Locke, it is not religion per se that inspires the political disturbances that surface in religion's name, but rather oppression and persecution; remove them through a regime of toleration and the sects will become peaceable. Locke advises the magistrate:

> Relinquish right in civil things equally to all citizens, and immediately you will no longer be afraid of religious gatherings: for if men plan anything seditious, it is not religion that induces them to it in their gatherings, but the misery of oppression. Just and temperate dominions *[imperia]* are everywhere quiet, everywhere safe; but where people are vexed by an unjust and tyrannical dominion, they always resist. I know that seditions are often raised, and frequently in the name of religion . . . but believe me, these do not belong to the peculiar character of churches or religious societies, but to *the common character [mors] of human beings everywhere,* who groan under an unequal *[iniquo]* burden and throw off the heavy yoke that holds their necks. (1963, 96, my emphasis)

We should not be fooled, Locke tells us, by the lofty, pious, and multifarious justifications in which seditious acts are clothed. Their true cause is baser and indicates, not an irreducible difference of a high order, but a common human nature. Religion is not naturally so important to human beings as the religious warfare tearing Europe apart would appear to indicate:

> Some in society make a community for trade and profit, others make leisure for gaiety; these come together in the same city, and shelter in the neighborhood of friends; those come together in religion for divine worship; but there is *one thing* that gathers people in sedition: oppression. (98, my emphasis)

Where their primary needs are met, where they are safe and secure, human beings take to religion in varying degrees, but never with the zeal of revolutionaries.

According to Locke's account of human nature, human beings seek their own security first. Human beings do not need to be scientists — natural or political — in order to do so; it is simply the sort of animals they are. Thus Locke is not being so devious as Fish suggests when he speaks of the "judgment of all mankind." When Fish quotes the passage from Locke about the "judgment of all mankind," he substitutes at the end a period for Locke's colon and omits Locke's explanation of what he means that immediately follows. According to Locke, doctrines that contradict the requirements of civil society are rarely found among the sects, "whose interest [res], peace, reputation, could not be safe" (1963, 94). The concerns of the sects are ultimately, in Locke's estimation, no more lofty, and therefore no more dangerous to civil society, than the concerns of individuals. Liberalism is made feasible by a common human nature, the same human nature that makes possible a judgment common to "all mankind." Thus, for Locke as for Hobbes, the high-order differences that Fish draws our attention to are in fact reducible. Indeed it is only because they are reducible that toleration can serve as a solution to the theologico-political problem.

So sure is Fish that liberalism begins with "irreducible difference" that he rushes past the genius of Locke's teaching. My point, however, is not to excoriate Fish for his reading of Locke and Hobbes. It is rather to show that liberalism cannot be equated with neutrality. I mean to suggest that Locke's teaching concerning toleration cannot be engaged decisively at the level of its purported neutrality, that it cannot be understood without recognizing the decidedly nonneutral understanding of human nature (which I have only begun to sketch here) that makes plausible the political effectiveness of toleration. I mean to suggest, in other words, that Locke at any rate was fully cognizant of the logical difficulties with moral neutrality on which Fish concentrates his energies.

Fish seems to acknowledge that liberalism cannot be identified with neutrality when he states that Stephen Carter "mistakes the essence of liberalism when he characterizes it as 'steeped . . . in skepticism, rationalism, and tolerance'" (1994, 137). Fish objects that "'tolerance' may be what liberalism claims for itself in contradistinction to other, supposedly more authoritarian views"; but since liberalism too must be intolerant, *tolerance* cannot lie at the heart of liberalism. Essentially the same point could be made with respect to identifying neutrality as the essence of liberalism. Fish seems to suggest that the essence of liberalism is not tolerance (or neutrality), but rationalism: "A liberalism that did not 'insist on reason as the only legitimate path to knowledge about the world' would not be liberalism."

But as Fish explains what he means by rationalism, it turns out to be just the sort of neutrality that he has shown to be impossible: "the principle of a rationality that is above the partisan fray (and therefore can assure its 'fairness') is not incidental to liberal thought; it *is* liberal thought, and if it is 'softened' by denying reason its priority and rendering it just one among many legitimate paths, liberalism would have no content." If, however, human beings cannot rise above the partisan fray, then there is no question of denying reason thus defined its priority. We cannot give priority to an impossibility. Fish, of course, sees this difficulty, as he continues: "Of course, it is my contention . . . that liberalism doesn't have the content it thinks it has." This leads to Fish's conclusion, which we saw in the previous chapter, that by its own self-definition "liberalism doesn't exist" (1994, 138).

This conclusion, however, skirts the issue that Fish raised with Carter: If the heart of liberalism is not what liberalism says it is, what is it? If Carter has mistaken the essence of liberalism as neutral toleration, must we not conclude for precisely the same reason that Fish has mistaken the essence of liberalism as neutral rationality? Fish provides some assistance out of this impasse in his account of Milton's Satan as a proto-liberal. At first, Fish states, "Satan had justified his rebellion by invoking freedom and liberty" (1999b, 244). Later, Satan defends himself "with a classic statement of rational empiricism":

That we were form'd . . . sayest thou?

. . . . . . . . . . . . . . . . .

. . . strange point and new!
Doctrine which we would know whence learnt: who saw?
When this creation was? remember'st thou
Thy making, while the Maker gave thee being?
We know no time when we were not as now;
Know none before us, self-begot, self-rais'd.

(5.853–60)

Fish rephrases Satan's contention thus: "seeing is believing, and since no one . . . has seen the moment of his creation, I don't believe it" (244). Here Fish identifies rationalism, not with neutrality — standing back from one's own beliefs, the "view from nowhere" — but with reserving full assent for what one sees *for oneself.* The rationalist thus understood may take the person who is willing to contradict what he sees with his own eyes — through, for example, faith in what Hobbes calls "invisible powers" — to be the one attempting, out of an unreasonable hope, to step back in some manner from his beliefs. Be that as it may, Fish here presents the beginning of an account of rationalism that is more plausible than neutrality to belief. Fish's account of "classic rational empiricism" is, in fact, much closer to Locke's own understanding of reason than is the neutral rationalism that Fish most often equates with liberal rationalism. In the *Essay Concerning Human Understanding* Locke distinguishes reason and faith in the following way:

> Reason therefore here, as contradistinguished to faith, I take to be the discovery of the certainty or probability of such propositions or truths which the mind arrives at by deduction made from such ideas which it got by the use of its natural faculties, viz., by sensation or reflection. Faith, on the other side, is the assent to any proposition, not thus made out of the deductions of reason, but upon the credit of the proposer, as coming from God in some extraordinary way of communication. This way of discovering truths to men we call "revelation." (4.18.2)

At the risk of oversimplifying, we may say that the difference between reason and faith is the difference between seeing for oneself and trusting the report of another.

Nevertheless, Fish hopes to show that this rationalism also fails by its own self-understanding. For Fish rightly claims that Satan's denial of God's creation, simply on the basis of his not having seen it, rests not on empirical evidence but on faith. He identifies in Satan's statement two distinct parts of "classic rational empiricism" (244): (1) seeing is believing, and (2) not seeing is disbelieving. Fish treats these as simply two sides of the same coin; yet this is not the case. Even if a rationalist cannot fully believe what he has not seen for himself, it would be absurd for him to disbelieve whatever he had only heard of.

Distinguishing (1) and (2) enables us to pose the difficulty for the rationalist more precisely than Fish does. If the empiricist (rationalist) cannot give full assent to something he has not seen for himself, he can never give full assent to creation. Yet it seems that he cannot rationally deny creation without proving its impossibility. Does this not mean that however he may live his life, and whatever he determines on the basis of what he sees for himself, must be said to rest on faith — on a non-evident assumption? Does not the fact that the first causes are hidden from human beings mean that every aspect of human life rests on faith? Is there any way to defend the life guided by reason without a completed and certain metaphysics? That, obviously, is a topic for another book. Here we can limit ourselves to the claim that Locke and his fellow Enlightenment rationalists were aware of this difficulty, and an adequate assessment of liberal rationalism would require an assessment of their responses to it. Antifoundationalism places an obstacle before such assessment. If genuine rationalism could only be the "view from nowhere," the arguments made in defense of any belief could only be a rationalization (rhetoric, in Fish's terminology) of unexamined and unexaminable prejudices. What incentive is there to examine seriously arguments (including our own) that we are convinced beforehand must be rationalizations?

It is true that we can no longer take liberal rationalism for granted. But that fact might have the benefit of enabling us to approach it with fresh eyes. It is only through a fresh approach to liberal rationalism, as it is found in the work of Hobbes, Locke, Spinoza, Montesquieu, Tocqueville, the American Founders, and others, that we may make either the acceptance or rejection of liberalism truly our own. Such an approach would mean in the first place an openness to the possibility that the liberal rationalists were right about human nature, religion, and political society. Such an approach would therefore mean suspending the prejudice encouraged by antifoundationalism against the possibility of a sober, reasoned assessment of any comprehensive view.

The antifoundationalists tell us that the various opinions about the whole are "incommensurable," by which they mean that we cannot understand the opinions of another society (or return to understand the thought of a previous age) as they are for those who hold them. All human thought is ultimately circular, and no human being can transcend his or her essentially historically bound opinions. But we could not know that the views of others were fundamentally inaccessible unless we first knew what those views were. In other words, "incommensurability" cannot be known, but remains an assertion. Where so much is at stake — the very foundations of our society and our way of life — we would do well not to accept the report of the antifoundationalists at their word, but to go and see for ourselves. Liberalism, precisely insofar as it is rational, not only sanctions but demands such inquiry.

# 8

## REASON, INDIFFERENCE,
## AND THE AIM OF
## RELIGIOUS FREEDOM

First and foremost I have intended to raise as a topic for serious discussion a question that should be of renewed interest for contemporary liberal theory: namely, the political significance of religion. This question seems to lie in a blind spot for much political theory today, despite the fact that, as it seems to me, it is in part the character of much political theory today that gives this question its renewed urgency. There is much talk among political theorists nowadays about the political significance of "identity," and religion may be listed among the multifarious mix — along with race, class, sex, and so forth — that is said to make up our various individual "selves." There is interest in the political significance of the components of our identity, which are said to be too easily dismissed by liberalism as merely private or personal. The political irrelevance of these things is challenged with such slogans as "the personal is the political." Why should there be a special, indeed unique, interest in the political significance of religion?

Many political theorists appear to be most comfortable in supposing that identity is so very complex and changing that none of the various components can be said to dominate. But it seems to me that, in general, the religion that accepts its place in such a scheme — democratically abstaining from any undue claims to authority — has already been transformed by liberalism; these anarchic selves are liberal selves, or at any rate have been shaped by liberalism. But (and Fish is good at making this clear) does not religion instruct us above all about how we should live? Does not Christianity, for example, claim unique authority over one's life in a way that being male, or heterosexual, or an attorney, does not? Would not a claim that "the personal is political" have to place the highest importance on the question of "the religious as political," precisely insofar as it seeks to be critical about liberalism?

Liberals too, of course, should be critical about liberalism. The liberal principles of religious freedom and disestablishment and the presuppositions underlying those principles are not self-evident, but in need of explanation. As Fish makes clear, the freedoms liberal government allows religion, while in many respects incomparable, are nevertheless limited. Religious freedom is *politically* limited. By what right do merely human institutions limit religion in this or any way? I state the matter provocatively only to suggest that simple and difficult questions regarding the liberal posture to religion are easily unearthed. Liberal principles require investigation and justification, even if we are predisposed to accept them as just. Insofar as we take the justice of liberal institutions for granted, we merely conform out of habituation. We do not yet make liberal principles our own, which would require recovering and reliving the arguments that aim to ground them. This, in turn, requires experiencing the arguments for liberal institutions in their controversial character and awakening to the problem they mean to address. Especially in the case of the religious question, this means also awakening to the need of rational arguments to ground liberal principles. Liberal rationalism supposes that only when liberal principles are grasped with one's own reason are they truly one's own, and therefore more firmly rooted than when accepted as a mere commitment or prejudice. And insofar as there are limitations to the liberal solution (and who would assert that liberalism is free of difficulties?), then it behooves us to awaken ourselves to them. In that way we would, in no trivial respect, free ourselves of those limitations.

It must be stressed that to recognize limitations in the liberal order, even radical limitations, need not mean that liberalism should be condemned or rejected in the absence of a superior alternative (cf. Owen 1999, 923). The practical superiority of liberalism in our circumstances is more readily evident than its fundamental soundness simply. Conversely, the practical superiority of liberalism in our circumstances should not induce us to ignore possible flaws in the liberal order's foundations and purposes.

Much liberal theory today wishes to turn away from liberalism's foundational questions. Rorty and Rawls are by no means anomalies in this respect. In the end, it is difficult to speak of Rorty and Rawls's cases against liberalism's rationalist foundations, since it cannot be said that they mean seriously to engage those foundations. This is their most fundamental failing. Rorty's critique of liberal rationalism, by his own admission, comes down to an assertion, to a deliberately "strong misreading." Rawls does not even go this far;

the foundational questions liberal theorists once saw the need to address are left silently behind. As liberals, both Rorty and Rawls remain heirs in one way or another of an older comprehensive liberalism. In seeking a postfoundational liberalism, they do not free this older liberalism of whatever challenges it faces. They merely free themselves of the responsibility of facing those challenges, challenges that willy-nilly remain, and even intensify, for their own de-rationalized liberalisms. The attempt on the part of contemporary liberal theorists such as Rorty and Rawls to ignore or somehow bypass liberalism's foundational questions in their full transhistorical frame leads to a liberalism characterized by dogmatism and conformism, neither of which is compatible with a political project of liberation. By offering a liberalism that "asserts itself without bothering to ground itself" (1991b, 176), while "consensus becomes the test of a belief" (1994, 5), Rorty's antifoundationalism is more self-conscious and explicit than Rawls's liberalism about what is at stake in the turn away from rationalism; but Rawls cannot avoid being implicated as well.

It is, however, only with Fish that the full import of the antifoundationalist challenge to liberal rationalism becomes evident, as the resources for reasonably distinguishing liberalism from either authoritarian or theocratic alternatives disappear. Fish thus helps us to feel the need to consider liberal foundations afresh, even while he asserts the impossibility of doing so. Yet a fully adequate defense, and indeed understanding, of liberalism would require a serious and reasoned consideration of those foundational questions that antifoundationalism eschews.


Fortunately, the antifoundationalist challenges are inadequate. They are based on a fundamental misconception of liberalism's rationalism, insofar as antifoundationalism understands rationalism to be substantively neutral, or above the fray of competing notions of the whole, the good life, and so forth. Rationalism does not seek to stand apart from, to take an example that is more than an example, religious orthodoxies, in order to encompass or incorporate them into some neutral framework. The critique of such neutrality is valid; but such neutrality does not belong to rationalism. Indeed, insofar as the critique serves to reveal an impossibility (the impossibility of neutrality with respect to life's great questions), and hence a corresponding necessity (the necessity as thinking beings of holding more or less adequate opinions on life's great questions), we may go so far as to say that the critique is *reason's* critique. Seeking self-knowledge to the highest degree, the rationalist must be aware that substantive neutrality is neither possible nor desirable, and therefore is not rational. Indeed, as Rawls's case makes clear, the attempt at a substantively neutral "viewpoint" is already a manifestation of the demise of rationalism, since such a "viewpoint" must be neutral in relation to, among other things, the question of reason's authority versus the claims of divine suprarational authority. Liberalism was not originally conceived as neutral — either in terms of its effects on moral and religious opinion or in terms of its theoretical basis.[1]

This does not mean, it is crucial to note, that the notion of neutrality with respect to the most important human questions is simply a creation of post-Enlightenment liberalism. It is, on the contrary, a product of liberalism's political strategy, which came to depend on a certain official state neutrality to religion. The freedom of religion does, after all, present itself as the freedom of religion as such. The liberal state appears to take no official theological stand. Is this not to say that liberalism is, after all, somehow theologically neutral? Official state neutrality with respect to religion, however, is not to be confused with the theoretical (and theological) justification or basis for that sort of "neutrality"; nor with the effects of that sort of "neutrality" on the character and substance of religion.

We can begin to see liberal religious neutrality for what it is by placing it in the context of liberalism's original political ambitions. The principal aim of liberal enlightenment in its early stages was to bring about a reasonable political order, by putting an end to the worst consequences of fanatical sectarianism — of the clash of "orthodoxies" — such as senseless persecution and bloodshed. If the warring sects are truly fanatical (i.e., in error), their moderation by whatever means serves a moral end. Liberalism sought to transform the character of religion, so as to sap those tendencies to zealotry that endanger civil peace. But, and here we must give our neutralist neoliberals their due, that transformation, not to say conversion, could not take place in the usual manner of religious conversions. To initiate one more sect, offering one more authoritative theological solution, would be no practical solution at all. Liberalism wishes to turn our political attention away from all such theological quarrels and sectarianism, with the effect of depoliticizing the sects. Liberalism must claim that the stuff of such sectarianism is none of its concern. It must transform while appearing to keep its hands off. It must distinguish all uniquely religious concerns from political concerns. It must separate church and state. It must, in a word, appear religiously neutral. The appearance of neutrality serves a nonneutral and eminently political end.

Consider Jefferson's comments on the non-establishment of Pennsylvania and New York: "They have made the happy discovery, that the way to silence religious disputes is to take no notice of them" ([1787] 1954, 161).[2] The way for government to silence religious disputes is not to settle them (as Jefferson doubted they could be settled), but to remain "neutral," to declare, in Locke's words, that "every church is orthodox to itself." The political consequence of maintaining that "every church is orthodox to itself" is to deny all "churches" the status of orthodoxy, which as such is authoritative over human affairs. The liberal state does not recognize orthodoxy. By its actions, it denies that God has spoken on matters of public concern.[3] Because liberalism cannot proceed effectively on the basis of that explicit claim, and because liberals do not wish to be dogmatic, liberalism maintains its own religious neutrality. Whether or not God has spoken is not an issue.

This strategy — a matter of policy rather than theory[4] — has proved to be a remarkable political success and is still at work in neoliberal theories of neutrality, such as Rawls's. That is, Rawls, in contradistinction to the founders of liberal thought, hopes to adopt as a theoretical strategy the disregard of religious disputes. Nevertheless, he still indicates his hope, as Jefferson appears to have done just prior to the statement quoted above, of the possibility of these high-order disputes continuing rationally, and thus even being aided by free and open discussion, albeit now on a subpolitical plane. Rorty, I believe, sees more clearly than Rawls that official public indifference to theological truth fosters private indifference.[5] For Rorty, this private indifference culminates in antifoundationalism, which denies our capacity to know and thereby emaciates the eros for knowledge before its quest can begin. Liberalism's rhetorical strategy, initiated by men who took the truth of religion with the utmost seriousness, has transformed itself into the basic theoretical premise of antifoundationalism, viz. that the highest theological and moral truths are unavailable to human understanding. The liberal rationalists did not themselves wish to avoid the question of what justifies ostensible governmental neutrality. Rorty, Rawls, and Fish, on the other hand, all attempt a metaphysical/theological neutrality. Each in his own way attempts a theoretical stance that is somehow stands above the fray of "metaphysics," "matters of ultimate importance" (Rorty), "comprehensive doctrine" (Rawls), or "first principles" (Fish). Antifoundationalism's critique of neutrality provides us with the tools for recognizing antifoundationalism's own inadequacy.

As the cases of Rorty, Rawls, and Fish make clear, however, the difficulty confronting a rational approach to foundational questions is not simply, or even primarily, theoretical. The objections of each are moral, as well. In the cases of Rorty and Rawls objections are made in the name of a distinctly liberal notion of justice: Each in his own way supposes that "foundationalism" of any sort is somehow linked to intolerance. We are therefore faced with the possibility that something inherent to liberalism itself places obstacles in the way of again taking seriously those questions that the founders of liberal thought, living in a preliberal age, were compelled to take seriously. This, perhaps, is the true demise of liberal rationalism, of which antifoundationalist theory is but a symptom. It is a difficulty of which serious liberals had better beware, lest the liberalism they would see defended induce them to neglect those foundational questions on whose basis alone the attachment to liberalism ultimately could be defended.

To some extent, as I have already suggested, a certain inclination toward indifference to such questions reigns in liberal society by design. Theological indifference was thought to provide a hedge against that fanaticism which endangers the civil peace and is too easily mistaken for genuine seriousness. For the sake of the low but solid and politically necessary good of civil peace, early liberals encouraged what they understood to be a healthy or natural indifference to what Jefferson called "metaphysical riddles." In a letter, Jefferson comments on his decision to permit seminaries (he had originally opposed them) at the University of Virginia: "by bringing the sects together . . . we shall soften and neutralize their prejudices, and make the general religion a religion of peace, reason and morality." A religion of reason, it would appear, pays no mind to "metaphysical riddles." In other letters, Jefferson stated that he was "confident . . . that the present generation will see Unitarianism become the general religion of the United States"; and "I trust that there is not a young man now living in the United States who will not die a Unitarian."[6] Jefferson saw clearly that a government that is ostensibly neutral or indifferent to theological truth does not have a neutral effect on the theological opinions of its citizens. No regime can be simply neutral to religion. Ostensible neutrality or indifference tends to erode diversity, and it does so in a special way. Precisely the regime's indifference tends to foster a private indifference, and with it a bland conformity. Jefferson had few illusions about the fact and saw it as politically salutary. In this respect, Richard Rorty really appears to be a child of Jeffersonian liberalism, as he claims to be. (He is, indeed, an unusually reflective one.) But is a child of Jeffersonian liberalism the same as a mature Jeffersonian liberal? How is such indifference compatible with enlightenment, and therefore with the genuine liberation that Jefferson hoped liberal society would also foster?

As Fish helps to show, and as the case of Rorty reveals, the indifference in question is not a simple indifference, but is rather supported by, and is therefore to a certain extent belied by, a set of moral opinions. The indifference too often fostered by liberal society is not the sort of indifference that Jefferson and the early liberal rationalists seem to have supposed natural to human beings. It is, rather, a peculiarly moralistic indifference, which therefore adds a peculiar obstacle to the awakening of our deepest natural human concerns. As Fish makes clear, this moralism is not the same as genuine moral seriousness. On the contrary, genuine moral seriousness becomes the enemy, apparently on the strange and humorless premise, not to say prejudice, that moral seriousness, indeed seriousness of any sort, embodies the vice of intolerance. This leaves liberals like Rorty "morally serious" only about realizing a world free of suffering, which would clearly not be a world of moral seriousness. But are we really to suppose that *political* toleration is incompatible with moral and intellectual seriousness?

Fish, for his part, does not share Rorty's intention in defending antifoundationalism. Rorty wishes to promote a "philosophical superficiality" or "light-mindedness" or "insouciance" regarding the most important questions (1991a, 193). For Fish, the knowledge of our own ignorance that antifoundationalism reveals "is at once our infirmity and our glory. It is our infirmity because it keeps us from eternity, and it is our glory because it sends us in search of eternity and keeps us from premature rest" (1994, 79). Unfortunately, this intention of Fish's tends to be overwhelmed by his repeated "assurance that what [antifoundationalism] is unable to give you — knowledge, goals, purposes, strategies — is what you already have" (1989, 355), the assurance that we are in no need of going in search of eternity.

The principle of religious freedom provides a basis superior to Fish's antifoundationalism for sensing the need and permanent possibility of that search, insofar as it represents precisely that need and possibility. Although Fish has usefully pointed out an unfortunate liberal tendency to trivialize religion (a tendency Rorty would radicalize), this is not the whole story of liberalism's self-presentation. It is not mere duplicity when liberals insist that religion is too important to be left to whatever chance ruler or popular majority happens to hold the political reins at the time. The private is not necessarily trivial, but can somehow transcend the political's necessary pre-occupation with the here and now. The principle of religious freedom, more-over, entails the recognition of the inherent dignity of owning the true reli-gion for oneself — owing to an examination fitting to the magnitude of what is at stake, rather than to the happenstance of having been born into this or that country, race, or family. The principle of religious freedom aims to pro-vide an unparalleled liberty to seek out and discover the truth for oneself in the needed conversation with the contending parties. The true religion is one's own only when it is embraced in full awareness of its truth. And liber-alism is ennobled when the human capacity thus to embrace the truth is affirmed. At the core of the freedom to seek out the truth for oneself is a recognition that human dignity is seated ultimately in the dignity of the mind. But we are apt to forget that the mere possession of political rights is insuffi-cient for realizing that dignity fully or truly. For the dignity to which liberal-ism points by its protection of religious liberty depends on our earnestly tak-ing advantage of that liberty to the extent we are capable.

APPENDIX:

A REPLY TO STANLEY FISH

A significant portion of the argument of chapters 6 and 7 appeared in the form of an article in the *American Political Science Review* (Owen 1999) alongside a reply from Professor Fish (Fish 1999a). In his reply, Fish took issue with two parts of my interpretation of his work. Since there is more at stake than a matter of interpretation, it is worthwhile taking up these two issues directly. Fish's first objection is that I conflate two assertions that he regards as distinct: "(1) that our convictions cannot be grounded in any independent source of authority and (2) that our convictions are ungrounded. I certainly assert the first, but never the second" (Fish 1999a, 925). My second mistake, according to Fish, is to suppose that his argument regarding the status of the grounds of beliefs and convictions — his antifoundationalism — has any consequences, or that he intends that antifoundationalism should have any consequences, outside the narrowly academic confines of theory. Or, as I put in my essay, according to Fish "the antifoundationalist insight is of no consequence for life" (1999, 918).

I will take up the second of these issues first, chiefly by underscoring points I made in my essay. In doing so, it is useful to distinguish at least two sorts of consequence antifoundationalism might be supposed to have. First, one might suppose that antifoundationalism would provide substantive guidance for our beliefs and actions. Antifoundationalism might be supposed, for example, to instruct us whether to be a theist or an atheist, orthodox or progressive, left-wing or right-wing, just or unjust. I do not argue that Fish hopes for this sort of consequence from antifoundationalism (though I do not believe that antifoundationalism is without implications in this regard). As I put Fish's contention in my essay, "the simple recognition of difference cannot reveal the difference to which one ought to be, or rather is, committed. . . . Antifoundationalism cannot lead us to the correct beliefs, for nothing in our power can do so. It 'offers you nothing but the assurance that what it is unable to give you — knowledge, goals, purposes, strategies — is what you already have' [Fish 1989, 355]" (1999, 917; see above, p. 142).

The passage I cite from Fish's *Doing What Comes Naturally* begins to indicate a second sort of consequence, for which, it seems clear to me, Fish does hope from antifoundationalism. Antifoundationalism, in Fish's view, does offer us assurance — assurance that we already know what we are about, what to do, and how to do it; assurance we do not necessarily have. This is no trivial matter in a moral world dominated by such liberal notions as toleration, rights, equality, impartiality, mutual respect, and neutral principle. These notions undermine such assurance and are thus the enemies of genuine moral intention and action, which Fish's relentless attack on them is meant to revive. Fish's attack reveals that life is "politics all the way down" (1999a, 17), by which Fish means an irresolvable conflict of incompatible moral (and theoretical) views. The antifoundationalist thesis should not be misconstrued as a critique of morality. On the contrary, the antifoundationalist critique reveals and thereby, in a manner, restores the centrality of morality:

> Politics . . . is what is usually opposed to morality, especially in the texts of liberal theorists. Politics, interest, partisan conviction, mere belief — these are the forces that must be kept at bay. What I have attempted here is a reversal of this judgment. Politics, interest, partisan conviction, and belief are the locations of morality. It is in and through them that one's sense of justice and of the "good" lives and is put into action. Immorality resides in the mantras of liberal theory — fairness, impartiality, and mutual respect — all devices for painting the world various shades of gray. (1999a, 242)

Antifoundationalism, by casting light on our true situation, would dispel the shadows and moral ambiguities. It would restore moral imperatives in vivid black and white. This restoration would, it is true, put us into fundamental conflict with one another. To be more precise, it would reveal our latent but ever-present conflicts which liberalism has done its best to garble and obscure. For if each of us could dispel the liberal confusions that dampen our moral thinking, we would not find ourselves in agreement. Our fundamental disagreements would once again (if not for the first time) be clear. But our disagreements would be clear only because we would now be certain of our moral ground and would be unwilling to sacrifice what is right for the sake of a dubious "mutual respect" for what is wrong. The fruit of liberalism is immorality.[1]

By this view, antifoundationalism undoes the immoral work of liberalism. This undoing is fairly called a consequence; and it seems to me a purpose that animates Fish's critique of liberalism. In his latest book (*The Trouble with Principle*, 1999b), the object of Fish's attack is principle — in particular, the liberal understanding of principle, or neutral principle: "The trouble with principle is, first, that it does not exist, and, second, that nowadays many bad things are done in its name. On the surface, this is a paradox: how can something that doesn't exist have consequences?" (Fish 1999b, 2). Liberalism (neutral principle) has consequences. Many bad things are done in its name. Fish cites numerous examples. In my essay (1999, 916 n. 9; chap. 6, note 6 above) I refer to one of Fish's examples, in which the editors of Duke University's student newspaper justified their decision to publish neo-Nazi propaganda by appealing to the neutral liberal principle of free speech. This principle was in fact not neutral (neutral principle doesn't exist), but served to benefit agents of immorality (a bad thing done in neutral principle's name). We cannot say for sure what the student editors would have done if they had learned the lesson of antifoundationalism. But we might expect that they would not have allowed liberal confusions about neutrality to cloud their moral thinking about what they ought to do. Because liberalism has consequences, the attack on liberalism has consequences, if only to undo liberalism's consequences. Antifoundationalism cannot give us convictions, but it can give us the courage of our convictions. I cite again a revealing passage that I cite in my essay: "In a world where nothing is fixed or permanent and the relationship between present urgencies and the ultimate ends is continually changing, one must not take one's constructs 'less seriously,' as [William] Corlett advises, but more seriously; for if we wait for constructs that are in touch with eternity we will fail to act in moments when action is possible for limited creatures" (1999b, 239).

This passage returns us to Fish's first objection. According to that objection, I conflate two assertions; one of which he regards as true, the other of which he regards as false:

The first (and true) assertion is that our convictions and beliefs cannot be grounded in any independent source of authority and validation, that is, in any neutral principle, impartial algorithm, master interpretive rule, sacred text, unimpeachable authority, and so on. The second (and false) assertion is that our convictions and beliefs are ungrounded. The second assertion would follow from (or necessarily accompany) the first only if the first were understood to deny the unavailability of all grounds rather than the unavailability of independent grounds. (1999a, 925)

What, then, does Fish mean by "independent grounds"? According to Fish, we find many incompatible beliefs and convictions vying for supremacy in the so-called marketplace of ideas. An independent ground would transcend that fray and stand as an authority for determining which belief or conviction is true. Such a ground would be something (or someone) one could appeal to in order to demonstrate or persuade adherents of other beliefs and convictions of the right one. It would therefore have to be, at the outset, an authority for everyone. This is "crucial," according to Fish, since if the authority is itself controversial, it would find itself in the fray as yet another belief or conviction. Fish states that "if a ground is to do its validating and disconfirming work from a position above the fray (as opposed to being in the fray), all combatants must acknowledge authority before any specific issue arises; only then will its pronouncements be authoritative for everyone and not be regarded at least by some (and one would be too many) as biased and partisan" (925). Such a ground would have to be an authority for everyone, just as he is, no matter his capacities, passions, prejudices, and willingness to listen. Such a ground, it seems, would not require education or the grace of God or a pure heart in order to feel its power.

Of course there is no such ground. But, one may wonder, who ever dreamt there was such a ground? If this is truly all Fish has ever meant to claim for antifoundationalism, then antifoundationalism seems not only uncontroversial (so that it is hard to identify a single "foundationalist," including Plato, Aquinas, Spinoza, and Hegel) but, as a theoretical contention, antifoundationalism seems vacuous, not to say inane. If we suppose that Plato is the paradigmatic foundationalist, then we must consider Socratic education. The very notion that wisdom depends on education presupposes that none of us begins wise and thus that there are no uncontroversial "grounds" that all recognize clearly at the outset. This also means that wisdom too — even a wisdom that is "in touch with eternity" — will remain radically controversial vis-à-vis the unwise. By Fish's definition of antifoundationalism here, Plato is an antifoundationalist.

In fact, Fish does claim more for antifoundationalism than that it makes the case against "independent grounds" as he defines them in his reply to my essay; and it is only because he claims more for it that his work is worthy of attention. For he does conclude from the fact of intractable and fundamental disagreement that no one is or can be "in touch with eternity." And from this he concludes that "the moral life rests on a base of nothing more than its own interpretations" (1994, 272). But clearly a belief could conceivably be grounded in something more than its own interpretation without being universally recognized. Fish seems to allow as much when he says that "in the absence of absolute certainty of the kind that can only be provided by revelation (something I do not rule out but have not yet experienced), we must act on the basis of the certainty we have so far achieved" (1994, 113). Yet why, by Fish's definition of "independent grounds," would revelation provide any greater certainty (of the foundationalist sort that is always at issue with Fish) than any other sort of opinion or knowledge? Is it because it would be absurd to deny that the mind of God counts as an "independent ground" of belief, even if it is not universally recognized? For it is the nature, as it were, of revelation not to be universally recognized, or even accessible to human beings as such. Has Fish even begun to show that the lack of universal recognition means that the ground of every belief of anyone whatever is nothing more than its own interpretation, i.e. nothing more than itself?

Fish and I agree to this extent: knowledge does not require universal recognition. But we disagree about what deserves to be called knowledge. Fish would like to give each of us (whoever we may be) the assurance that we already have knowledge. Fish has an unusually low standard for what counts as knowledge. I have an unusually high one, in part because I maintain a strict distinction between knowledge and opinion. This distinction is almost wholly absent from Fish's antifoundationalism. One can, it seems to me, safely define the rationalist (and so too the "foundationalist" as I mean to defend him) as one who is radically aware of the irreducible difference (to use a Fishian phrase) between knowledge and opinion — between what he knows and what he merely opines — and who seeks ever to move from opinion to knowledge. In Fish's account, no such movement is necessary on anyone's part. Everyone may or should suppose that his opinions are "sufficient —

they tell us what is and what to do quite nicely, thank you" (1999a, 926). Antifoundationalism shields our opinions by "assuring" us that, whatever our opinions may be, they are sufficient.

I also agree with Fish that the universal agreement of the "independent grounds" he speaks of would not be essentially superior, and would indeed be inferior, to the controversial opinions with which we begin. For universal agreement is not the same as knowledge. Universally held opinion may be right or wrong. The independent ground Fish speaks of issues "authoritative pronouncements" (1999a, 925). It provides "extra justification for deeply held convictions" (928). It does not lead toward knowledge or instruct. Its universal character would be inferior from the point of view of knowledge, since we might not become aware of the inadequacy of our opinions if we were not confronted with radical disagreement. Awareness of this disagreement provides the incentive for the quest for knowledge. The voice of reason is awakened by the awareness of "difference." Antifoundationalism is a concerted effort to silence the voice of reason, to assure us that "difference" does not matter, should not matter.

It should go without saying that reason as I understand it is not neutral but is concerned with what is truly right and what is truly good. It is not content with providing "justification for deeply held convictions." Neutral principle as Fish describes it has more in common with Fish's antifoundationalism than it does with reason as I understand it.

Something notably absent from Fish's reply to my essay was any direct comment on the theme of my essay — the implications of his antifoundationalism for the separation of church and state. He does not comment, for example, on the following characterization of his position:

> Liberalism confronts religion as a competing faith. When believers accept the separation of church and state, they bow to the political establishment of an alien faith. . . . According to Fish's logic every act of legislation is the establishment of some faith or other, so we are compelled to conclude that, in a manner of speaking, there is no such thing as the separation of church and state. There would appear to remain no principled reason for believers not to seek expressly religious establishment. (Owen 1999, 917–18; see above, p. 144)

This, it seems to me, is the climax of his critique of liberalism. I only make explicit the implications of Fish's statement that the believer "should not seek accommodation with liberalism; he should seek to rout it from the field" (1999b, 250). His most extended treatment of the topic is entitled "Mission Impossible: Drawing the Just Bounds between Church and State" (1997b). Yet the most radical implication of his argument is that the primary problem is not drawing the just bounds between church and state but rather separating them in the first place. I cannot say if Fish's silence on this point in his reply can safely be read as confirmation of my interpretation. If, however, anti-foundationalism removes all reasonable obstacles to overturning the separation of church and state, then one cannot seriously maintain that the anti-foundational argument is without consequence.

# NOTES

## CHAPTER ONE

1. See also Seidman and Tushnet 1996, 200–201, and Powell 1993.
2. See the context of the quotation from Levinson, where he states that the faith of a community "can collapse almost literally overnight" (1988, 52).
3. See, e.g., Berns 1985; McCabe 1997; and Neuhaus 1992.
4. See, e.g., Carter 1987, 1993; Gedicks 1991, 1995; Gedicks and Hendrix 1991; McConnell 1992, 1993; Mensch and Freeman 1987, 1992; and Smith 1995. Not all of those listed endorse antifoundationalism in toto.
5. In *The Culture of Disbelief,* Carter repeatedly reassures the reader that he supports liberal institutions (see, e.g., 8, 78, 85, 231, 234, 259, 287), and his genuinely liberal sentiments are evident throughout. The radical kernels of thought on which I focus attention here are thus obscured.
6. The quotation Smith cites is from Augustine's *Correction of the Donatists.*
7. On the political resurgence of religions around the world, see Kepel 1994; on the struggle in the United States between the religious many and the secular few, see Hunter 1991.

## CHAPTER TWO

1. For Dewey's defense of this claim, see [1910] 1965, 8; 1939, 114.
2. That Dewey overestimated the novelty of this "change in point of view" is evident from the definition of science presented by Hobbes at the founding of liberal political philosophy: "Whereas sense and memory are but knowledge of fact, which is a thing past and irrevocable, Science is the knowledge of consequences, and dependence of one fact upon another, by which, out of that we can presently do, we know how to do something else when we will, or the like, another time; because when we see how anything comes about, upon what causes, and by what manner, when the like causes come into our power, we see how to make it produce the like effects" (*Leviathan,* 5.17). This definition applies to political as well as natural science, according to Hobbes (see Hobbes's table of the classification of the sciences, chapter 9). I see nothing in Hobbes's definition of science with which Dewey would disagree. For a comparison of the political doctrines of Hobbes and Dewey, see Nichols 1990, 380–82.

   On the subject of pragmatism's originality, also consider Tocqueville's account of "The Philosophical Method of the Americans" ([1835] 1945, 2:3–8).

3. As science and the scientific attitude drop out of Rorty's pragmatism, education ceases to be a focus. It seems plausible that these two shifts in Rorty's pragmatism are related. But much more would have to be said (after all, regimes not devoted to science are dependent on education, too), and Rorty says too little on the subject of education to allow for more than speculation.

4. Although Dewey frequently speaks of "religion" in the singular, he offers the following caveat: "There is no such thing as religion in the singular. There is only a multitude of religions. . . . It is probable that all the peoples we know anything about have had a religion. But the differences among them are so great and so shocking that any common element that can be extracted is meaningless" (1934, 7–8).

5. Some years earlier, in a less conciliatory spirit, Dewey had stated: "Intellectually, religious emotions are not creative but conservative. They attach themselves readily to the current view of the world and consecrate it. They steep and dye intellectual fabrics in the seething vat of emotions; they do not form their warp and woof" ([1910] 1965, 3).

6. Cf. Heidegger, "Phenomenology and Theology" (1976); "Letter on Humanism" ([1947] 1977, 226–31).

7. Cf. Bacon's *Advancement of Learning:* "It is not yet known in what case and how far effects attributed to superstition do participate of natural causes: and therefore howsoever the practice of such things is to be condemned, yet from the speculation and consideration of them light may be taken, not only for the discerning of the offences, but for the further disclosing of nature" ([1605] 1915, 71).

8. This is not to say that mystical religion is a problem, from James's point of view. On the contrary, he sees it as evidence of man's link to what transcends him. Although James seems to concede a great deal to those who argue that the causes of religion are strictly natural, he identifies himself in the postscript to *The Varieties of Religious Experience* with "the supernaturalists of the piecemeal or crasser type" — those who "admit miracles and providential leadings, and find no intellectual difficulty in mixing the ideal and the real worlds together by interpolating influences from the ideal region among the forces that causally determine the real world's details" ([1902] 1982, 521–52). Regarding "mystic states," however, though they are the "root and centre" of "the personal religious experience," James admits: "my own constitution shuts me out from their enjoyment almost entirely, and I can speak of the subject only at second hand" (379).

9. For most human beings through history, Dewey argues, the insecurity of what

they most value has led them to trust in the invisible powers of the gods, which is effectively to leave matters to chance. The philosophers of old, however, responded to the same insecurity by denying that what was insecure could possibility be of value. They longed for security so much that they determined that whatever was certain (knowledge of eternal forms) was also of the highest value. Dewey finds this solution highly artificial. This, Dewey claims, is the origin of the contemplative life. See 1929, 26–48. By delivering the security for which human beings long, modern progress, on this view, would presumably eliminate, or tremendously weaken, the root of both belief in divine supernatural powers and philosophic contemplation.

10. These comments led Harvey Mansfield to say: "[Rorty] is the one who has given up on America. Some Deweyan" (1988, 36).

11. Dewey does, however, seem to admit that the objectivity of method, even if it is the best we can do, must somehow be qualified: "Every proposition concerning truths is really in the last analysis hypothetical and provisional, although a large number of these propositions have been so frequently verified without failure that we are justified in using them as if they were absolutely true. But, logically, absolute truth is an ideal which cannot be realized, at least not until all the facts have been registered, or as James says 'bagged,' and until it is no longer possible to make other observations and other experiences" ([1931] 1963, 24). This raises the question of whether objective knowledge in an unqualified sense, the ideal of science, must not be knowledge of permanent truths. Compare Newton's Fourth Rule of Reasoning in Philosophy (Newton [1687] 1995): "In experimental philosophy we are to look upon propositions collected by general induction from phaenomena as accurately or very nearly true, notwithstanding any contrary hypothesis that may be imagined, till such time as other phaenomena occur, by which they may either be made more accurate, or liable to exceptions. This rule we must follow, that the argument of induction not be evaded by hypotheses."

12. Rorty asks rhetorically, "Is it unreflective of us contemporary secularists, brought up on Dewey, not to ponder the evidences of the Christian religion?" (1986, xvii).

13. Cf. Friess 1950, 110: "Social inquiry, [as conceived by Dewey], is clearly not a matter of applying some exact, self-contained technique from above to social subject matter. It is a complex, groping phase of social processes and relations themselves."

14. For an extended articulation of a similar argument, see Feyerabend 1975.

15. Elsewhere Rorty admits that such a complete naturalism remains something hoped for (1991a, 114).

CHAPTER THREE

1. See also Rorty 1989, 88: "On my definition, an ironist cannot get along without the contrast between the final vocabulary she inherited and the one she is trying to create for herself. Irony is, if not intrinsically resentful, at least reactive. Ironists have to have something to have doubts about, something from which to be alienated." Cf. Bhaskar 1991, 87; Fraser 1990, 309–10.

2. Rorty will speak of "commonsensical nonmetaphysicians" (see 1989, 87ff.). To the mind of Thomas Aquinas, according to whom metaphysics is the most difficult of the sciences, the science furthest removed from ordinary experience, and reserved in the progression of philosophic education until relatively late in life, a term such as "commonsensical nonmetaphysicians" would likely seem a pleonasm (see Aquinas 1986, Lect. 1; 1996, 5.1). Metaphysics is, as a matter of course, far removed from common sense. Rorty, however, gives the name of "metaphysics" to any claim to objective truth, however far removed from philosophy. The rudest bumpkin is a metaphysician. Rorty hopes that liberalism will someday produce "commonsensical nonmetaphysicians," who instinctively view all questions of truth as good liberals view questions of theology — as either private or futile and uninteresting.

3. But see 1989, 144, where Rorty speaks of the "metaphysicians" as "people who have never had any doubts about the final vocabulary they employ."

4. By changing the subject and leaving the plane of the perennial philosophic debates, however, Rorty seeks effectively to end the "conversation" regarding the principal questions of philosophy by declaring them pointless. It is hard to see philosophy's concern with the highest truth as a threat to its vitality rather than the very source of its vitality. However that may be, "keeping the conversation going" as the *sole* end of philosophy would be purchased at the price of turning away from those questions which have kept the philosophic conversation alive for thousands of years. In fact, however, as I have already noted, Rorty does not simply change the subject.

5. But see Dewey [1910] 1965, 10–14. Dewey points out that for Greek philosophy the eternal forms, or species, are part of our experience of the world — tree, white, love, and so forth. The very word "form" *(eidos)* indicates appearance — surface, not substratum. Aristotle speaks of matter, in contrast, as a substratum *(hē prōtē hekastō hupokeimenē hulē)*; and he contends that "nature is more [the form] than the matter" (*Physics* 193a29, b7–8, my translation). Ordinary human experience is not only, or even principally, of the ephemeral. "Treeness" gives every appearance of being fixed. In contrast, the radical evolution of the biological species, and hence of nature, was (and arguably still is) hidden and has only recently (by

Darwin) been discovered (although Aristotle defends teleology against the proto-Darwinism of Empedocles, *Physics* 198b17f.). Cf. Rorty 1996, 6.

6. Charles Taylor points out that Rorty seems arbitrarily to identify realist epistemology with representationalism. It seems to be Rorty's supposition, for which he never argues, that all "realists" must ultimately hold some version of representationalism. Taylor argues that Rorty thereby stacks the deck in favor of his argument for the incommensurability of worldviews. Taylor asks: "How could you know in general that this kind of question [regarding the differences between worldviews] can't be adjudicated by reasoned argument with a view to the truth? Well, you could know this if you had a lot of confidence in some general theory of what knowing was; for example one that told us that we all only know the world mediately, through a screen of representations which each of us forms in the mind. On this view stubborn differences in representation would be inarbitrable, because no one would ever be able to get behind our pictures into contact with the world out there" (1990, 260). Taylor points out that, for Rorty, epistemology must follow this model, or nothing at all. A sign of the difficulty is present in the title *Philosophy and the Mirror of Nature*. The immediate intellectual perception suggested by the philosophic tradition's "ocular metaphor," which Rorty wishes to drop, is silently replaced by Rorty with a metaphor of the mediated perception of a "mirror." While I share some of Taylor's dissatisfaction with identifying epistemology with representationalism, I am here trying to be as faithful to Rorty's own presentation as possible.

7. See Rorty 1989, 3ff.

8. Cf. Hobbes's *Leviathan* 1.4: "All which qualities called sensible are in the object that causeth them but so many several motions of the matter, by which it presseth our organs diversely. Neither in us that are pressed are they anything else but divers motions (for motion produceth nothing but motion). But their appearance to us is fancy, the same waking that dreaming. And as pressing, rubbing, or striking the eye, makes us fancy light, and pressing the ear produceth a din, so do the bodies also we see, or hear, produce the same by their strong, though unobserved action. For if those colours and sounds were in the bodies, or objects, that cause them, they could not be severed from them, as by glasses, and in echoes by reflection, we see they are, where we know the thing we see is in one place, the appearance in another."

9. Cf. Caputo 1985, 257.

10. According to David Vaden House 1994, 129: "Rorty, as I have indicated, distinguishes between the world which we don't make, and the truth which we do. However, the world, as he says, is not part of the mechanism; it seems to have

no function at all. Rorty is right to criticize the useless problematics of *Vorstellung* and *Ding an sich*. However, in distinguishing between the world and the truth in the manner in which he does, he simply reinstates those very problematics. Rorty's 'solution' to the Kantian problematic seems to consist in little more than a different set of labels buttressed by adamant refusals to offer any account of what possible relevance the world might have for the truth." Cf. Farrell 1995, 163.

11. See Vaden House 1994, 119: "On the one hand, [Rorty] seems to be telling us that the causal narrative is just one human vocabulary among others — it has no privileged relation to reality. It is one humanly constructed truth. On the other hand, we are invited to see our own self-assertive, creative constructions as the outcome of contingent causal forces."

12. Aristotle's own view on the relation between teleology and intelligent purpose is much more difficult to determine. See *Physics* 198b9–199b33. See also Bolotin 1998, 31–51. Aristotle, of course, did not believe in Creation; he taught the eternity of the world.

13. See Newton's *Principia*, Book 3, General Scholium (Newton [1687] 1995).

14. The judgment of the success of such prediction would still depend upon the recognition of the thought predicted, the *thought* not understood as the firing of neurons. The very notion of the prediction of thought through the firing of neurons thus presupposes that thought cannot be reduced to the firing of neurons. Thought remains primary. Similarly with chairs, Rorty's saying that we have various purposes for a chair, or in describing a chair, does not affect his ability to pick out a chair when he enters a room. In some sense, we are forced to say that Rorty does know what a chair *is*. And this, in turn, points to a priority of the being of "chairness" defined in terms of being sat upon rather than in terms of being made of wood, plastic, atoms, etc. It points, in other words, to the priority of "form."

15. Cf. Rorty 1979, 354: "Physicalism is probably right in saying that we shall someday be able, 'in principle,' to predict every movement of a person's body (including those of his larynx and his writing hand) by reference to microstructures within his body."

16. MacIntyre reasonably asks, "if [Rorty] is offering us . . . conclusions detached from any rational grounds, why should we be interested?" (1990, 710).

CHAPTER FOUR

1. Cf. Beiner 1993; Goodheart 1996, 231; Shusterman 1994, 400–403. Rorty 1998 may seem to provide evidence to the contrary.

2. Note Rorty's use of "we atheists" quoted above.

3. McCarthy observes: "'Our' settled convictions include things like basic human

rights, human dignity, distinctions between mores and morals, justice and prudence — and most of the other things Rorty wants to get rid of" (1990, 365).

4. By speaking of liberalism's "suspicion" of ethnocentrism, Rorty puts the liberal rejection of ethnocentrism as backwards and immoral remarkably mildly, presumably in order to soften the tension he is trying to finesse.

5. For Loyola, leaving others to stand or fall spiritually as they might, while one pursues one's own private fantasies, may well seem an extreme of cruelty. As for Nietzsche, he beckons us to "reconsider cruelty and open our eyes," recognizing the fundamental place of cruelty in "almost everything we call 'higher culture'" (*Beyond Good and Evil,* aph. 229).

6. In a reply to Rorty, Lyotard writes: "Richard Rorty is afraid that I no longer have confidence in liberal democracy. I am pleased that he is afraid. I would like to transmit to him my fear, or my loss of confidence. . . . We must, in fact, question democracy again — not democracy in the usual sense of the term, democracy in the sense in which it is opposed to despotism, but democracy in just the sense that it is *not* opposed to despotism. . . . I ask Richard Rorty to revise his excessive confidence in democracy, even liberal" (Lyotard and Rorty 1985, 582–83, my translation).

7. See Rorty 1987, 12: "My own hunch is that we have to separate individual and social reassurance, and make both sublimity and *agape (but not tolerance)* a private, optional matter. That means conceding to Nietzsche that democratic societies have no higher aim than what he called 'the last men' — the people who have their 'little pleasures for the day and their little pleasures for the night.' . . . Such societies should not aim at the creation of a new breed of human being, or anything less banal than evening out people's chances of getting a little pleasure out of their lives." (my emphasis)

8. Fish 1997a. See chap. 6 below.

9. For an extended comparison of Nietzsche and Rorty on this issue, see Lutz 1997.

10. Rorty looks back on Rousseau as "one of us" (1991a, 219). Yet Rorty's political and moral project, the project of what Rorty calls "postmodern bourgeois liberalism," would undoubtedly have revolted Rousseau. Rousseau describes just the sort of man Rorty announces that postmodernism permits us to be with a clear conscience: "Always in contradiction with himself, always floating between his inclinations and his duties, he will never be either man or citizen. He will be good neither for himself nor for others. He will be one of these men of our days: a Frenchman, an Englishman, a bourgeois. He will be nothing" (Rousseau 1979, 40). Note that Rousseau's critique of the bourgeois is compatible with pragmatist standards of evaluation: the bourgeois soul does not "work."

11. But cf. Jefferson [1787] 1954, 223, where in Virginia's Act for Establishing Religious

Freedom, Jefferson states that "our civil rights have no dependence on our religious opinions, more than on our opinions in physics or geometry."

12. In a context somewhat different from our own, Strauss wrote: "When liberals became impatient of the absolute limits to diversity or individuality that are imposed by even the most liberal version of natural right, they had to make a choice between natural right and the uninhibited cultivation of individuality. They chose the latter. . . . But it is practically impossible to leave it at the equality of all preferences or choices. . . . In order to live, we have to silence the easily silenced voice of reason, which tells us that our principles are in themselves as good or bad as any other principles. The more we cultivate reason, the more we cultivate nihilism: the less we are able to be loyal members of society. The inescapable consequence of nihilism is fanatical obscurantism" (1953, 5–6).

CHAPTER FIVE

1. See Rorty 1991b, 175–96.

2. But cf. Rawls 1996, 62, top of the page.

3. Even without considering the crucial question, broached by Sandel, with respect to the claims that these bonds — morality or justice — place on us, we may wonder what it could mean to say that we choose our ends. A general, for example, does not choose victory as his end, but chooses rather the means (he hopes) to victory. The end is prior to, and in this sense determines, his choice. If a general were to choose a course of action he believed would lead to defeat, we would have to ask why he so chose — with a view to what end. A choice not guided by an end cannot be intentional, and an unintentional choice is no choice. See Aristotle *Nicomachean Ethics* 1111b26–30.

4. Cf. Tocqueville [1835] 1945, 1:323–24: "The two great dangers which threaten the existence of religion are schism and indifference. In ages of fervent devotion men sometimes abandon their religion but they only shake one off in order to adopt another." Such is the situation Rorty wishes to avoid: the replacement of one "divinization" for another, even, presumably, if the new "religion" is fervent devotion to Enlightenment rationalism. Tocqueville continues: "Such, however, is not the case when a religious belief is secretly undermined by doctrines which may be termed negative, since they deny the truth of one religion without affirming that of any other. Prodigious revolutions then take place in the human mind, without the apparent co-operation of the passions of man, and almost without his knowledge. Men lose the objects of their fondest hopes as if through forgetfulness. . . . In ages which answer to this description men desert their religious opinions from lukewarmness rather than from dislike; they are not rejected, but they fall away." Tocqueville, unlike Rorty, believes this falling away

"plunges them into despair." Rorty's attention is focused, not on the loss of our fondest hope, but on the hope for a "liberal utopia" which is served by such forgetfulness.

5. This prompts Patrick Neal to state that "Rawls is not anti-foundationalist, but simply a-foundationalist," since he "is simply not speaking to these issues" (Neal 1994, 87, 81).

6. This is not to say that the liberalism of *A Theory of Justice* (1973) was a liberalism of enlightenment. It suffices to mention the veil of ignorance. As Clifford Orwin and James Stoner put it, "Rather than lifting the veil of convention to reveal the truth about nature (and hence the necessity and limits of convention), the original position is itself a convention that by means of the 'veil of ignorance' abstracts from our natural awareness of the world" (Orwin and Stoner 1990, 441). Cf. Barry 1973, 92–96; Mansfield 1978, 92–93.

7. Rawls does allow: "Reasonable comprehensive doctrines, religious or nonreligious, may be introduced in public political discussion at any time, provided that in due course proper political reasons — and not reasons given solely by comprehensive doctrines — are presented that are sufficient to support whatever the comprehensive doctrines introduced are said to support" (1997, 784). Nothing may be said that cannot be reiterated in terms of public reason, and even then only what is put in terms of public reason is "properly political." Public reason remains sovereign.

8. In making his distinction between public and private reason, Kant seems to have had in mind that private individuals as believers may have their reasoning limited by some, probably religious, doctrine or dogma. But no such doctrine or dogma may legitimately limit the use of reason in public affairs. Thus Kant's and Rawls's intentions are not as altogether different as they may at first appear. The fact that their teachings concerning public reason appear opposed is the result of their different notions of reason, such that Rawls can consider strict adherence to doctrine or dogma to be the product of the free use of reason (see 1996, xxvi; 1997, 765).

9. Patrick Neal states: "While it is true that Rawls does not deny that [justice as fairness] might be true, it does not follow that Rawls affirms, in even the slightest degree, the truth of [justice as fairness]" (Neal 1994, 89).

10. But compare Rawls's statement that it is unreasonable to expect any one reasonable comprehensive doctrine to be affirmed by citizens generally "in the *foreseeable* future" (1993, xviii).

11. Macedo adds that the forms of reasoning and evidence relevant to public justification should not be "(if possible) too deeply at odds with firmly held and not unreasonable views" (1990, 49). In this, he resists the full reach of Rawls's

doctrine, even as expressed in the supporting footnote. There Rawls says that public reason's "guidelines and rules *must* be specified by reference to the forms of reasoning available to common sense, and by the procedures and conclusions of science when not controversial." The conclusions of science too must bow to the desire for consensus.

12. But recall that it is Rawls's contention that these doctrines are arrived at by the free use of reason.

13. Cf. Sandel 1994, 1788.

14. Rawls seems to forget this when he characterizes the rational as "egoistic" and being "ready to violate [fair terms of cooperation] as suits their [own] interests when circumstances allow" (49n, 50). That is, he slips into contrasting the public-spirited reasonable with the self-interested rational, despite acknowledging that it is the rational, rather than the reasonable, who look to the good of the whole. Rawls's doctrine is complicated by the fact that what he seems to ask us to subordinate is not our own good but our very notion of what is good, including what is good for the public (one is tempted to say our notion of what is just), which is of course public spirited. It is true that we get the sense that, in Rawls's view, to insist on our own notion of the public good is to be somehow selfish or narrow, or at any rate not public spirited.

15. To desire progress in the understanding is to desire to become better oneself; and this presupposes superior and inferior human states and a lack of toleration and respect for one's own ignorance as an inferior state.

16. Rawls does, however, maintain that "a public and shared basis of justification that applies to comprehensive doctrines is lacking in the public culture of a democratic society. But such a basis is needed to mark the difference, in ways acceptable to a reasonable public, between comprehensive doctrine as such and true comprehensive doctrine" (1996, 61).

17. There arises the obvious question of how Macedo's account of liberalism's "transformative agenda" fits with his endorsement of Rawls's political liberalism. Macedo has repeatedly criticized the notion of liberal neutrality on the grounds that "the soul and religion need to be shaped in accordance with political imperatives," liberal imperatives (1998, 64). Liberalism, according to Macedo, fosters or needs to foster a set of peculiarly liberal moral opinions, which properly rule all aspects of our lives, even our most private lives. Liberalism thus is not substantively — morally and religiously — neutral. Yet when the question turns to how we should understand the substance of this non-neutral liberalism, Macedo proposes something very close to Rawls's political liberalism. Macedo is not unaware of the tension and attempts to resolve it by proposing "civic liberalism."

Civic liberalism is to extend the principles of political liberalism beyond the narrow confines of Rawls's political realm, reaching much further into the "subpolitical" realm of moral and religious opinion, the support of which is necessary for political liberalism. Political liberalism does, I believe, depend on this support; but this only goes to show that political liberalism cannot maintain the narrow and substantively neutral understanding of the political that *defines* political liberalism. Macedo's difficulty is evident in the following sentence: "While I have also argued for the value of casting liberalism as something *less than a fully comprehensive* philosophical system, there is no question that the civic liberalism I have defended has broad implications for *the shape of people's lives as a whole* " (2000, 275, my emphasis). Macedo is right about the fact of liberalism's nonneutrality, but either he is wrong about liberalism's substance or liberalism's substance is confused.

18. Cf. Fish 1997b, 2311–12.

19. Cf. Kautz 1995, 178–79.

20. Cf. Aristotle *Politics* 1252a1–7; *Nicomachean Ethics* 1294a26–b11.

21. Tocqueville observed that in America, "each sect adores the Deity in its own peculiar manner, but all sects preach the same moral law in the name of God" ([1835] 1945, 1:314).

22. See Macedo 2000, 4: "The fact is that from the standpoint of the great moral alternatives that humans have faced throughout history, or even over the course of the American republic, today's celebrations of diversity and difference are often superficial, for they are often about celebrations of the broad extensions of freedom and the fuller realization of equality."

23. A further problem of justice, beyond that posed by the fact of partisanship, goes unaddressed by Rawls — the perennial question that Rorty attempts to overcome: "why is it in one's interest to be just?" (Rorty 1989, xiii), or the tension between "private perfection and human solidarity" or "justice" (xiv). No one can be unaware of this tension. Rawls identifies people as reasonable who seek "social cooperation," but he does not even raise the question of the choiceworthiness or goodness of social cooperation for those who seek it. Does political liberalism ask us to pursue our "self-interest rightly understood," or more simply our good? Or does it ask us to subordinate our good to social cooperation or justice? If Rawls is asking us to subordinate our own good, is it not reasonable to wonder, at least, why we should do so? Madison's solution does not ask people to subordinate their interests. Cf. Kautz 1995, 179–80.

24. Cf. Macedo 2000, 183: "Political liberalism asks of fundamentalists only what it asks of others, including proponents of secular ideals such as Dewey's humanism:

to put reasonably contestable comprehensive ideals to one side in the political realm, and to focus on values such as mutual tolerance and freedom that can be shared by reasonable people."

CHAPTER SIX

1. 827 F. 2d 1058 (6th Cir. 1987). For an extended discussion of the case and what is at stake in it, see Stolzenberg 1993.
2. 827 F. 2d 1058, 1063 (6th Cir. 1987), quoted at Fish 1999b, 157.
3. Cf. Nagel 1991, 10ff.
4. See, e.g., D'Souza 1995, 385.
5. This statement, while at first glance shockingly illiberal, appears in the context of a defense of affirmative action, a policy designed with a view to the liberal moral principle of colorblind equality.
6. Fish presents the following example of how liberal principles can obscure moral commitment in the essay "There's No Such Thing as Free Speech" (1994, 102–19). The editors of Duke University's student newspaper, *The Chronicle,* accepted an advertisement of neo-Nazi propaganda, a denial of the Holocaust presented in scholarly garb. The students defended their decision to publish, despite acknowledging that they believed the views and claims in the advertisement were pernicious and false, in an editorial appealing to the universal right of free speech and free press. Fish comments: "When it happens that the present shape of truth is compelling beyond a reasonable doubt, it is our moral obligation to act on it and not to defer action in the name of an interpretive future that may never arrive. By running the First Amendment up the nearest flagpole and rushing to salute it, the student editors defaulted on that obligation and gave over responsibility to a so-called principle that was not even to the point" (113).
7. Cf. Aristotle *Topics* 101a36–b4: "[the treatise on dialectical reasoning] has a use besides these in relation to the chiefest of the principles regarding each science. For on the one hand, it is impossible to say something about them from principles belonging to the science being put forward, since indeed they are the chiefest principles of everything; but on the other hand, it is necessary to discuss what is held in opinion regarding each. And this is peculiar to or belongs most of all to dialectics; for being capable of examination, it holds the way to the principles of all inquiries" (my translation).
8. Martha Nussbaum is thus mistaken when she states that Fish advocates the "suspension of normative judgment" (1994, 726). According to Fish, no such suspension is possible, even for a moment. Nor is she correct in stating that Fish is "critical not only of dogmatic ethical views that claim to derive from first principles, but also from any form of ethical or legal argument that makes a

definite recommendation for what society and law should do" (727). These too, in Fish's view, are unavoidable.

9. Thus Fish's "pragmatism," which he arrives at via Rorty's postmodernization of Dewey, has turned the pragmatism of Peirce, James, and Dewey entirely on its head. See Fish 1999b, 293–308. For critiques of Fish's argument against the "consequences of pragmatism" and of theory generally, see Abrams 1995, 601–605; Moore 1989, 912–17; Barber 1991.

10. It must be noted that Rortian liberalism would not be metaphysical according to the philosophic tradition's understanding of metaphysics as scientific speculation, as opposed to faith-based opinions, about what is. The philosophic tradition that took the science of metaphysics seriously did not, however, suppose that political society could ever be "metaphysical." Metaphysics was understood to be a private, subpolitical, or, more precisely, suprapolitical study.

11. See, e.g., Benhabib 1996; Honig 1993; Mouffe 1993; and Young 1990.

12. Cf. Bruell 1995, 103: "Despite its best or worst intentions, [multiculturalism] reveals itself as an heir of the liberal universalism it would like to discard. This becomes evident the minute one considers its very concern for the self-assertion of groups as such: this is not a concern of any of the particular groups themselves, each of which, precisely as self-assertive, is preoccupied with the promotion of its own 'agenda'; rather it presupposes a universalistic perspective. Such a perspective is apparent also in the emphasis the movement places on the harmony and mutual respect of the groups: harmony and mutual respect are, from the particularistic perspective of any one group, merely tactical or at best secondary goals. But it is above all the movement's confidence that the self-assertion of groups is not incompatible with their harmony and mutual respect that reveals its universalistic perspective. For that confidence, as much at odds as it is with liberalism's fears, shows the newer movement to be in conscious or unconscious agreement with liberalism that no difference which might divide us — and, in particular, no differing stands we might take on questions about which we disagree — can ever be so important as to *deserve* to call into question the goal we are all taken to share of living in peace and harmony together. In fact, the agreement is more likely to be unconscious than conscious; for it is precisely the newer movement's lack of awareness of its own distance from a genuinely particularistic or group perspective — its ignorance, that is, of what such a perspective truly entails — that enables it to be so sanguine with regard to the consequences of the fostering of particularity. Liberalism, by contrast, being more consciously universalistic, is also more aware of the alternative to universalism; as a result its political instinct is far sounder than that of the movement which would replace it."

13. As William James put it in another context, "Knowledge about a thing is not the thing itself. You remember what Al-Ghazzali told us in the Lecture on Mysticism, — that to understand the causes of drunkenness, as a physician understands them, is not to be drunk" (1982, 488). James warns, however, against one potential consequence of "theory" for "practice": "breadth of knowledge may make one only a dilettante in possibilities, and blunt the acuteness of one's living faith" (489). Knowledge of "drunkenness" and "drunkenness" may be incompatible.

14. See Marsden 1994, postscript.

15. Marsden makes the following response to Fish: "I do not say that since there are no standards for truth Christianity should be accepted as intellectually as good as the next thing. Rather I say that because the *mainstream academy* lacks universal standards for truth, it is not in a good position to marginalize traditional religious perspectives on the old scientistic grounds that such perspectives have failed to meet some objective standards to which all educated people should assent" (1996, 3).

16. Carter seems to endorse the liberal wariness of "those who take their religion too seriously" (1993, 8).

17. Fish does not deny that it may be in the interest of a given faith to play by liberal rules as a matter of prudent strategy. But if it is done well, such a strategy is performed with a view to winning. Elsewhere, Fish praises McConnell's brief in *Rosenberger v Rector* (1995) for doing just that, for manipulating liberal principles in order to get the public policy his beliefs demand. See 1999b, 224.

18. Cf. Perry 1991, 1993; Smolin 1991.

19. Compare Fish's statement with Locke's comments in the *Essay Concerning Human Understanding* on the irremovable uncertainty surrounding even allegedly directly received revelation (4, esp. 16.14, 18.8, 19.4). See also Spinoza's *Tractatus Theologico-politicus,* chaps. 1 and 2.

20. Such a denial is, as we have already seen, not Fish's intention. It may nevertheless be the case that antifoundationalism leads to such a denial. See Fish 1994, 204, where Fish, with apparent approval, describes Richard Posner's pragmatism: "authorities do not come ready made in the form of pure calculus or a scriptural revelation." See also 1989, 485: "As I write, the fortunes of rhetorical man are on the upswing, as in discipline after discipline there is evidence of what has been called the interpretive turn, the realization (at least for those it seizes) that the givens in any field of activity — including the facts it commands, the procedures it trusts in, and the values it expresses and extends — are socially and politically constructed, are fashioned by man rather than delivered by God or Nature."

21. It is here that one's suspicions that Fish's doctrine culminates in nihilism reemerge, precisely where he attempts to explain how morality can have a "content." For

if morality's "content" "rests on a base of nothing more than its own interpretations," it is separated from the complete absence of meaning (emptiness) only by our blind commitment. If, as Fish attests, we cannot live nihilism, if we cannot live a life devoid of meaning, if we must live by some *commitment*, this would not show that nihilism is false, but only that we cannot live a life that is not a lie. Or are we to take the lesson that it is impossible truly to believe in antifoundationalism? Cf. Schanck 1992, 2547–48.

22. There is the following difficulty with my interpretation: If Adam and Eve knew right and wrong (good and evil), what did they gain from the fruit?

23. See especially chapters 5 and 6. The great complexity of the relationship between knowledge and morality is also evident in Fish's interpretation: "[Eve] still has the presence of mind to remember the divine command and thus to protect herself against a surrender to wonder"; "finally, . . . she fails to remember what she knows" (248, 249; cf. 243, 245).

24. See Fish 1999b, 245–46 and 1967, 10, referring to Satan's "morality"; also 1967, 210n.

25. Plato also found no place for willful wrongdoing (for acting badly despite knowing what is good) when he concluded that vice is ignorance. But that conclusion, unlike the doctrine of conflicting "moralities," was traced from the inadequate opinion concerning willful wrongdoing. It is not the product of a typically modern reduction. See *Apology* 25d8–26a7; *Republic* 336b2–337a2, 330d4–331b7; *Apology* 40c4f.

CHAPTER SEVEN

1. Ronald Beiner, himself a critic of liberalism, has made a similar objection to communitarianism. He asks, which community? Are not many communities worse than liberal society? See Beiner 1992, 29.

2. See chapter 6, note 5 above.

3. As evidence of that power, consider the following statement of Justice William Brennan, quoted in his obituary in the *New York Times:* "Asked in a 1986 interview to name his hardest case, [Justice Brennan] cited his concurring opinion in the 1963 Schempp case, one of the early decisions prohibiting organized prayer in the public schools. 'In the face of my whole lifelong experience as a Roman Catholic,' he said in the interview, 'to say that prayer was not an appropriate thing in public school, that gave me quite a hard time. I struggled.' But he added that at the moment he joined the Court, 'I had settled in my mind that I had an *obligation* under the Constitution which could not be influenced by any of my religious *principles*" (July 25, 1997; my emphasis). Here liberalism can be seen doing just what Fish decries, viz. displacing the authoritative status of religious principles while claiming to leave those principles intact. Yet Justice Brennan also brings out

liberalism's moral force. Sanford Levinson, in contrast to Fish, goes so far as to raise Constitutionalism to the status of America's "civil religion," while continuing to recognize liberalism's fundamental tension with religious commitment. On that tension, see Levinson 1990.

4. See Fish 1994, 137; 1999b, 157.

5. *Leviathan* 11.26; 12.1.

6. Thus Hobbes is more a friend of toleration than is commonly recognized. For, while the Hobbesian ruler does have an absolute right over matters of speech, worship, etc., he has no interest in using his power for the salvation of souls or any purpose other than securing the peace.

7. *Essay Concerning Human Understanding*, book 1, 3.1. Cf. *Reasonableness of Christianity*, sect. 252.

8. But see Fish 1967, 218.

9. This is Locke's version of Hobbes's "that which every man calleth in himself religion, and in them that worship or fear the [invisible] power otherwise than they do, superstition" (*Leviathan*, 11.26).

10. Fish cites the Popple translation of 1689.

11. This is the same problem of the allegedly inevitable circularity of justification that Rorty emphasizes. See chapter 4 above.

12. The political importance of Locke's epistemology becomes evident here. What is it to know? What can we know? And above all, what is the difference between knowledge and faith, or trust in what cannot be known? Compare the "Epistle to the Reader" preceding the *Essay Concerning Human Understanding*, where Locke recounts that he thought to pursue the subject of the *Essay* during a meeting with some friends. They were, Locke says, "discoursing on a Subject very remote from this, [and] found themselves quickly at a stand, by the Difficulties that rose on every side. After we had puzzled our selves, without coming any nearer a Resolution of those Doubts which perplexed us, it came into my Thoughts, that we took a wrong course; and that, before we set our selves upon Enquiries of that Nature, it was necessary to examine our own Abilities, and see, what Objects our Understandings were, or were not fitted to deal with" ([1693] 1975, 7). James Tyrrell, who was present at the meeting, annotated this passage in his copy of the book, identifying the subject of the conversation as "the Principles of morality and revealed Religion" (xix).

CHAPTER EIGHT

1. The fact that rationalism cannot be neutral does not in itself, of course, justify rationalism. The most basic task for rationalism is to justify itself as necessary for human beings before and in conversation with more serious challenges than

that of antifoundationalism to the authority of reason, including above all the challenge of revealed (as opposed to natural) religion.

2. Cf. Montesquieu [1748] 1961, 2:163: "One attacks religion more surely by favor, by the commodities of life, by the hope of fortune; not by what averts, but by what makes one forget; not by what makes one indignant, but by what casts into lukewarmness, when other passions agitate the soul, and those that are inspired by religion are silent. General rule: in making a change of religion, invitations are stronger than penalties" (my translation).

3. See Rawls 1996, 153: "Of course, we do not believe the doctrine believers here assert [the denial of "reasonable pluralism"], and this is shown in what we do." See also Berns 1985, 48: "Congress does not have to grant an exemption [from military service] to someone who follows the command of God rather than a command of the law because the Congress established by the Constitution of the United States denies — to state the matter harshly, as the court has forced us to do — *that God has issued any such commands.*"

4. To claim that religion has a distinct and separate purpose from government is, after all, to make a theoretical, indeed theological, claim.

5. See Rorty 1989, 85–86; 1991, 193.

6. Quoted in Pangle 1988, 83. It is tempting to dismiss Jefferson's predictions about the spread of Unitarianism as manifest folly. Unitarianism remains a tiny sect. Transformation, however, is not quite the same as conversion. In assessing Jefferson's prediction, therefore, it is necessary to take a somewhat broader view of Unitarianism. Unitarianism places little importance on doctrine, creed, and theology, and a very high importance on toleration. By that standard most Presbyterians and Methodists, for example, are much closer to the Unitarians of Jefferson's day than to the Presbyterians and Methodists of Jefferson's day. Ask a typical Methodist what the important doctrinal differences are between him and a Presbyterian that lead him to profess Methodism, and he will likely have very little to say. It seems that Jefferson's scheme has largely, if not entirely, succeeded.

### APPENDIX

1. Not only does neutral principle obscure morality, it thereby becomes a form, it would almost appear *the* form, of immorality. Fish thus speaks of "the immorality of principle" ("At the Federalist Society," 1996, 724).

# BIBLIOGRAPHY

Abrams, Kathryn. 1995. "The Unbearable Lightness of Being Stanley Fish." *Stanford Law Review* 47 (3): 595–614.

Aquinas, Thomas. 1986. *The Division and Methods of the Sciences: Questions V and VI of his* Commentary on the *De Trinitate* of Boethius. Translated by Armand Maurer. Toronto: Pontifical Institute of Medieval Studies.

———. 1996. *Commentary on the Book of Causes.* Translated by Vincent Guagliardo, Charles Hess, and Richard Taylor. Washington, D.C.: Catholic University Press.

Bacon, Francis. [1605] 1915. *The Advancement of Learning.* London: Everyman's Library.

Barber, Sotirios A. 1991. "Stanley Fish and the Future of Pragmatism in Legal Theory." *University of Chicago Law Review* 58:1033–43.

Barry, Brian. 1973. *The Liberal Theory of Justice.* Oxford: Oxford University Press.

Beiner, Ronald. 1992. *What's the Matter with Liberalism?* Berkeley: University of California Press.

———. 1993. "Richard Rorty's Liberalism." *Critical Review* 7 (1): 15–31.

Benhabib, Seyla, ed. 1996. *Democracy and Difference.* Princeton, N.J.: Princeton University Press.

Berns, Walter. 1985. *The First Amendment and the Future of American Democracy.* Washington, D.C.: Regnery Gateway.

Bernstein, Richard J. 1987. "One Step Forward, Two Steps Backward: Richard Rorty on Liberal Democracy and Philosophy." *Political Theory* 15 (November): 538–63.

———. 1990. "Rorty's Liberal Utopia." *Social Research* 57 (1): 31–72.

Bhaskar, Roy. 1991. *Philosophy and the Idea of Freedom.* Oxford: Basil Blackwell.

Bloom, Harold. 1997. *The Anxiety of Influence.* 2d ed. New York: Oxford University Press.

Bolotin, David. 1998. *An Approach to Aristotle's Physics.* Albany: State University of New York Press.

Bruell, Christopher. "On Reading Plato Today." In *Political Philosophy and the Human Soul: Essays in Memory of Allan Bloom,* edited by Michael Palmer and Thomas Pangle, 95–108. Lanham, Md.: Rowman and Littlefield.

Bullert, Gary. 1983. *The Politics of John Dewey.* Buffalo, N.Y.: Prometheus Books.

Caputo, John D. 1985. "The Thought of Being and the Conversation of Mankind: The Case of Heidegger and Rorty." In *Hermeneutics and Praxis,* edited by Robert Hollinger, 248–71. Notre Dame, Ind.: University of Notre Dame Press.

Carter, Stephen. 1987. "Evolutionism, Creationism, and Treating Religion as a Hobby." *Duke Law Journal.* 977–96.

———. 1993. *The Culture of Disbelief.* New York: Basic Books.

Cohen, Joshua. 1993. "Moral Pluralism and Political Consensus." In *The Idea of Democracy,* edited by David Copp, Jean Hampton, and John Roemer, 270–91. Cambridge: Cambridge University Press.

D'Souza, Dinesh. 1995. *The End of Racism.* New York: Free Press.

Dewey, John. [1910] 1965. *The Influence of Darwin on Philosophy.* Reprint, Bloomington: Indiana University Press.

———. 1929. *The Quest for Certainty: A Study of the Relation of Knowledge and Action.* New York: Minton, Balch, and Company.

———. [1931] 1963. *Philosophy and Civilization.* Reprint, New York: Capricorn Books.

———. 1934. *A Common Faith.* New Haven, Conn.: Yale University Press.

———. 1939. *Freedom and Culture.* New York: G. P. Putnam's Sons.

Elshtain, Jean Bethke. 1992. "Don't Be Cruel: Reflections on Rortyian Liberalism." In *The Politics of Irony,* edited by Daniel W. Conway and John E. Seery, 199–217. New York: St. Martin's Press.

Farrell, Frank B. 1995. "Rorty and Antirealism." In *Rorty and Pragmatism,* edited by Herman J. Saatkamp, Jr., 154–88. Nashville, Tenn.: Vanderbilt University Press.

Feyerabend, Paul. 1975. *Against Method.* London: New Left Books.

Fish, Stanley. 1967. *Surprised by Sin.* Berkeley: University of California Press.

———. 1989. *Doing What Comes Naturally.* Durham, N.C.: Duke University Press.

———. 1994. *There's No Such Thing as Free Speech.* New York: Oxford University Press.

———. 1995. *Professional Correctness: Literary Studies and Political Change.* Oxford: Clarendon Press.

———. 1996. "At the Federalist Society." *Howard Law Journal* 39: 719–35.

———. 1997a. "Boutique Multiculturalism, or Why Liberals Are Incapable of Thinking about Hate Speech." *Critical Inquiry* 23 (2): 378–95.

———. 1997b. "Mission Impossible: Settling the Just Bounds between Church and State." *Columbia Law Review* 97 (December): 2255–333.

———. 1999a. "A Reply to J. Judd Owen." *American Political Science Review* 93 (4): 925–30.

———. 1999b. *The Trouble with Principle.* Cambridge: Harvard University Press.

Fott, David. 1991. "John Dewey and the Philosophical Foundations of Democracy." *Social Science Journal* 28 (1): 29–44.

Fraser, Nancy. 1990. "Solidarity or Singularity? Richard Rorty between Romanticism and Technocracy." In *Reading Rorty,* edited by Alan R. Malachowski, 303–21. Oxford: Basil Blackwell.

Friess, Horace L. 1950. "Social Inquiry and Social Doctrine." In *John Dewey: Philosopher of Science and Freedom,* edited by Sidney Hook, 106–17. New York: Barnes and Noble.

Gedicks, Frederick Mark. 1991. "The Religious, the Secular, and the Antithetical." *Capital University Law Review* 20:113–145.

———. 1995. *The Rhetoric of Church and State: A Critical Analysis of Religion Clause Jurisprudence.* Durham, N.C.: Duke University Press.

Gedicks, Frederick Mark, and Roger Hendrix. 1991. *Choosing the Dream: The Future of Religion in American Public Life.* New York: Greenwood Press.

Goodheart, Eugene. 1996. "The Postmodern Liberalism of Richard Rorty." *Partisan Review* 63 (2): 223–35.

Hamilton, Alexander, James Madison, and John Jay. 1961. *The Federalist,* edited by Jacob E. Cooke. Middleton, Conn.: Wesleyan University Press.

Heidegger, Martin. [1947] 1977. "Letter on Humanism." In *Basic Writings,* edited by David Farrell Krell, 193–242. New York: Harper and Row.

———. 1976. "Phenomenology and Theology." In *The Piety of Thinking,* edited by James Hart and John Maraldo, 5–21. Bloomington: Indiana University Press.

Hobbes, Thomas. [1651] 1994. *Leviathan.* Indianapolis: Hackett.

Honig, Bonnie. 1993. *Political Theory and the Displacement of Politics.* Ithaca, N.Y.: Cornell University Press.

Hook, Sidney. [1939] 1995. *John Dewey: An Intellectual Portrait.* Reprint, Amherst, N.Y.: Prometheus Books.

Hunter, James Davison. 1991. *Culture Wars: The Struggle to Define America.* New York: Basic Books.

James, William. [1902] 1982. *The Varieties of Religious Experience.* New York: Penguin Books.

Jefferson, Thomas. [1787] 1954. *Notes on the State of Virginia.* Chapel Hill: University of North Carolina Press.

———. 1943. *The Complete Thomas Jefferson.* Edited by Saul K. Padover. New York: Tudor.

Johnson, Phillip. 1984. "Concepts and Compromise in First Amendment Doctrine." *California Law Review* 72:817–46.

Kant, Immanuel. [1784] 1970. "An Answer to the Question 'What is Enlightenment?'" In *Political Writings,* 54–60. Cambridge: Cambridge University Press.

Kautz, Steven. 1995. *Liberalism and Community.* Ithaca, N.Y.: Cornell University Press.

Kepel, Gilles. 1994. *The Revenge of God: The Resurgence of Islam, Christianity, and Judaism in the Modern World.* University Park: Pennsylvania State University Press.

Levinson, Sanford. 1988. *Constitutional Faith.* Princeton, N.J.: Princeton University Press.

———. 1990. "The Confrontation of Religious Faith and Civil Religion: Catholics Become Justices." *DePaul Law Review* 39:1047–81.

———. 1994. "The Multicultures of Belief and Disbelief." *Michigan Law Review* 92: 1873–92.

Locke, John. [1689] 1963. *A Letter Concerning Toleration: Latin and English Texts.* Edited by Mario Montuori. The Hague: Marinus Nijhoff.

———. [1693] 1975. *An Essay Concerning Human Understanding.* Edited by Peter H. Niddich. Oxford: Clarendon Press.

———. [1695] 1965. *The Reasonableness of Christianity.* Chicago: Henry Regnery.

Lutz, Mark. 1997. "Socratic Virtue in Post-Modernity: The Importance of Philosophy for Liberal Democracy." *American Journal of Political Science* 41 (4): 1128–49.

Lyotard, Jean-François, and Richard Rorty. 1985. "Discussion entre Jean-François Lyotard et Richard Rorty." *Critique* 41:581–84.

McCabe, David. 1997. "John Locke and the Argument against Strict Separation." *Review of Politics* 59 (2): 233–58.

McCarthy, Thomas. 1990. "Private Irony and Public Decency: Richard Rorty's New Pragmatism." *Critical Inquiry* 16 (Winter): 355–70.

McConnell, Michael W. 1992. "Religious Freedom at a Crossroads." *University of Chicago Law Review* 59:115–94.

———. 1993. "'God is Dead and We Have Killed Him!': Freedom of Religion in the Postmodern Age." *Brigham Young University Law Review,* 163–88.

Macedo, Stephen. 1990. *Liberal Virtues.* Oxford: Clarendon Press.

———. 1995. "Liberal Civic Education and Religious Fundamentalism: The Case of God v. John Rawls?" *Ethics* 105 (3): 468–96.

———. 1998. "Transformative Constitutionalism and the Case of Religion: Defending the Moderate Hegemony of Liberalism." *Political Theory* 26 (1): 56–80.

———. 2000. *Diversity and Distrust.* Cambridge: Harvard University Press.

MacIntyre, Alasdair. 1985. "Moral Arguments and Social Contexts: A Response to Rorty." In *Hermeneutics and Praxis,* edited by Robert Hollinger, 222–23. Notre Dame, Ind.: University of Notre Dame Press.

———. 1990. Review of *Contingency, Irony, and Solidarity,* by Richard Rorty. *Journal of Philosophy* 87 (12): 708–11.

Mansfield, Harvey C., Jr. 1978. *The Spirit of Liberalism.* Cambridge: Harvard University Press.

———. 1988. "Democracy and the Great Books." *The New Republic,* April 4, 33–37.

Marsden, George M. 1994. *The Soul of the American University: From Protestant Establishment to Established Nonbelief.* New York: Oxford University Press.

———. 1996. Letter to the editor. *First Things,* June/July, 3.

Mensch, Elizabeth, and Alan Freeman. 1987. "Religion as Science/Science as Religion:

Constitutional Law and the Fundamentalist Challenge." *Tikkun* 2 (5): 64–71.

———. 1992. "Losing Faith in Public Schools." *Tikkun* 7 (2): 31–36.

Montesquieu, Charles de Secondat. [1748] 1961. *De l'Esprit des Lois.* 2 vols. Paris: Editions Garnier Frères.

Margaret Moore. 1993. *The Foundations of Liberalism.* New York: Oxford University Press.

Moore, Michael S. 1989. "The Interpretive Turn in Modern Theory: A Turn for the Worse?" *Stanford Law Review* 41 (4): 874–957.

Mouffe, Chantal. 1993. *The Return of the Political.* London: Verso.

Nagel, Thomas. 1991. *Equality and Partiality.* New York: Oxford University Press.

Neal, Patrick. 1994. "Does He Mean What He Says? (Mis)Understanding Rawls's Practical Turn." *Polity* 27 (1): 77–111.

Neuhaus, Richard John. 1992. "A New Order of Religious Freedom." *George Washington Law Review* 60: 620–33.

Newton, Isaac. [1687] 1995. *The Principia.* Translated by Andrew Motte. Amherst, N.Y.: Prometheus Books.

Nichols, James H., Jr. 1990. "Pragmatism and the U. S. Constitution." In *Confronting the Constitution,* edited by Allan Bloom, 369–88, 529–32. Washington, D.C.: AEI Press.

Nietzsche, Friedrich. [1886] 1966. *Beyond Good and Evil.* Translated by Walter Kaufmann. New York: Vintage Books.

Norris, Christopher. 1985. *The Contest of Faculties: Philosophy and Theory after Deconstruction.* London: Metheun.

Nussbaum, Martha C. 1994. "Skepticism about Practical Reason in Literature and the Law." *Harvard Law Review* 107 (3): 714–44.

Orwin, Clifford, and James R. Stoner, Jr. 1990. "Neoconstitutionalism? Rawls, Dworkin, and Nozick." In *Confronting the Constitution,* edited by Allan Bloom, 437–70, 539–41. Washington, D.C.: AEI Press.

Owen, J. Judd. 1997. Review of *Professional Correctness* by Stanley Fish. In *Books in Canada: The Canadian Review of Books.* 26 (8): 32–34.

———. 1999. "Church and State in Stanley Fish's Antiliberalism." *American Political Science Review* 93 (4): 911–24.

Pangle, Thomas L. 1988. *The Spirit of Modern Republicanism.* Chicago: University of Chicago Press.

———. 1992. *The Ennobling of Democracy.* Baltimore: Johns Hopkins University Press.

Perry, Michael J. 1991. *Love and Power: The Role of Religion and Morality in American Politics.* New York: Oxford University Press.

———. 1993. "Further Thoughts — and Second Thoughts — on Love and Power." *San Diego Law Review* 30 : 702–28.

Powell, Jefferson. 1993. *The Moral Tradition of American Constitutionalism: A Theological Interpretation.* Durham, N.C.: Duke University Press.

Rawls, John. 1971. *A Theory of Justice.* Cambridge, Mass.: Harvard University Press, Belknap Press.

———. 1985. "Justice as Fairness: Political not Metaphysical." *Philosophy and Public Affairs* 14 (3): 223–51.

———. 1996. *Political Liberalism.* New York: Columbia University Press.

———. 1997. "The Idea of Public Reason Revisited." *University of Chicago Law Review* 64 (3): 765–807.

Raz, Joseph. 1990. "Facing Diversity: The Case of Epistemic Abstinence." *Philosophy and Public Affairs* 19 (1): 3–46.

Robbins, J. Wesley. 1993. "A Neopragmatist Perspective on Religion and Science." *Zygon* 28 (3): 337–49.

Rorty, Richard. 1979. *Philosophy and the Mirror of Nature.* Princeton, N.J.: Princeton University Press.

———. 1982. *The Consequences of Pragmatism.* Minneapolis: University of Minnesota Press.

———. 1986. Introduction to *John Dewey: The Later Works, 1925–1953,* vol. 8, edited by Jo Ann Boydston. Carbondale: Southern Illinois University Press.

———. 1987. "Posties." *London Review of Books,* September 3, 11–12.

———. 1988. "That Old-Time Philosophy." *The New Republic,* April 4, 28–33.

———. 1989. *Contingency, Irony, and Solidarity.* Cambridge: Cambridge University Press.

———. 1991a. *Objectivity, Relativism, and Truth.* Vol. 1 of *Philosophical Papers.* Cambridge: Cambridge University Press.

———. 1991b. *Essays on Heidegger and Others.* Vol. 2 of *Philosophical Papers.* Cambridge: Cambridge University Press.

———. 1993a. "Human Rights, Rationality, and Sentimentality." *Yale Review* 81 (4): 1–20.

———. 1993b. "Trotsky and the Wild Orchids." In *Wild Orchids and Trotsky,* edited by Mark Edmundson, 31–50. New York: Penguin Books.

———. 1994. "Religion as Conversation-Stopper." *Common Knowledge* 3 (1): 1–6.

———. 1995. "Dewey between Hegel and Darwin." In *Rorty and Pragmatism,* edited by Herman J. Saatkamp, 1–15. Nashville, Tenn.: Vanderbilt University Press.

———. 1996. "Who Are We? Moral Universalism and Economic Triage." *Diogenes* 44 (173): 5–15.

———. 1998. *Achieving Our Country: Leftist Thought in Twentieth-century America.* Cambridge, Mass.: Harvard University Press.

Ross, Andrew. 1992. "On Intellectuals in Politics." *Dissent* 39 (2): 263–65.

Rousseau, Jean-Jacques. 1979. *Emile.* Translated by Allan Bloom. New York: Basic Books.

Sandel, Michael. 1982. *Liberalism and the Limits of Justice.* Cambridge: Cambridge University Press.

———. 1994. Review of *Political Liberalism* by John Rawls. *Harvard Law Review* 104: 1765–94.

Schanck, Peter C. 1992. "Understanding Postmodern Thought and its Implications for Statutory Interpretation." *Southern California Law Review* 65 (6): 2505–97.

Seidman, Louis Michael, and Mark Tushnet. 1996. *Remnants of Belief: Contemporary Constitutional Issues.* New York: Oxford University Press.

Sherry, Suzanna. 1989. "Outlaw Blues." *Michigan Law Review* 87:1418–37.

Shusterman, Richard. 1994. "Pragmatism and Liberalism between Dewey and Rorty." *Political Theory* 22 (3): 391–413.

Smith, Steven D. 1995. *Foreordained Failure: The Quest for a Constitutional Principle of Religious Freedom.* New York: Oxford University Press.

Smolin, David. 1991. "Regulating Religious and Cultural Conflict in Postmodern America: A Response to Professor Perry." *Iowa Law Review* 76:1067–1104.

Spinoza, Benedictus de. 1989. *Tractatus Theologico-politicus.* Translated by Samuel Shirley. Leiden: E. J. Brill.

Stolzenberg, Nomi Maya. 1993. "'He Drew a Circle that Shut Me Out': Assimilation, Indoctrination, and the Paradox of a Liberal Education." *Harvard Law Review* 106: 582–667.

Strauss, Leo. 1953. *Natural Right and History.* Chicago: University of Chicago Press.

———. 1965. "Comments on *Der Bergriff des Politschen* by Carl Schmitt." In *Spinoza's Critique of Religion,* 331–51. New York: Schocken Books.

———. 1968. "An Epilogue." In *Liberalism Ancient and Modern,* 203-23. Chicago: University of Chicago Press.

Taylor, Charles. 1990. "Rorty in the Epistemological Tradition." In *Reading Rorty,* edited by Alan R. Malachowski, 257–78. Oxford: Basil Blackwell.

Tocqueville, Alexis de. [1835] 1945. *Democracy in America.* 2 vols. Edited by Phillips Bradley. New York: Vintage Books.

Tushnet, Mark. 1988. *Red, White, and Blue: A Critical Analysis of Constitutional Law.* Cambridge, Mass.: Harvard University Press.

Vaden House, David. 1994. *Without God or His Doubles: Realism, Relativism, and Rorty.* Leiden: E. J. Brill.

Wittgenstein, Ludwig. [1921] 1961. *Tractatus Logico-philosophicus.* Translated by D. F. Pears and B. F. Guiness. New York: Humanities Press.

Young, Iris Marion. 1990. *Justice and the Politics of Difference.* Princeton, N.J.: Princeton University Press.

# INDEX

Abrams, Kathryn, 193 n.9
"Act for Establishing Religious Freedom"
 (Jefferson), 95, 96
*Advancement of Learning* (Bacon), 182 n.7
affirmative action, 192 n.5
Age of Reason. *See* Enlightenment
antifoundationalism/foundationalism:
 convictions and beliefs, 56, 146, 152,
 163, 173–74; "correspondence" or
 "representationalism," 49, 64; critique
 and challenges, 3, 48–51, 56, 64, 90, 131,
 167, 174; decline and failure, 56, 105;
 definition and significance of, 2, 13, 49,
 90, 105–6, 135, 143, 146–48, 173–75, 176–
 77; knowledge and, 2, 48–51, 169, 171;
 liberalism, 3, 12, 14, 74–75, 135, 138–42,
 143, 167, 174–75; liberal rationalism, 2–
 3, 163–64, 170; moral issues and, 148–
 51, 174–75; neutrality and, 71, 103, 167,
 169–70; ontology and, 63; pragmatism
 and, 13, 194 n.20; rationalism and, 2–3,
 7, 11, 64, 135, 167; reality and, 13; reason
 and, 11, 13, 143, 178; religion and secularism, 4–9, 13, 67, 89–90, 131, 145; toleration, 138; truth and, 105, 152, 169; true
 world and, 49, 54–55, 56; worldviews
 and, 10, 142. *See also* Carter, Stephen L.;
 Fish, Stanley; Rawls, John; Rorty, Richard
*Apology of Socrates* (Plato), 195 n.25
Aquinas, Saint Thomas, 176, 184 n.2
Aristophanes, 11
Aristotle: creation, 186 n.12; Enlightenment and, 45; matter as substratum,

184 n.5; need for rhetoric, 111–12; rationalism, 10, 62–63; references, 188 n.3,
 191 n.20; science, 192 n.7
atheism and atheists, 65–66, 69–70, 74, 81,
 139–40
Augustine, Saint, 6, 181 n.6

Bacon, Francis, 19, 45, 182 n.7
Barber, Sotirios A., 193 n.9
Barry, Brian, 189 n.6
Beiner, Ronald, 91, 186 n.1, 195 n.1
beliefs. *See* convictions and beliefs
Bellah, Robert, 74
Benhabib, Seyla, 193 n.11
Berns, Walter, 181 n.3, 197 n.3
Bernstein, Richard, 82, 85, 93
*Beyond Good and Evil* (Nietzsche), 43, 91,
 187 n.5
Bhaskar, Roy, 184 n.1
Bible, 62
Bloom, Harold, 30
Bolotin, David, 186 n.12
Brennan, William, 195 n.3
Bruell, Christopher, 193 n.12
Bullert, Gary, 31

Caputo, John, 49, 185 n.9
Carter, Stephen L.: antifoundationalism,
 142; criticism of liberalism, 4–5, 9, 161,
 181 n.5; dispute over creation and evolution, 5; liberal neutrality, 6; religion
 and, 4, 5, 30, 69, 70, 71, 143, 194 n.16;
 and Rorty, 70